Crafting Law
on the Supreme Court

The Collegial Game

In *Crafting Law on the Supreme Court*, Forrest Maltzman, James Spriggs, and Paul Wahlbeck use material gleaned from internal memos circulated among justices on the Supreme Court to account systematically for the building of majority opinions. The authors argue that at the heart of this process are policy-seeking justices who are constrained by the choices made by the other justices. By strategically using threats, signals, and persuasion, justices attempt to influence the behavior of their colleagues on the bench. Evidence derived from the recently released papers of justices Brennan, Douglas, Marshall, and Powell is used to test the authors' theory of opinion writing. The portrait of the Supreme Court that emerges stands in sharp contrast to the conventional portrait where justices act solely on the basis of the law or their personal policy preferences. This book provides a fascinating glimpse of how the Court crafts the law.

Forrest Maltzman is Associate Professor of Political Science at George Washington University. He was the 1991–1992 Robert F. Hartley Fellow in Government Studies at the Brookings Institution, as well as a 1994–1995 American Political Science Association Congressional Fellow. Maltzman has authored articles in numerous journals, including *American Political Science Review*, *American Journal of Political Science*, and *Journal of Politics*. He is the author of *Competing Principals: Committees, Parties, and the Organization of Congress* (1997) and a contributor to *Supreme Court Decision-Making* (1999).

James F. Spriggs II is Associate Professor of Political Science at the University of California at Davis. Spriggs is author of articles in *American Journal of Political Science*, *Journal of Politics*, *Political Research Quarterly*, and *American Politics Quarterly*. He is a contributor to *Supreme Court Decision-Making* (1999).

Paul J. Wahlbeck is Associate Professor of Political Science at George Washington University. A member of the bar in Illinois, Wahlbeck has published articles in *American Political Science Review*, *American Journal of Political Science*, *Journal of Politics*, and *Law and Society Review*. He also contributed to *Supreme Court Decision-Making* (1999).

Crafting Law on the Supreme Court

The Collegial Game

FORREST MALTZMAN

George Washington University

JAMES F. SPRIGGS II

University of California at Davis

PAUL J. WAHLBECK

George Washington University

CAMBRIDGE
UNIVERSITY PRESS

PUBLISHED BY THE PRESS SYNDICATE OF THE UNIVERSITY OF CAMBRIDGE
The Pitt Building, Trumpington Street, Cambridge, United Kingdom

CAMBRIDGE UNIVERSITY PRESS
The Edinburgh Building, Cambridge CB2 2RU, UK   http://www.cup.cam.ac.uk
40 West 20th Street, New York, NY 10011-4211, USA   http://www.cup.org
10 Stamford Road, Oakleigh, Melbourne 3166, Australia
Ruiz de Alarcón 13, 28014 Madrid, Spain

© Forrest Maltzman, James F. Spriggs II, Paul J. Wahlbeck   2000

First published 2000

Printed in the United States of America

Typeface Ehrhardt 10/13 pt.   *System* QuarkXPress 4.04 [AG]

A catalog record for this book is available from the British Library.

Library of Congress Cataloging in Publication data

Maltzman, Forrest, 1963–
    Crafting law on the Supreme Court: the collegial game/Forrest Maltzman, James F.
Spriggs II, Paul J. Wahlbeck.
        p.   cm.
    ISBN 0-521-78010-1 (hc) – ISBN 0-521-78394-1 (pbk.)
    1. United States. Supreme Court – Decision making.   2. Judicial process – United States.
3. Judges – United States – Attitudes.   4. Law and politics.   5. Collective behavior.   I.
Spriggs, James F., 1966–   II. Wahlbeck, Paul J., 1961–

KF878 .M285 2000
347.73'5 – dc21   99-047720

ISBN 0 521 78010 1 hardback
ISBN 0 521 78394 1 paperback

In memory of my aunt,
Carol Adler
– *Forrest*

To Cam, Rylie, Jeremy, and Adrienne
– *Jim*

To Janice, Matthew, and Katie
– *Paul*

Contents

Tables and Figures

TABLES

ix

FIGURES

Acknowledgments

We subtitled this book "The Collegial Game" with two purposes in mind. First, it describes our view of how justices interact on the United States Supreme Court. Although each justice pursues his or her goals, each is also required to work within a collegial setting, with no single view of policy determining the final shape of the law. But, second, we believe the subtitle nicely captures a key characteristic of our profession. Life in the academy is also in many respects a collegial game. Despite harboring a diversity of goals and views, each of us is called upon to interact with colleagues with different goals, with conflicting visions of what constitutes good political science, and with alternative theoretical approaches for explaining similar events. Nowhere is this more clear to us than in the many colleagues and students who have given us advice and assistance in writing this book. Not all of these scholars have seen eye-to-eye with us in terms of their epistemological orientation or their understanding of life on the bench. Yet the fact that so many have been willing to play this collegial game reaffirms to us our decisions to become political scientists.

Much of the material in this book was initially presented as conference papers. In presenting our work and writing the final manuscript, we have benefited from the comments of Larry Baum, Sarah Binder, Lee Epstein, Roy Flemming, John Gates, Tim Johnson, Rich Pacelle, Ed Schwartz, Lee Sigelman, Elliott Slotnick, Harold Spaeth, and Sandra Wood. Saul Brenner and Jeff Segal not only read and commented on conference paper versions of many of the book's chapters, they also read from cover to cover the completed manuscript. We are particularly grateful for the support they have given us on this and other projects. Steve Balla, Neal Beck, Eric Lawrence, Langche Zeng, and Chris Zorn have provided us with methodological advice. Along the way, we have also received advice from Chris Deering, Scott Gartner, Larry Heimann, Robert Jackman, Jim Levobic, Chuck Shipan, Randy Siverson, Steven Smith, Isaac Unah, and Jack Wright. We also appreciate the opportunity to present arguments in this book to seminars at Columbia University, George Washington University, Texas A&M, U.C. Davis, and U.C. Berkeley. The comments and suggestions from seminar participants have vastly improved the book.

We have also benefited from research assistance and interactions with graduate students at U.C. Davis and George Washington University, including Rachel Caufield, Mary DeCamp, Dan Else, Chris Nemachek, Jennifer Saunders, and Tressa Tabres. Tom Hansford, in addition to commenting on various conference versions of book chapters, also read the entire manuscript. Of course, graduate students themselves need to eat. Thus, we are grateful for the research support provided by the National Science Foundation (SBR-9512817), the George Washington University Facilitating Fund, the George Washington University Junior Scholar Incentive Award, the Committee on Research of the Davis Division of the Academic Senate of the University of California, the U.C. Davis Program on Economy, Justice, and Society, the U.C. Davis Washington Center, and the U.C. Davis Institute for Governmental Affairs. We further appreciate technical assistance and computer support provided by the U.C. Davis Social Science Data Service. Without the support of these programs, this project would never have been completed.

This project has required several years of data collection. In addition to several cross-country trips for Spriggs, it has involved several years of daily trips to the Library of Congress's Manuscript Division for Maltzman and Wahlbeck. At the library we benefited from the helpful staff. The superb care they give to the national treasures in their custody is something for which we are grateful. We are particularly appreciative of Justice William Brennan's willingness to provide us access to his personal papers. As the reader will soon discover, without access to Brennan's circulation records, this project would not have been possible. In addition to the Brennan papers, at the library we relied extensively upon the papers of Justice William O. Douglas and Justice Thurgood Marshall. We are thankful that each of these justices recognized the importance of providing the public with access to his papers and thus an understanding of the Court. Finally, we made extensive use of Justice Lewis Powell's papers that are housed at his alma mater, Washington and Lee University. We are grateful for both Justice Powell's willingness to give us access to his papers and to John Jacob's assistance in using this collection.

At Cambridge University Press, Alex Holzman, Alissa Morris, and Brian MacDonald each helped shepherd this project. Malcolm Litchfield and Chuck Myers were also extremely helpful in transforming our manuscript into a book. We are grateful for their support.

The antecedents of this book are many. We presented a version of Chapter 2 at the 1998 annual meeting of the American Political Science Association, Boston. Chapter 3 is a modified version of "Bargaining on the U.S. Supreme Court: Justices' Responses to Majority Opinion Drafts" (Spriggs, Maltzman, and Wahlbeck 1999). Versions of Chapter 4 were presented at the 1997 and 1998 annual meetings of the Midwest Political Science Association, Chicago, and the 1997 annual meeting of the Law & Society Association, St. Louis. Finally, Chapter 5 was presented at the 1996 annual meeting of the American Political Science Association, San Francisco, and the 1996 annual meeting of the Scientific Study of Judicial Politics, St. Louis.

Of course, writing this book required more than great data, advice, and assistance. We have also relied upon a strong supporting cast. Thus, we conclude by acknowledging the love and support that Sarah and Noa provided Forrest, that Cam, Rylie, Jeremy, and Adrienne gave Jim, and that Janice, Matthew, and Katie gave Paul.

1

Introduction

On June 18, 1990, the Supreme Court ruled in *Pennsylvania v. Muniz* that although a drunk driving suspect had not been advised of his right to remain silent, as mandated by *Miranda v. Arizona* (1966), the prosecution could introduce at trial a videotape of his slurred speech taken as he answered questions during his booking. Writing for the Court, Justice William Brennan explained that the videotape was not "rendered inadmissible by *Miranda* merely because the slurred nature of his speech was incriminating." Instead, the Court ruled "the physical inability to articulate words in a clear manner" was akin to physical evidence, such as a blood test, rather than testimonial evidence, and thus was not covered by the Fifth Amendment's protection against self-incrimination. Eight justices supported this portion of the Court's opinion. Justice Thurgood Marshall was the lone dissenter.

Once the Court's opinion upheld the right to use the videotape, the Court turned its attention to the more contentious issue of whether the questions asked of the defendant were permissible under *Miranda*. In addressing this issue, Brennan's opinion drew a distinction between routine questions about the suspect's name and address and questions intended to check Inocencio Muniz's analytical ability. After arresting Muniz, the police asked him in what year he had turned six. Even though Muniz could answer the routine booking questions, albeit in a slurred manner, he was unable to determine the year of his sixth birthday. The Brennan opinion made clear that a criminal suspect's response to a question requiring this sort of calculation was testimonial in nature and thus infringed upon the suspect's Fifth Amendment rights. That is, Muniz's inability to make the rather simple calculation about the year of his sixth birthday potentially communicated his guilt by permitting someone to infer that his mental state was impaired. While Justice Marshall supported the majority on this point, four justices, including Chief Justice Rehnquist, dissented.

In allowing questions about Muniz's name and address, Justice Brennan's opinion recognized a "routine booking question" exception to *Miranda v. Arizona* (1966). Based on the reasoning in *Muniz*, police can ask questions regarding biographical information without giving a *Miranda* warning. Importantly, this case represents the first time the Supreme Court explicitly recognized such an exception to a criminal suspect's constitutional right not to incriminate himself. Thus, Muniz's answers to the questions regarding his age, weight, height, and the like were admissible at trial because they fell within this exception, while his answer to the question about his sixth birthday was inadmissible. This portion of the opinion, however, did not receive majority support. Justice Marshall dissented, and Chief Justice Rehnquist with three other justices (White, Blackmun, and Stevens) concurred in the result, but found the exception unnecessary as they believed none of the responses to the booking questions were testimonial.

On its face, the outcome in *Muniz* was not entirely surprising. Since the appointment of Chief Justice Warren Burger in 1969, the Court has issued rulings in favor of the prosecution in 71.6 percent of the 162 cases that pertain to *Miranda*-related issues.[1] Indeed, in 1990, the median justice, Byron White, supported prosecutors in 75.2 percent of these cases.

Brennan's ruling was extraordinary, though, for several different reasons. Coming only two weeks before he was to retire from the bench, the decision appears inconsistent with the historically broad interpretation that Brennan had given to the Fifth Amendment. Of the *Miranda*-related cases that were decided while Brennan served on the Court (1956–1990), Brennan voted with prosecutors only 28.0 percent of the time. Brennan was considered a consistent voice in favor of protecting an individual's *Miranda* rights. Moreover, Brennan's defense of defendants' rights was historically supported by his ideological ally, Justice Thurgood Marshall. Indeed, in the 146 *Miranda*-related cases in which both Marshall and Brennan participated, the two justices voted alike 93.2 percent of the time. In *Muniz*, however, Justice Marshall agreed to

---

[1]   *Miranda v. Arizona* (1966) establishes a right to remain silent, the presence of counsel at interrogations, and knowledge of one's rights. To calculate the percentage of cases where the Court rules with the prosecution, we rely on Spaeth (1998) to establish the Court's behavior in orally argued, signed, and per curiam opinions that delve into issues of self-incrimination, right to counsel, and *Miranda* warnings.

join his ideological ally on only one point. In contrast, the justices who supported Brennan's opinion in *Muniz* agreed with Brennan, on average, in only 28.7 percent of these cases.

Why did Brennan author an opinion that restricted individual liberties? And why did Marshall refuse to join his ideological ally, while Brennan's usual adversaries chose to join his opinion? The answers become clear when we delve into the personal papers of the justices. In a letter to Marshall dated June 7, 1990, Justice Brennan informed Marshall that although "everyone except you and me would recognize the existence of an exception to Miranda for 'routine booking questions,' . . . I made the strategic judgment to concede the existence of an exception but to use my control over the opinion to define the exception as narrowly as possible" (Brennan 1990a). In this letter, Brennan admitted that even though he personally opposed his newly created exception to *Miranda*, he voted with the majority to control the breadth of the legal rule being developed in the opinion.[2]

Indeed, in his first draft of the *Muniz* majority opinion, Brennan argued that the routine booking question exception should not be applied in this case because the state had not demonstrated an administrative need to ask the questions. He held that the case should be remanded to establish whether such a need necessitated these questions (Brennan 1990b). Justice O'Connor responded to this draft by writing a note to Brennan in which she characterized herself as "in accord with much of [his] opinion" (O'Connor 1990), but she took issue with the doubts Brennan expressed about its application in this case. O'Connor particularly objected to the administrative needs test articulated by Brennan, concluding with a threat to withhold support from Brennan's opinion. Brennan immediately responded by circulating a draft that both acknowledged the presence of a routine booking question exception and removed the doubt he previously expressed about the admissibility of the videotape of the defendant's answers to these questions (Brennan 1990c).

In a subsequent letter Brennan sent to Marshall after seeing Marshall's *Muniz* dissent, Brennan wrote: "Thanks, pal, for permitting me to glance at your

---

[2] Brennan had a disproportionate ability to shape the majority because he was in a position as the senior associate justice to assign it to himself. Even though the chief justice assigns the majority opinion when he votes with the majority, in this instance Chief Justice Rehnquist did not support the majority position in all respects. Although Rehnquist joined the majority's ruling on the use of the videotape at trial, he dissented on the "birthday question" and concurred on the "routine booking question" exception without joining that part of Brennan's opinion.

dissent in this case. I think it is quite fine, and I fully understand your wanting to take me to task for recognizing an exception to *Miranda,* though I still firmly believe that this was the strategically proper move here. If Sandra had gotten her hands on this issue, who knows what would have been left of *Miranda*" (Brennan 1990d).

Pennsylvania v. Muniz raises a theoretical puzzle for scholars of the Supreme Court. The dominant explanations of Supreme Court decision making – the legal and attitudinal models – leave little room for such strategic positioning and calculation by the justices. Scholars who adhere to the legal approach to decision making generally attribute case outcomes and thus the behavior of individual justices to particular factual circumstances, the present state of the law, or other legally relevant factors. The legal model would therefore predict that legal precedent or modes of legal analysis (such as original intent) would explain Brennan's vote and opinion in this case.

Political scientists attempting to explain judicial outcomes tend to dwell on the ideological proclivities of individual justices. According to what has become known by political scientists as the attitudinal model, judicial outcomes reflect a combination of legal facts and the policy preferences of individual justices. As Segal and Spaeth characterize the model, "Simply put, Rehnquist votes the way he does because he is extremely conservative; Marshall voted the way he did because he is extremely liberal" (1993, 65). The attitudinal model suggests that Brennan's vote in *Muniz* resulted from his ideological orientation. Because the model's main proponents indicate that empirical evidence only supports the notion that a justice's final vote on the merits should be attributed to a justice's policy preferences, the model does not explain how opinions are crafted (Segal and Spaeth 1994).

Brennan's actions and correspondence in *Muniz* reveal that more than his understanding of legal precedent or his ideology shaped his final vote and the opinion he crafted for the Court. Indeed, Brennan's actions reflected his strategic calculation about what steps could be taken to curtail the erosion of *Miranda v. Arizona* (1966) favored by a majority of the Court. Both policy preferences and rational calculation mattered in this case. Yet, although the strategic nature of Brennan's actions in *Pennsylvania v. Muniz* are clear, we know little about how frequently or under what conditions justices are prone to play this strategic game. The primary focus of this book is strategic calculation on the Supreme Court. Such an approach, we argue, represents a significant departure from the dominant paradigm favored by political scientists, the attitudinal model. As we hope to show, shifting our substantive focus from casting votes to crafting opinions requires that we adapt our theoretical lenses as well.

COURT OPINIONS MATTER

Brennan's actions in *Muniz* highlight a point that is obvious to legal scholars but often underestimated by political scientists: Court opinions matter. Brennan worried more about how the opinion in *Pennsylvania v. Muniz* would be framed than about casting a vote against the defendant. Political scientists who study judicial process and politics tend to focus on the disposition of cases, because that is where the most readily available data exist. In contrast, scholars who approach the study of the Court from a legal perspective recognize that it is the legal rules articulated in Court opinions that give the Court its most powerful legal weapon. Thus, to understand fully the political dynamics of the Court, we need to move beyond the study of voting alignments to explore the multiple strategies that produce Court opinions. It is this premise that motivates our study of the modern Supreme Court.

Creating expectations about future Court behavior and sanctions for noncompliance, Supreme Court opinions have implications for the behavior of private parties and decision makers in all three branches of government (Spriggs 1996; Wahlbeck 1997; Epstein and Knight 1998). Court opinions influence subsequent rulings by lower courts (Rohde and Spaeth 1976; Segal and Spaeth 1993, 261; Johnson 1987a; Songer, Segal, and Cameron 1994), provide guideposts or targets for subsequent congressional behavior (Eskridge 1991a, 1991b; Ignagni and Meernik 1994), and even affect executive branch decision making (Spriggs 1996, 1997). In addition to influencing political decision makers, Court opinions provide private parties and organizations with information about future Court actions and thus influence private behavior as well. As Hurst explains, "legal procedures and tools and legal compulsions . . . create a framework of reasonable expectations within which rational decisions could be taken for the future" (1956, 10–11).

Judicial scholars, of course, have recognized the importance of Supreme Court opinions. As Rohde and Spaeth explain, "The Opinion of the Court is the core of the policy-making power of the Supreme Court. The vote on the merits in conference determines only whether the decisions of the court below will be affirmed or reversed. It is the majority opinion which lays down the broad constitutional and legal principles that govern the decision in the case before the Court, which are theoretically binding on lower courts in all similar cases, and which establish precedents for future decisions of the Court" (1976, 172). But journalists and scholars, recognizing the importance of opinions, usually offer only anecdotal evidence about the crafting of particular opinions (Woodward and Armstrong 1979; B. Schwartz 1985, 1988, 1996). Such detailed case studies highlight the vast array of tactics and factors that may influence Court opinions but offer little theoretical grounding for framing our understanding of Court dynamics.

In contrast, the most theoretically rich and empirically robust studies by judicial scholars generally focus on explaining case outcomes (e.g., who wins or loses) or the behavior of individual justices. For instance, we know much about what factors influence the Court's decision to grant certiorari (Caldeira and Wright 1988; McGuire and Caldeira 1993; Perry 1991; Provine 1980; Tanenhaus et al. 1963; Ulmer 1984), and we can account for the voting patterns of individual justices or the Court (Pritchett 1948; Rohde and Spaeth 1976; Schubert 1965, 1974; Segal et al. 1995; Segal and Cover 1989; Segal and Spaeth 1993). Although such studies have been instrumental in furthering our understanding of the Court, they leave unexamined the factors that shape Court opinions and thus ultimately the law. The new challenge for students of the Court, it seems clear, is to offer a theoretically grounded and empirically rich portrait of the multiple strategies that together yield the Court's most powerful weapon. That is the challenge we take up in this book.

THE OPINION-WRITING PROCESS

Supreme Court opinions are shaped sequentially by four elements of the opinion-writing process: the initial assignment of the case, the writing of the first opinion draft, the response of the justices to the opinion author's drafts, and the subsequent reply of the opinion author to his or her colleagues on the bench. We consider each of these influences in turn.

After oral arguments are heard, the justices meet in conference, which provides them an opportunity to cast an initial vote and to provide their colleagues with the legal justification for their vote. The purpose of the conference vote and discussion is, as Justice Rehnquist (1987, 295) put it, "to determine the view of the majority of the Court." Although these votes provide an indication of the direction in which the Court is likely to rule, the votes are nonbinding. Indeed, justices' final votes do not necessarily resemble their initial conference votes (Brenner 1995; Brenner, Hagle, and Spaeth 1989; Dorff and Brenner 1992; Hagle and Spaeth 1991; Howard 1968; Maltzman and Wahlbeck 1996a). In this sense, the conference discussion resembles a form of "cheap talk," or communication through costless words (Crawford 1990; Farrell and Gibbons 1989). Justices thus can articulate positions at conference without necessarily binding themselves to that position in the future.

A justice voting with the majority in conference is normally selected to craft the majority opinion. According to Court custom, if the chief justice votes with the majority, he has the right to assign the majority opinion (Schwartz 1993, 152; Rehnquist 1987, 296). If the chief justice sides with the conference minority, the most senior associate justice in the majority assigns the majority opinion (Brennan 1963; Hughes 1966, 58–59; Segal and Spaeth 1993, 262). Because of their control over the shape of the opinion, majority opinion authors are traditionally considered to wield considerable influence over Court opinions (Rohde and Spaeth 1976, 172). A large part of the assigned author's influence stems from his or her position as an agenda setter (see Riker 1982, 1986; Hammond 1986; Shepsle and Weingast 1987). The opinion circulated by the author is almost always the first move in the case. Other justices wait to circulate dissenting or concurring opinions until they have at least seen the majority opinion draft. By virtue of this position, then, the assigned author enjoys an agenda-setting advantage, given his or her ability to propose a policy position from the range of available policy alternatives. This advantage is enhanced by the costs associated with writing a competing opinion. Because justices encounter time and workload constraints, a justice who disagrees with portions of an opinion may simply join to avoid the costs associated with writing an alternative opinion.[3]

This agenda-setting effect makes the assignment of the opinion a particularly strategic choice. As much was suggested by Justice Frankfurter in 1949 when he noted, "perhaps no aspect of the 'administrative side' that is vested in the Chief Justice is more important than the duty to assign the writing of the Court's opinion" (Frankfurter 1949, 3; Clark 1959, 51). Or, in the words

---

[3] Justices call this type of grudging assent a "graveyard dissent." As Justice White wrote to Justice Marshall in *Department of Justice v. Tax Analysts* (1989): "I was the other way, but I acquiesce, i.e., a graveyard dissent" (White 1989).

of Justice Fortas, "If the Chief Justice assigns the writing of the Court to Mr. Justice A, a statement of profound consequence may emerge. If he assigns it to Mr. Justice B, the opinion of the Court may be of limited consequence" (Fortas 1975, 405). Political scientists, of course, have also long recognized that one of the chief justice's most important tools is his prerogative to assign the Court's opinion when he is in the majority (e.g., Danelski 1968; Murphy 1964; Ulmer 1970a; Rohde 1972a; Rohde and Spaeth 1976; Slotnick 1978, 1979a; Segal and Spaeth 1993). Likewise, such assignment power has led some scholars to argue that the senior associate justice is also more powerful than his colleagues because of his occasional role in assigning the majority opinion (Johnstone 1992).

Although the majority opinion author may have a disproportionate ability to shape the majority opinion, the majority opinion author "is not, however, a free agent who can simply write the opinion to satisfy solely his own preferences" (Rohde and Spaeth 1976, 172). Because outcomes on the Supreme Court depend on forging a majority coalition that for most cases must consist of at least five justices, there is good reason to expect that final Court opinions will be the product of a collaborative process, what we call the collegial game. As Chief Justice William Rehnquist put it, to get an opinion for a majority of the Court, "some give and take is inevitable. . . . Judging inevitably has a large individual component in it, but the individual contribution of a good judge is filtered through the deliberative process of the court as a body" (Rehnquist 1992, 270). Or, as Rehnquist wrote elsewhere, "While of necessity much latitude is given to the opinion writer, there are inevitable compromises" (Rehnquist 1976, 643). The institutional structure of the Court's opinion-writing process – including such informal rules as the chief assigning cases when voting with the majority or Court opinions constituting precedent only when supported by a majority of the justices – creates the context in which the collegial game is played.

After opinion assignment, the collegial game is played in three additional phases. The first phase occurs as the opinion author crafts a first draft of the majority opinion.[4] At this stage, opinion authors frequently take into account any discussion that occurred in the initial justices' conference following the oral argument. In many respects, the initial conference serves as an opportunity for each justice to communicate information to the majority opinion

---

[4]   As is well known, contemporary Supreme Court justices generally use law clerks to help craft the first draft of an opinion (Rehnquist 1987). For an examination of the stylistic effect clerks have on opinions, see Wahlbeck, Spriggs, and Sigelman (1999).

writer about his or her preferences regarding the legal outcome and reasoning for each case. Although the conference discussion constitutes "cheap talk," it may nevertheless allow justices to coordinate their positions and enable the author to pen an opinion that will gain support among the justices (see Crawford 1990). In other words, an opinion author is likely (and wise) to use the information gleaned at conference to try to draft an opinion that reflects both his or her own policy goal and the preferences of the expected majority coalition.

The other postassignment phases of the collegial game begin after a first draft opinion is circulated. Now a process of give-and-take occurs among the justices. Court custom is for the justices to respond to the draft opinion in writing (B. Schwartz 1996; Rehnquist 1987). Once a draft is circulated, other justices who initially voted with the majority have a range of options. They can proceed to "join" the opinion, make suggestions (sometimes friendly, sometimes hostile) for recommended changes, announce that they are unprepared to take any action at that time, or decide to abandon the majority and write a concurring or dissenting opinion. These reactions signal to the majority opinion author whether and in what manner to respond to the multiple demands of his or her colleagues. The final phase occurs as opinion authors circulate additional draft opinions in response to their colleagues' concerns.

The importance of the signals sent during the second postassignment phase is made apparent by the office manual Justice Lewis Powell prepared for his new clerks. Powell explains that after circulating the first draft: "You then wait anxiously to see what reaction this initial draft will prompt from other Justices. Subsequent drafts may be sent around to reflect stylistic revisions, cite checking changes, or accommodations made in the hope of obtaining the support of other Justices" (Powell 1975). This portrait of the Court's decision-making process resembles Justice Rehnquist's. Rehnquist notes that while he tries to write a first draft that comports with the conference discussion, "the proof of the pudding will be the reactions of those who voted with the majority at conference" (Rehnquist 1987, 301).

Eventually, every justice writes or joins an opinion, and the opinion that commands the support of a majority of the justices becomes the opinion of the Court. Although the final majority opinion is most regularly authored by the justice who was initially assigned the opinion, on rare occasions another justice's concurrence or dissent is transformed into the Court's majority opinion. Justice William Brennan explains, "Before everyone has finally made up his mind [there is] a constant interchange among us . . . while we hammer out the final form of the opinion" (Brennan 1960, 405). Justice Brennan's description of the opinion-writing process is consistent with Justice Tom Clark's observation that once the opinion draft is circulated, "the fur begins to fly" (1959, 51, as quoted in O'Brien 1996, 307). Thus, although the assignment of the majority opinion is a first critical step in shaping the final opinion, the responses of the other justices and the subsequent replies of the majority opinion author also play a dramatic and influential role in shaping the Court's opinion. Understanding the political dynamics of these interchanges among the justices – and offering a coherent theoretical perspective to account for such strategic interaction – is our task in this book.

THE (POLITICAL SCIENCE) TEXTBOOK COURT

Whereas adherents to the legal approach tend to attribute case outcomes to case facts and the law (see Levi 1949; Segal 1984), the textbook justice according to most political scientists votes in a manner that reflects his or her sincere policy preferences (Segal and Spaeth 1993). Those scholars who suggest that policy preferences shape judicial behavior subscribe to the attitudinal model: justices cast votes based exclusively on their policy preferences. If a justice prefers policy Y and a lower court strikes down that policy, the attitudinal model predicts that the justice will vote to reverse the lower court. As Segal and Cover succinctly put it: "The Court's structure grants the justices great freedom 'to base their decisions *solely* upon personal policy preferences'" (1989, 558, quoting Rohde and Spaeth 1976, 72).

Empirical support for the attitudinal model is widespread. As numerous scholars successfully document, justices' votes are consistent with their policy preferences (Hagle and Spaeth 1992, 1993; Segal and Spaeth 1993; Segal et al. 1995; Segal and Cover 1989). Although the attitudinal approach has been fruitfully employed to explain justices' final votes on case dispositions, its applicability to other, and potentially more important, forms of judicial behavior is unclear. Modern proponents of the attitudinal model, for example, insist that it is only applicable to Supreme Court justices' final votes on the merits (see Segal and Spaeth 1994, 11).[5] Indeed, even Harold Spaeth, the

---

[5] Although Segal and Spaeth (1994) claim that the model does not attempt to explain choices other than the votes on the merits, other scholars have interpreted the model as attempting to explain much more than justices' final votes on the merits (Knight 1994). This interpretation

scholar most closely associated with the attitudinal model, has noted that "opinion coalitions and opinion writing may be a matter where nonattitudinal variables operate" (Spaeth 1995a, 314).

In many respects, the attitudinal approach is the culmination of the behavioral revolution as applied to the study of politics (see Segal and Spaeth 1993, 73). As is well known, the behavioral revolution, which began to flourish in the early 1950s, radically altered the study of politics. Rather than merely describing historical events and formal institutions (e.g., constitutions), political scientists sought to identify and understand empirical regularities. The behavioral approach represented a marked departure from political science's normative and anecdotal origins (Dahl 1961; Polsby, Dentler, and Smith 1963), placing political scientists who articulated and tested hypotheses with empirical data at the forefront of the discipline. The behavioral revolution, in short, ushered in the scientific study of politics.

The signal distinction between behavioralists and their predecessors was the behavioralists' abandonment of political science's earliest roots: the study of political institutions. In the words of Kenneth Shepsle, "institutions were, in the thinking of many behavioralists, empty shells to be filled by individual roles, statuses and values" (1989, 133; Clayton 1999). Indeed, the leading behavioral studies of the electorate (Berelson, Lazarfeld, and McPhee 1954; Campbell et al. 1960), Congress (Fenno 1962, 1966; Matthews 1960; Manley 1970), and the judiciary (Schubert 1965; Spaeth 1963) almost always embraced sociological or psychological explanations of behavior. Such psychological and sociological theories of human behavior shared two important tenets. First, both portrayed human action as basically free from real choices. Instead, human action was said to be dictated by sociological or psychological forces beyond the immediate control of any individual. Sociological and psychological explanations, in other words, were deterministic at their core. Second, both approaches viewed individuals as "fundamental building blocks" (Shepsle 1989, 133). Under such a rubric, political outcomes were no more than "the aggregation of individual actions" (Shepsle 1989, 133).

Although some of the earliest works that embraced the attitudinal approach had explicit links to sociological and psychological theories dominant in the

is obviously based on the amount of attention that Segal and Spaeth (1993) devote to stages in the Court decision-making process that precede the final votes. Regardless of Segal and Spaeth's intentions, their empirical findings suggest that the attitudinal model consistently explains only the final vote on a case's merits.

1950s and 1960s (see Nagel 1961, 1962; Schmidhauser 1961; Schubert 1961, 1962, 1965; Spaeth 1961, 1963; Ulmer 1970b, 1973a; Vines 1964), the attitudinal approach took a significant turn in the 1970s with the advent of rational choice analysis. Supreme Court justices were now seen as maximizers of exogenously determined preferences. This new attitudinal perspective suggested that preferences, not roles or backgrounds, shaped behavior. Drawing on this new perspective, Rohde and Spaeth (1976) placed the psychometric attitudinal model within a rational choice framework. Somewhat similar to Schubert (1965), Rohde and Spaeth maintained that justices cast votes by thinking about the facts of a case – the dominant legal issue and the types of litigants – in light of their attitudes and values. They went on to argue, though, that justices are free to vote their attitudes because of the insulating nature of the Court's institutional features, specifically because of justices' lifetime tenure, their lack of ambition for higher office, and the Court's position as the court of last resort.

Although the attitudinal approach articulated by Spaeth and his collaborators builds from a different theoretical base than the earlier versions of the attitudinal approach, it has two very important links to its sociological and psychological roots. First, the attitudinal model continues to view the votes of justices as shaped by forces (in particular, preferences) exogenous to the strategic context of the Court. Second, the attitudinal approach continues to view individuals as the analytical building blocks and outcomes as the aggregated preferences of a Court majority. For this reason, Baum observes that "students of judicial behavior generally focus on individual judges, building explanations of collective choices from the individual level" (1997, 7). In many respects, then, the attitudinal model as articulated since the 1970s represents the culmination of the behavioral revolution as applied to the study of judicial politics. As Segal and Spaeth explain, "The behavioral school of political science that began to flower in the 1950s and continues to bloom today brought it [the attitudinal model] to fruition" (1993, 73).

INSTITUTIONS AND JUDICIAL BEHAVIOR

In recent years, judicial scholars have begun to incorporate into their explanations the role of institutions (Baum 1997; Brace and Hall 1990, 1995; Clayton and Gillman 1999; Epstein and Knight 1998). "Institutions are the rules of the game in society or, more formally, are the humanly devised constraints that shape human interaction" (North 1990, 30). Institutions, in other words, provide the structure within which decision making occurs and thereby affect the choices that can be made. This book fits squarely in this theoretical tradition. Rather than viewing justices as unconstrained actors whose behavior is dictated by their policy preferences, recent work has suggested that justices are strategic actors operating in an environment defined by institutional constraints. As Baum explains, "Judges who vote strategically take into account the effects of their choices on collective results when they vote on outcomes and write or support opinions. . . . Because of this motivation, the positions they take may differ from the positions that they most prefer" (1997, 90).

In many respects, the strategic approach directly contradicts the two tenets of the behavioral tradition: that human behavior is predetermined and that individual action can be aggregated to account for political outcomes. In contrast, a strategic explanation places rational political actors back into their institutional context, recognizing that rational calculation entails consideration of the strategic element of the political game. Instead of deterministically responding to psychological or sociological forces beyond their control, rational actors understand that they face a number of constraints imposed by the actions of other political actors and by the institutional context in which they act. Justices as strategic actors must take into consideration these constraints as they attempt to introduce their policy preferences into the law.[6]

Among judicial scholars, the intellectual origins of a model of strategic interaction were offered by Murphy in his pathbreaking *Elements of Judicial Strategy* (1964). According to Murphy, justices are constrained by the actions and preferences of their colleagues, as well as by decision makers and influences outside of the Court. Murphy did not view each justice as an independent actor. Nor did he think outcomes were the aggregation of individual preferences. Instead, Murphy argued that justices' behavior was shaped by the actions taken by the other justices and the potential for action by Congress, the president, and the general public. In short, Murphy saw that justices are constrained by institutional features internal, as well as external, to the Court.[7]

---

[6] Although we argue that a justice's principal goal is policy, at times justices may pursue other goals, such as legitimacy of the Court (Epstein and Knight 1998; Baum 1997).

[7] Scholars have investigated whether justices strategically respond to actors external to the Court, but the results have been mixed. While some scholars suggest that the Court acts strategically either in specific cases (Knight and Epstein 1996a) or under particular conditions (Hansford and Damore n.d.), others argue that the political environment does not systemat-

Institutional constraints often take the form of formal rules or informal norms that limit the choices available to political actors (Knight 1992; North 1990; March and Olsen 1984, 1989).[8] Formal rules can be in the form of constitutional provisions, legislative statutes, or even court opinions. Informal rules and procedures include, for example, the chief justice assigning the majority opinion when in the conference majority, or a Court opinion setting precedent only if supported by a majority of the sitting justices. Rules provide the context in which strategic behavior is possible by providing information about expected behavior and by signaling sanctions for noncompliance (Knight 1992; North 1990). Institutions therefore mediate between preferences and outcomes by affecting the justices' beliefs about the consequences of their actions. Because the heart of strategic action is interdependency – with justices' choices being shaped, at least in part, by the preferences and likely actions of other relevant actors – justices must possess information about how other justices are likely to behave. Formal or informal rules facilitate this process, providing the requisite information for successful strategic action. Of course, while justices respond to the anticipated or observed choices of others, strategic justices will not necessarily act insincerely. If the political context favors the justice's preferred course of action, a strategic justice's behavior will be the same as it would be without constraints.[9]

In this book, we are concerned with the rules, procedures, and norms, internal to the Court, that constrain justices' capacity to translate their preferences into legal policy outcomes.[10] The Court's agenda-setting, opinion-as-

---

ically constrain the justices (Segal 1997). Although extrainstitutional constraints are theoretically plausible and interesting, we focus on the intra-Court collegial game.

[8] There are other definitions of institutions. Historical institutionalism, sociological institutionalism, and other institutionally focused approaches to the study of politics provide alternative concepts of institutions. In fact, neoinstitutionalism incorporates a variety of theoretical and empirical perspectives. For an overview of the political economy of institutions, see the edited volumes by Alt and Shepsle (1990) and Knight and Sened (1995). For alternative theoretical approaches, see, for example, March and Olsen (1984, 1989) and Smith (1988, 1996). Distinctions between rational choice and non-rational-choice institutionalism are discussed in detail by Orren and Skowronek (1994) and Smith (1996).

[9] In other words, sophisticated behavior (i.e., acting contrary to one's most preferred course of action) is a sufficient, but not necessary, condition for a justice to have been subject to strategic constraints. Again, the essence of a strategic explanation is the interdependency of choice among actors (see Elster 1986).

[10] In addition to the rules we examine, there are other institutions that affect judicial behavior: rules establishing three-judge federal appellate panels (Atkins 1970, 1972), rules for assigning judges to federal appellate panels (Atkins and Zavoina 1974), rules for assigning opinions to judges (Brace and Hall 1990; Hall and Brace 1989, 1992), rules for seniority-ordered vot-

signment, and opinion-writing norms and policies each affect justices' success in converting policy goals to legal doctrine (see Epstein and Knight 1998). As a result of these informal rules, justices engage in strategic behavior as they attempt to shape the Court's policy output into conformance with their policy goals. The intra-Court strategic game thus results from the institutional rules and practices of the Court arena.

Perhaps the most important institutional feature of the Court is its collegial character. Contrary to a portrait of the Court as "nine small, independent law firms" that have little interaction with one another (Powell 1976), the strategic approach recognizes that the behavior of individual justices is shaped in part by the actions and preferences of their brethren. As a result, a justice's choices during the opinion-writing process will depend in large part on the choices made by the other justices (see Rohde 1972b, 1972c). Decision making is thus interdependent because justices' ability to have majority opinions reflect their policy preferences depends in part on the choices made by other justices.

The first important, post-oral-argument informal rule that constrains the ability of justices to see their individual preferences converted into legal policy is the process by which opinions are assigned on the Supreme Court. As we have already noted, since the tenure of Chief Justice Roger Taney (Schwartz 1993, 152), the custom has been for the chief justice to assign opinions when in the conference majority; otherwise, the most senior associate justice in the conference majority assigns the opinion. This norm provides an opportunity for opinion assignors to attempt to affect the Court's decisions (Epstein and Knight 1998; Baum 1998). This influence may be achieved by assigning the case to a justice who will represent the assignor's preferences. After all, as we previously discussed, the opinion author occupies an agenda-setting position and can write an opinion draft that proposes a policy position from the range of alternatives available in a case.

The Court's informal rule that before carrying the imprimatur of the Court an opinion must gain the support of a majority of justices is another reason that judicial behavior is interdependent. Opinions that fail to gain the necessary

ing by judges (Brace and Hall 1993), informal norms of adhering to precedent (Knight 1993; Knight and Epstein 1996b; Spriggs and Hansford 1998), rules governing the number of justices required to grant certiorari (Perry 1991), rules for selecting judges (Brace and Hall 1995), and norms of consensus on the Supreme Court (Walker, Epstein, and Dixon 1988; Caldeira and Zorn 1998).

support will not be seen as speaking for the Court, although they may announce the judgment of the Court, and their precedential impact may be lessened (Johnson and Canon 1984; Segal and Spaeth 1993).[11] Thus, because outcomes on the Supreme Court generally depend on the agreement of at least five justices, Murphy (1964) argues that justices do not simply vote their policy preferences. Instead, he characterizes the Supreme Court's deliberative process as a struggle among the justices to shape the content of opinions. At the heart of this process are policy-oriented justices who employ a "mixture of appeals, threats, and offers to compromise" (1964, 42) to encourage their colleagues to support legal rulings that reflect their policy preferences. As we show in this book, the choices justices make reflect the role of this informal rule.

In this book, we systematically explore what happens after the justices hold an initial vote on a case's merits and prior to the release of the Court's opinion. We seek to show the extent to which institutional constraints endogenous to the Court shape the opinion-writing process and thus ultimately the law. More specifically, we seek to explain under what conditions, and to what extent, the choices that justices make in the process of writing opinions result from strategic interdependencies on the Court.

STRATEGIC INTERACTION AND THE
OPINION-WRITING PROCESS

The strategic model implies that final Court opinions cannot be exclusively attributed to justices' strict reading of the law, simple accounting of justices' policy preferences, or strategic calculations about the response (or nonresponse) of political actors exogenous to the Court. The hallmark of this approach is its focus on the interdependencies inherent in judicial decision making. To achieve policy outcomes as close as possible to their own preferences, justices must at a minimum take into account the choices made by

---

[11] Traditionally, a plurality opinion (i.e., one lacking majority support) did not establish a legal precedent. In 1977, however, the Supreme Court, in *Marks v. United States,* ruled that "the holding of the Court may be viewed as that position taken by those members who concurred in the judgments on the narrowest grounds." Thus, it is possible that a plurality opinion might create a precedent, provided it is the opinion in the case decided on the narrowest grounds (see Thurmon 1992). Of course, deciphering exactly which opinion rules on "the narrowest grounds" is often no easy task. Thus, strategic justices generally prefer having their views written into law by a majority opinion.

their colleagues, with whom they ultimately must negotiate, bargain, and compromise.

In the spirit of earlier work, our strategic model of judicial decision making is based on two postulates. These postulates broadly define the contours of what we view as the collegial court game. Both postulates stem from institutional features of the American legal system. The first postulate touches upon two principles that are at the heart of the legal and attitudinal models.

Outcome Postulate: Justices prefer Court opinions and legal rules that reflect their policy preferences.

Reflecting the tenets of the legal model, this postulate recognizes the importance of Court opinions to members of the bench. Consistent with the attitudinal model, this postulate asserts that justices are principally motivated by their policy preferences. Even though the attitudinalists do not believe that Supreme Court opinions constrain the justices' decisions as precedent (Segal and Spaeth 1993; Spaeth and Segal 1999), they do recognize that the Court's opinions produce its most profound policy contributions (Rohde and Spaeth 1976, 172). Thus, some have argued that having justices prefer legal rules that conform to their preferences is consistent with the attitudinal model (Wahlbeck 1997, 1998).

The second postulate recognizes that even though justices hope to see their policy preferences implemented into law, the Court's institutional structure constrains the choices that justices are likely to make. The most important of these constraints is an acknowledgment that Supreme Court decision making is a collective enterprise among all of the justices. Contrary to the portrait of the Court as nine separate law firms that have little interaction with one another, our model of strategic interaction recognizes that the behavior of individual justices is determined in part by the actions and preferences of their brethren.

Collective Decision-Making Postulate: Justices will try to secure opinions that are as close as possible to their policy positions by basing their decisions in part on the positions and actions of their colleagues.

Indeed, a recognition that in a collegial setting strategic action is necessary might lead justices to support positions that deviate from their ideal policy outcome. In many respects, the collective decision-making postulate constitutes what we consider to be the heart of the collegial game. As we have already alluded to, our definition of strategic behavior touches on these two postulates. A strategic justice is one who pursues his or her policy preferences within constraints determined by the interdependent nature of decision making on the bench.

If one accepts the principles that justices care more about the content of the Court's opinion than the actual decision to vacate, reverse, or affirm the lower court's decision and that opinions crafted by the Court reflect justices' interaction with one another, then it seems reasonable to suspect that neither an understanding of the law nor the policy preferences of justices alone can account for their behavior. Instead, Court outcomes depend on a combination of the preferences held by the justices and the strategic moves of the justices in their efforts to ensure that the final opinion represents, as much as possible, their policy views. These postulates lead us to ask how and when the actions of each justice are constrained by the concurrent actions of his or her colleagues on the bench.

In subsequent chapters, we articulate and test a series of hypotheses consistent with the postulates that structure the collegial game on the Court. These hypotheses should help us determine to whom cases are likely to be assigned, the tactics justices are likely to pursue to shape majority opinions, the likely response of opinion authors to such bargaining, and the justices' final decisions to join majority opinions. Although the primary focus of this book is to demonstrate how the collegial nature of the Court influences justices' ability to pursue their policy preferences, we recognize that it is not the only constraint that shapes judicial behavior. Other contextual constraints, such as workload capacity and the Court's calendar, may affect the choices justices make. Because any explanation of behavior that ignores such relevant contextual constraints would be underspecified, it is important for us to recognize and control for such factors. Therefore, even though the purpose of this book is to explore how the Court's collegial character affects the development of the law, we also discuss several variables that do not emanate from the collegial game.

Explaining Justices' Choices

Our primary argument is that Supreme Court justices are strategic actors who pursue their policy preferences within the strategic constraints of a case and the Court. As our two postulates make clear, within constraints imposed by the collegial nature of the institution, justices attempt to secure legal rulings that comport as much as possible with their preferred outcomes. Two sets of hypotheses explicitly derive from our postulates, one pertaining to justices' preferences and the other relating to strategic constraints on choice.

Consistent with our first postulate, we expect a justice's policy preferences to guide the decisions he or she makes in a case. A justice's choices in a case depend on both the proximity of his or her policy views to the policy outcome preferred by the other justices and the overall level of policy agreement among the justices. For example, we expect a justice whose views clearly differ from the majority of the Court to be more willing to author a separate opinion and less willing simply to agree with the Court majority. Likewise, if an opinion draft is inconsistent with a justice's values, we also anticipate a strategic justice will aggressively pursue changes to the opinion.

Strategic justices take into consideration not only the proximity of their policy views to those of their brethren, but also the level of policy cohesion among the justices. The importance of a coalition's ideological heterogeneity is based on Axelrod's observation that "the less dispersion there is in the policy positions of the members of a coalition, the less conflict of interest there is" (1970, 169). When there is a great deal of conflict among the justices, each justice will understand that such disagreements will help shape the final opinion.

It is the importance of policy preferences that led Murphy to argue that the strategic justice's "initial step would be to examine the situation on the Court. In general three sets of conditions may obtain. There may be complete coincidence of interest with the other justices, or at least with the number of associates he feels is necessary to attain his aim. Second, the interests of the other justices, or a majority of them, may be indifferent to his objective. Third, the interests of his colleagues may be in opposition to his own" (1964, 37). A justice's ideological position relative to that of his colleagues and a justice's understanding of the ideological preferences of his or her colleagues relative to each other is thus the first factor likely to influence the decisions on any particular case before the bench. The notion that ideological compatibility affects justices' decisions is consistent with Axelrod's argument that "the amount of conflict of interest in a situation affects the behavior of the actors" (1970, 5).

Given the Court's institutional rules, our second postulate suggests that justices must take into consideration the preferences and choices of their colleagues deciding the same cases. The decisions made by each justice are therefore likely to vary with the positions and signals that are sent by the other justices. As previously discussed, Supreme Court decision making is interdependent because the costs or benefits any one justice receives from a particular decision depend in part on the choices made by the other justices. For example, the size of the winning coalition that exists at the initial conference on a case's merits affects the decisions each of the justices may subsequently make. Indeed, in a 5–4 case, the chief justice may be more reluctant to jeopardize the majority coalition by assigning the opinion to an extreme colleague than in a 7–2 case. Likewise, an opinion author's willingness to accommodate a colleague is likely to be greater in a 5–4 case than a 7–2 case. As observed by Chief Justice William Rehnquist:

> The willingness to accommodate on the part of the author of the opinion is directly proportional to the number of votes supporting the majority result at conference; if there were only five justices at conference voting to affirm the decision of the lower court, and one of those five wishes significant changes to be made in the draft, the opinion writer is under considerable pressure to work out something that will satisfy the critic. (1987, 302)

In both scenarios, the fragility of the minimum winning coalition will affect the justices' calculations.

Of course, tentative votes cast at initial conferences are only one of many ways that justices signal their brethren. Throughout the opinion-writing process, justices circulate memos announcing their willingness or reluctance to accept a particular opinion draft or their intention to circulate dissenting or concurring opinions. Because opinion authors lack perfect information about each justice's preferred position, such signals sent between the justices are critical to the process of forming the final majority opinion and its supporting coalition (see Austen-Smith and Riker 1987; Crawford and Sobel 1982). For example, once a majority of justices has announced its support for an opinion, the author learns that there is little to be gained by further attempts at accommodation. For this reason, Justice Powell (1984a, 18) argued: "A Justice is in the strongest position to influence changes in an opinion before other justices have joined it. Once an opinion is supported by a 'Court' (a 'majority'), it is virtually impossible to negotiate a change."

Strategic justices recognize another form of interdependency of choice – the nature of the cooperative relationship between pairs of justices. Because justices are engaged in long-term relationships with their colleagues, over time justices presumably learn to cooperate and engage in reciprocity, rewarding those who have cooperated with them in the past and punishing others (E. Schwartz 1996; see also Axelrod 1984). Thus, the extent of past cooperation between sets of justices results in a specific strategic context likely to affect those justices' decisions in a case. For example, if Justice X regularly accommodates Justice Y, Justice Y might realize that there is no reason to antagonize a regular ally by not accommodating Justice X. Alternatively, justices may punish colleagues who have previously been uncooperative with them. According to Segal and Spaeth, for instance, Justice Sandra Day O'Connor's difficulty in forming majority opinion coalitions (as seen by the frequency with which she authored plurality opinions) occurred in part because of her unwillingness to suppress her concurring opinions, which "may have exacerbated the intransigence of those who specially concurred when she was assigned the opinion of the Court" (Segal and Spaeth 1993, 294–295).

Even though we are principally concerned with exploring the strategic nature of Supreme Court decision making, contextual factors independent of other justices' preferences or choices may shape the choices a justice makes. Judicial scholars often suggest that contextual factors, such as experience, case importance, or workload, may affect justices' choices (see Murphy 1964; Maltzman and Wahlbeck 1996a; Wahlbeck, Spriggs, and Maltzman 1999; Baum 1997; McGuire 1993a, 1993b; Hagle 1993). While these factors do not explicitly derive from the two postulates that are the basis of the collegial game, we include them in our analyses because they allow us to examine competing explanations for the justices' decisions. By pitting alternative explanations against those that are derived from the collegial game, the reader's confidence in the support we find for the collegial game should be enhanced (Green and Shapiro 1994, 37). The contextual hypotheses we include have been selected because they have strong intuitive appeal and a long tradition in the literature on judicial politics. Thus, these constraints can and do provide interesting and worthwhile information about how Supreme Court justices decide cases.

Although these constraints are "nonstrategic," this does not mean that they are "nonrational." A justice who has multiple goals (Baum 1997) and limited time and resources could easily make a rational calculation to take what we label as a "contextual" variable into account. What distinguishes our contextual hypotheses from those we portray as stemming from a model of strategic interaction is that they do not tap the heart of strategic interdependency – that one justice's choice depends on the choices of other justices. We examine four types of contextual features: the importance of a case, the complexity of a case, the institutional position of a justice, and the competing time pressures justices encounter.

The first contextual factor suggests that judicial choices depend on the importance of the issue or case at hand. As Murphy (1964, 37) recognized, justices are occasionally indifferent to the wording of the legal rule. We expect justices to be more concerned about the content of an opinion dealing with important issues and having widespread consequences (see Epstein and Knight 1995; Spaeth and Segal 1999). Anecdotal evidence of just these sorts of calculations abounds. For example, a 1971 memo from Chief Justice Warren Burger to Justice Hugo Black about Black's opinion in *Astrup v. Immigration and Naturalization Service* (1971) illustrates the trade-offs justices are willing to make. Even though Burger disagreed with Black, Burger perceived that the potential benefit of writing separately was not worth the costs: "I do not really agree but the case is narrow and unimportant except to this one man," noted Burger, ". . . I will join up with you in spite of my reservations" (Burger 1971a). A memo Justice Sandra Day O'Connor circulated in *Roberts v. United States Jaycees* (1984) also highlights such variance in case salience: "I continue to have some concerns in this case because of its implications in so many future cases" (O'Connor 1984a). Because justices have limited resources and time, their choices will vary as a function of the importance or salience of any given case.

A second contextual factor, the difficulty of the case, also varies by case. Although some court opinions are straightforward, others involve multiple and unusual issues. These cases are more complex and may lead to different patterns of behavior among the justices. The effect of case complexity is illustrated by Justice John Paul Stevens's response to Chief Justice William Rehnquist's proposal to assign majority opinions to those justices who were "current" in their work. Stevens claimed that if the Rehnquist proposal was implemented and "[i]f I am assigned three opinions, one of them requiring a study of the record and considerable research and two that can be written on the basis of little more than a careful review of the briefs, which should I work on first? To get my fair share of assignments, I should probably do the . . . [easy] cases right away and save the hard one until my desk is clear" (Stevens 1989). Stevens's memo demonstrates that some cases are harder than others and that this may influence his work habits.

A third contextual factor results from a justice's institutional position on the Court. Here, leadership positions are paramount. As head of the Court, a chief justice may feel greater pressure than his colleagues to protect and enhance the Court's reputation by producing unanimous opinions, suppressing conflict, and otherwise facilitating harmony on the Court (Brenner and Hagle 1996; Ulmer 1986; Danelski 1968). Likewise, the chief justice may feel a greater sense of responsibility than the senior associate justice to ensure that opinions are distributed in an equitable fashion (Johnstone 1992).

Another dimension to justices' institutional position is their experience and skills, which depend on the amount of time they have spent on the bench and the experience gained during prior service. With regard to the former, the process of new justices assimilating to the Court may affect their decisions in a case. Scholars often suggest that a justice's institutional position as a "freshman" matters in that new justices require a few years to acquire experience and become comfortable in their new setting (Brenner and Hagle 1996; Hagle 1993; Howard 1968; Wood et al. 1998). This process of adjustment may, for example, lead justices to adopt a "following rather than a leading" (Howard 1968, 45–46) approach and thus avoid conflict, vote more moderately, or exhibit somewhat unstable voting patterns (Howard 1968; Snyder 1958; Ulmer 1959; Walker et al. 1988). If, for example, a new person (Justice Z) joins the bench, other justices (such as Justices X and Y) may try to secure the support of Justice Z by joining her opinions when she is the author. As Murphy explains, "When a new justice comes to the Court, an older colleague might try to charm his junior brother" (1964, 49). With regard to the latter, a justice's substantive expertise in an area of the law is likely to affect his or her decisions (Brenner and Spaeth 1986). If, for instance, a justice has substantive expertise in the area dealt with by a case, then it is more likely such a justice will be unwilling to defer to other justices' positions in the case.[12] In short, the institutional position of the chief as the leader of the Court, a freshman as a new member, and policy experts are likely to affect the choices they and other justices are likely to make in a case.

Fourth, justices' choices will be affected in part by the competing time pres-

---

[12] Because experts have the capacity to inform their less knowledgeable colleagues, specialization is frequently seen as a solution to problems of uncertainty (Gilligan and Krehbiel 1989, 1990; Krehbiel 1991). Kingdon (1981) notes that members of Congress recognize that their colleagues specialize and that these specialists provide important voting cues.

sures they encounter. Time pressures result from two sources, the workload of a justice and the amount of time left in the term to complete that work. For example, if an opinion is crafted late in the Court's term, a justice's ability to pursue changes to the opinion is limited by time pressures that would not have existed at the outset of the term. Justice Ginsburg, for example, wrote that: "some judges are more prone to indulge their individuality than others, but all operate under one intensely practical constraint: time" (1990, 142).

Likewise, workload considerations may encourage justices to concentrate on one opinion rather than another. A letter from Justice Black to Justice Brennan illustrates the weight of workload in shaping justices' decisions: "I voted to reverse these cases and uphold the ICC's action. . . . I have decided to acquiesce in your opinion and judgment unless someone else decides to write in opposition" (Black 1970). Black was willing to dissent only if someone else would incur the costs of writing an opinion. These types of contextual factors, shaped by the Court's calendar and the justices' workload, are thus likely to alter the costs a justice incurs in pursuing a particular tactic on the bench.

The influence of time pressures takes on added significance when one recognizes that bargaining outcomes depend in part on the cost associated with delay (Baron and Ferejohn 1989). When the costs associated with delay are steep, the individual who controls the agenda has more power (see Rubinstein 1982; Binmore 1986). In the opinion-writing process, the opinion author controls the agenda. The costs of delay are shaped in large part by the amount of time available for negotiation. In the context of the Court's term, time available is shaped by the Court's calendar. Toward the end of the Court's term, the opinion author is less likely to accommodate colleagues' signals, as he or she is advantaged by the Court clock. As the Court approaches its traditional July 1 recess, the incentive for the author to accommodate his or her colleagues diminishes rapidly.

Each of these factors varies across the cases that justices place on their docket and across the justices in particular cases. Thus, to varying degrees they affect the choices made by the justices in assigning majority opinions, in responding to opinions that have been drafted and circulated, in accommodating the preferences of their colleagues on the bench, and in joining opinions. Most importantly, ideological relationships, coalition size, signals sent by the justices, and contextual factors themselves vary within the time frame of deciding a particular case. None of these forces are necessarily fixed throughout the writing of the Court's opinion. This means, of course, that justices must constantly reevaluate their options as Court opinions are drafted and polished. In other words, strategic interaction is dynamic and complex. Yet, as we hope to show in this book, justices' choices follow predictable and testable patterns for us to observe and explain.

EMPIRICAL TESTS

Journalistic and historical accounts of Supreme Court decision making have occasionally provided empirical support for a strategic conception of the Court (Woodward and Armstrong 1979; Biskupic 1995; B. Schwartz 1985, 1988, 1996). But few systematic studies have explored the patterns underlying such interdependent behavior. Scholars such as Murphy (1964) attempted to examine claims that justices act strategically, but they have generally relied upon case studies whose generalizability is questionable (see Epstein and Knight 1995).[13] Recently, Epstein and Knight (1998) have furthered our understanding of strategic interaction by documenting the patterns of such interdependent behavior. In particular, they persuasively demonstrate that justices' overriding goal in deciding cases is securing opinions that as closely as possible resemble their policy preferences.

No one has yet, however, systematically tested a multivariate model of strategic interaction. In other words, social scientists possess little theoretical or empirical understanding of the factors affecting whether, when, and to what extent justices decide to bargain, negotiate, or compromise in the process of writing opinions. Epstein and Knight, whose book is among the recent works exploring strategic behavior by justices, "encourage researchers to pick up where we have left off and invoke the strategic account to understand the choices justices make: to accommodate the concerns of other justices in majority opinions, to bargain . . . , to engage in persuasion, and, yes, to vote in a particular way" (1998, 185).

The fundamental barrier to studies of the opinion-writing process has been the lack of data (Epstein et al. 1994, 1), forcing scholars to rely largely upon stylized case studies rather than more systematic evidence. Indeed, those

---

[13] One notable exception is Perry (1991, chap. 6), who interviewed justices and their clerks to establish that, although bargaining and negotiating are rare on certiorari decisions, they occur during the opinion-writing process.

scholars who more systematically analyze the Court's decision-making process have tended to limit their focus to areas with more readily available data: namely, the final votes in cases (Rohde and Spaeth 1976; Segal 1984; George and Epstein 1992). To test our model of strategic interaction, we rely on three sources of original data from the private papers of Supreme Court justices: assignment sheets, docket sheets, and circulation records. To determine which justice was assigned to write the majority opinion, we use the assignments sheets that the chief justice circulates and are contained in the papers donated by Justices William Brennan and Thurgood Marshall to the Library of Congress. These sheets indicate who assigned the opinion and to whom and when the opinion was assigned.

To explain when and how justices attempt to influence the majority opinion author and how willing majority opinion authors are to accommodate their colleagues, we use the documentary history of each case during the Burger Court, relying on the detailed circulation records maintained by Justice Brennan.[14] These records list all majority opinion drafts, non-majority-opinion drafts, and letters and memoranda written by every member of the Court and circulated to the conference.[15] Because the strategic moves a justice is likely to make vary along with the tentative votes cast at the initial conference on a case's merits, we use also Justice Brennan's docket sheets to determine the makeup of the initial coalition.

Finally, we also rely on the judicial databases that Spaeth (1994) and Gibson (1997) have assembled and freely share with scholars through the Inter-University Consortium for Political and Social Research. These data provide valuable information about the types of cases before the court, the parties involved in each case, and final outcomes. By combining these data with the

[14] After circulating an opinion draft, the author commonly receives replies regarding the draft from other justices on the Court. Court custom is for a justice to make suggestions or threats, or to announce positions taken to the writer in a letter (Rehnquist 1987, 302). Since the Burger Court, justices exchange their views almost exclusively in writing (B. Schwartz 1996, 7). A copy of these letters is usually sent to the entire conference and thus included in Brennan's circulation records. Both Brennan's docket and circulation records are available in the Manuscript Division of the Library of Congress, Washington, D.C.

[15] As Epstein and Knight (1995, 29–30) note, scholars cannot obtain all private memoranda that may have been circulated between two justices but not sent to the entire conference. These memos are excluded from our analysis, as Brennan's circulation records do not consistently record them prior to the 1982 term. We should also note that when Brennan's circulation records do record these private memoranda, only those written by or sent to Brennan are listed. Although including private memoranda would obviously introduce substantial bias because they are only recorded for Brennan, it is important to note that excluding such memoranda has the possible effect of underestimating the amount of strategic action that occurs.

original data we collected, a better understanding of the opinion-writing process can be gleaned.

Our task is to use these data to explain systematically the internal dynamics of Supreme Court decision making. Only by delving into the justices' original records, we maintain, can we truly show the power of the strategic model to account for the political dynamics of the opinion-writing process. By relying on data that span throughout the entire Burger Court, we are able to demonstrate that the hypotheses we articulate are generalizable beyond a single case or even a single term. Of course, although the papers of the justices provide us a means of understanding intra-Court dynamics, we are highly dependent on the reliability of the data. In Appendix 1, we confirm the accuracy of these data sources. The conclusions we draw from our empirical tests, we argue, are based on what we believe to be the most reliable and comprehensive record of Supreme Court decision making yet to be uncovered and mined.

OUTLINE OF THE BOOK

Although the actions of the Court are a collective enterprise of all the justices, there is little doubt that majority opinion authors tend to have disproportionate influence over the shape of final opinions. Thus, to understand how opinions are crafted requires us to explore first the politics of opinion assignment. In Chapter 2 we look at the criteria used by either the chief justice or the most senior associate justice in the majority to select a justice to author the majority opinion.

In Chapters 3 through 5 we turn our analytical focus to the interchange and bargaining that occur among the justices. In Chapters 3 and 4 we investigate the tactics that justices pursue to shape the Court's majority opinion. Chapter 3 explains how justices try to shape the opinions drafted by their colleagues, while Chapter 4 explores the response of the majority opinion author to such tactics. In Chapter 5 we examine how the process of writing the majority opinion affects the formation of the final majority coalition. In Chapter 6 we review our findings and discuss their implications for Court decision making.

Finally, two caveats are in order about our claims for the power of a strategic interaction model. First, in crafting the model, we seek to explain only a portion of the many factors likely to shape final Court opinions. Although we believe that almost every decision a justice makes is shaped in part by what we broadly term the collegial game, we are not so naive to believe that this perspective can account for every action of every justice. Inevitably, justices have numerous goals, only one of which is at the heart of a model of strategic interaction – securing their policy preferences. Moreover, we do not doubt that justices' decisions on the bench may sometimes reflect concerns other than those embraced by our explicitly strategic perspective. A justice's understanding of the law, strategic concerns that stem from factors exogenous to the bench, and even random or idiosyncratic events are likely to shape judicial behavior. Still, we hope to show that after controlling for many of these "nonstrategic" influences, our model of strategic interaction robustly explains a wide range of choices made by justices of the Supreme Court.

Second, we test our model by applying it only to the few stages of the judicial process that affect the content of final opinions. Although our results are generalizable for these stages, we neglect many other important aspects of the judicial process. For example, we do not systematically test whether the decision to grant certiorari or even the initial vote a justice casts on a case's merits stem from strategic considerations. We make no claims about the generalizability of our model to these other areas of judicial interaction, but we suspect that strategic considerations permeate these choices as well (see Epstein and Knight 1998). Application of our strategic model to other stages of the judicial process, other courts, and other times we leave to the future.

2

Selecting an Author: Assigning the Majority Opinion

On December 17, 1971, Chief Justice Warren Burger assigned the majority opinion in *Roe v. Wade* (1973) to Justice Harry Blackmun. Justice William Douglas immediately lodged a protest to this assignment in a memo to the chief justice on December 18. Douglas's principal complaint was that the chief justice assigned the majority opinion despite being a member of the minority coalition in the Court's conference discussion of *Roe*. What is more, according to Justice Douglas, the assigned author was also a member of the three-justice conference minority. Douglas concluded that "to save future time and trouble, one of the four, rather than one of the three, should write the opinion" (Douglas 1971).[1] Chief Justice Burger disputed Douglas's account of the conference discussion. He responded to Douglas in a memo by stating: "At the close of discussion of this case, I remarked to the Conference that there were, literally, not enough columns to mark up an accurate reflection of the voting in either the Georgia or the Texas cases. I therefore marked down no votes and said this was a case that would have to stand or fall on the writing, when it was done" (Burger 1971b).

When the Court later chose to set *Roe v. Wade* for reargument the following term, Justice Douglas took the unusual step of drafting an opinion to dissent from that decision.[2] Although this opinion was never published, Douglas

---

[1] Seven justices participated in the consideration of *Roe v. Wade* during the 1971 term. At the time of oral arguments, there were two vacancies that were eventually filled by Justices Powell and Rehnquist.

[2] Chief Justice Burger had pushed for the case to be held over until a complete Court with nine justices could consider the issue. Justice William Douglas (1972a) argued that Burger's move was a strategic choice to influence the legal outcome: "The plea that the cases be reargued is merely another strategy by a minority to somehow suppress the majority view with the hope that exigencies of time will change the result. That might be achieved of course by death or conceivably retirement. But that kind of strategy dilutes the integrity of the Court." During

circulated it privately to Justice Brennan. Justice Douglas used this outlet to denounce Burger's use of the assignment process to further his own policy goals. Douglas thought that Blackmun, then seen as a Court conservative, would favor an opinion that would at best articulate a narrow statement of a woman's right to abortion. Douglas asserted:

The Chief Justice represented the minority view in the Conference and forcefully urged his viewpoint on the issues. It was a seven-man Court that heard these cases and voted on them. Out of that seven there were four who initially took a majority view. Hence traditionally the senior Justice in the majority – who in this case was not myself – should have made the assignment of the opinion. For the tradition is a longstanding one that the senior Justice in the majority makes the assignment. The cases were, however, assigned by The Chief Justice. . . .

Perhaps the purpose of the minority in the *Abortion Cases* is to try to keep control of the merits. (Douglas 1972a)[3]

Not all justices see opinion assignments as a strategic instrument through which Court outcomes can be influenced. Chief Justice William Rehnquist's stated criteria for assignment stand in contrast to Justice Douglas's portrait of Burger's criteria in *Roe*. On November 24, 1989, Chief Justice Rehnquist circulated a memo to the conference forewarning his brethren that he was changing the criteria used to assign majority opinions. Rather than trying to distribute majority opinion assignments equally, Rehnquist explained that opinion assignments would now be made "to avoid the annual 'June Crunch,'" at which time so much of our work piles up" (Rehnquist 1989). Rehnquist was explicit about his plans:

One step we can take, I think, is to try to get as much of our work as possible done before late spring. During the past three terms, the principal rule I have followed in assigning opinions is to give everyone approximately the same number of assignments of opinions for the Court during any one term. But this policy does not take into consideration the difficulty of the opinion assigned or the amount of work that the "assignee" may currently have backed up in his chambers. . . . it only makes sense in the

---

the next term, one of the two new Nixon appointees, Justice Powell, cast a pro-choice vote and Justice Blackmun wrote a broad statement of a woman's right to have an abortion.

3   One might question Douglas's claim in this passage that he was not the senior associate justice who was entitled to make the assignment. After all, he was the senior justice of those voting to affirm the lower court's decision. Douglas explained: "The reason that Bill Brennan, not I, represented the consensus at the first Conference on the Abortion Cases was that I thought at the time that the cases – at least Georgia's – could be disposed of on Equal Protection grounds – a theory that did not hold up on further study" (Douglas 1972b).

assignment of additional work to give some preference to those who are "current" with respect to past work. (Rehnquist 1989)

Rehnquist's memo suggests the importance of contextual factors in shaping his opinion assignments. Importantly, it does *not* suggest he used his power of assignment to further his own policy goals. Rehnquist claims instead to have made assignments to ensure the smooth operation of the Court. In other words, Rehnquist's memo lends credence to the influence of nonpolicy factors (what in this book we generally refer to as contextual variables) on his decisions. It does not support the outcome or collective decision-making postulates articulated in Chapter 1. Rehnquist, that is, does not suggest that opinion assignments result from the desire to produce opinions that resemble his policy preferences (the Outcome Postulate) or the necessity of basing decisions on the choices of other justices (the Collective Decision-Making Postulate). In contrast, Rehnquist claims that his assignments were likely to be shaped by the difficulty of each case and each justice's capacity to complete his or her work in a timely manner, rather than the policy preferences of each justice. If such contextual factors determine the chief's assignments, such a justice would not be playing the collegial game.

Rehnquist and Douglas thus suggest two different explanations for opinion assignments. Are assignments made to advance the assignor's policy objectives? Or are assignors constrained in the pursuit of policy goals by, for example, the Court's need to complete its work in a timely, equitable, and expert manner? If assignors understand the collegial game, we expect them to systematically adopt an approach to opinion assignments that takes into account the likely influence of an assignment on the ultimate legal ruling in a case. According to the collegial game, the assignor's policy preferences and the strategic environment will influence to whom an opinion is assigned. To test this idea adequately, we need to control for contextual factors that are likely to influence opinion assignments too. As the Court's taskmaster, the chief, for example, faces constraints not operating on other justices, such as the equitable distribution of opinions.

Recall from Chapter 1 that one of the Court's informal institutional rules states that the chief justice assigns the opinion when voting with the majority at conference. If, however, the chief does not vote with the majority, then the most senior member of the majority assigns the opinion. In addition to modeling the chief's assignments, this chapter examines the assignments made by associate justices. Although we show that associate justices, like chief justices, pursue their policy preferences by assigning opinions to more ideologically proximate justices, we also contend that they are less constrained by contextual forces. Strategic factors, such as the size of the majority coalition in conference, can affect all assignors, but only the chief seems likely to be constrained by contextual factors such as workload, equity, and expertise. Although pursuing the collegial game, the chief still shoulders institutional demands in his role as the Court's "task leader" (see Danelski 1968, 1986).

ASSIGNING THE COURT'S OPINION

The chief justice is the dominant figure in the opinion assignment process because he assigns the vast majority of Court opinions. The assignment sheets circulated by Chief Justice Burger (and discussed in Chapter 1) reveal that he assigned 85.9 percent of the majority opinions during his tenure on the Court. Table 2.1 reports the number of opinions assigned by every justice who made an assignment during the 1969–1985 terms of the Court. In comparison to the chief justice, we see that associate justices made relatively few assignments. The justice with the second highest assignment total was William Brennan, whose 182 assignments trail far behind the chief's. Although this dominance in opinion assignment may occur because Burger became part of the dominant ideological coalition on the Court, as Douglas's draft dissent in *Roe v. Wade* (1973) makes clear, even chief justices who are ideologically in the minority may control the assignment process by voting in a sophisticated fashion. For example, Epstein and Knight's (1998, 129) analysis of Justice Brennan's and Justice Powell's conference notes suggests that, in spite of the norm that the chief justice casts the first vote in conference, during the 1983 term Chief Justice Burger "cast more pass votes during conference than any other justice" (cf. Maltzman and Wahlbeck 1996a, 589). Inevitably, one reason Burger is likely to have deferred his vote was to see what position would prevail so he might cast a vote that would allow him to assign the majority opinion.

In spite of his dominant part in opinion assignment, the chief justice's administrative role is sometimes characterized as virtually powerless. Indeed, as Justice Rehnquist noted before he was elevated to chief, the chief justice "presides over a conference not of eight subordinates, whom he may direct or instruct, but of eight associates who, like him, have tenure during good behav-

Table 2.1. *Opinion Assignors on the Burger Court*

Assigning Justice	Number of Assignments	Percentage of all Assignments
Chief Justice Warren Burger	1,891	85.9
Justice William Brennan	182	8.3
Justice William Douglas	68	3.1
Justice Potter Stewart	22	1.0
Justice Hugo Black	21	1.0
Justice Byron White	13	.6
Justice John Harlan	2	.1
Justice Thurgood Marshall	2	.1
Total	2,201	100.1

ior, and who are as independent as hogs on ice" (Rehnquist 1976, 637). This view, however, overlooks the important strategic value of opinion assignment as a form of agenda setting. Normally, Court scholars focus the discussion of agenda setting on the Court's vote on whether to place a case on its docket (see Caldeira and Wright 1988). Yet, because any individual case raises numerous issues that can potentially be addressed in an opinion (Murphy 1964, 85–87; Wenzel 1994; McGuire and Palmer 1995), agenda setting occurs in at least two other decision-making stages: the assignment of the majority opinion and the writing of that opinion.

The power of agenda setting should not be underestimated. Numerous scholars have, of course, recognized that outcomes are determined in part by the order in which alternatives are considered (see Riker 1982, 1986). For instance, Shepsle and Weingast (1987) suggest that congressional committees are able to control legislative outcomes due to their control over the final proposal, the conference report. Hammond (1986, 385) maintains that the agenda setter in bureaucracies may be the official who occupies the position given responsibility for recommending a policy position from among a set in a multidimensional space. So, too, should we expect the author of a majority opinion to exercise substantial agenda-setting powers. First, opinion authors have the opportunity to put issues on the agenda that otherwise might have been ignored. Second, because it is customary for the first draft of a majority opinion to be circulated prior to concurrences and dissents, the majority opinion author can frequently secure commitments from his or her colleagues prior to the circulation of any competing opinions. As we will see in the next chapter, justices frequently join the first draft of the majority opinion. Although these justices are entitled to change their vote at any stage prior to the release of the Court's opinion, justices who regularly change their vote after committing to an earlier draft would incur reputation costs that might undermine their leverage in future cases.

Third, the assigned author's proposals are even more potent in the face of the obstacles associated with developing policy alternatives. To propose an alternative to supplant the one circulated by the assigned author, a justice must draft a separate opinion. Drafting separate opinions, moreover, requires an investment of time and energy by an opinion author, and they are therefore costly. To be sure, justices can take other actions to modify the assigned author's opinion, such as making suggestions for changes in an opinion. Still, these are not designed to be competing policy alternatives but rather are intended to make the existing opinion draft more acceptable to the individual justice. Of course, justices do circulate separate opinions, and occasionally one of these competing opinions gains enough support to become the Court's opinion. But that is rare, occurring on average only three times each term during the Burger Court.

The power of opinion assignment as agenda setting is seen in the *Pennsylvania v. Muniz* (1990) case discussed in Chapter 1. Because Chief Justice Rehnquist supported the conference minority on some issues raised in the case, Justice Brennan was the senior justice in the majority. He assigned himself the opinion, taking the opportunity to draft a proposed opinion that conformed most closely to his policy objectives. In fact, he wrote a cover letter that accompanied his first draft, stating that among the conference majority "there was some disagreement as to the proper disposition of the case based on these conclusions. Although I originally voted to affirm the judgment of the state court, I now believe that the proper disposition of the case, given our conclusions, is to vacate the judgment and remand for further proceedings. Accordingly, I have styled the draft opinion in this manner" (Brennan 1990e). This opinion, with its narrow view of a routine booking question exception to *Miranda*, represented the opening proposal in the case. Ultimately, Justice O'Connor forced Brennan to alter his opinion or face the loss of her support, but, by exercising the agenda-setting prerogative, he discouraged Court conservatives from proposing a policy alternative that would have carved out a broad exception to the *Miranda* rules.

If the justice assigned the majority opinion has an agenda-setting advantage, we would expect assignors to take advantage of the opportunity to assign opinions to justices ideologically closer to them. In this way, the policy proposal contained in the opinion draft would be more likely to approximate the assignor's preferences. Indeed, political scientists have characterized the chief's opinion assignments as motivated by the chief's personal attitudes and policy preferences (Segal and Spaeth 1993). This is not to say that the chief is entirely free to make assignments to ideological allies. Rather, chief justices are said to assign opinions to advance their policy objectives, while at the same time being constrained by the needs of the Court as an organization (Baum 1985, 150; Maltzman and Wahlbeck 1996b; Rehnquist 1987; Wood et al. forthcoming). Nevertheless, empirical research on the chief justice's assignment decisions has not definitively established the extent to which assignors are constrained by either strategic or contextual forces. Indeed, what scholars have discovered is that in some cases the chief's assignments appear to be designed to further his policy objectives, while in other cases assignments reflect concerns about the smooth operation of the Court (Slotnick 1978, 1979a; Segal and Spaeth 1993; Davis 1990; B. Schwartz 1996; Steamer 1986; Maltzman and Wahlbeck 1996b). Moreover, no published research provides a systematic explanation, or even presents descriptive data, of the underlying determinants of associate justice assignments. If justices are as sophisticated as the collegial game suggests, then opinion assignors' assignment of cases should systematically vary along with the strategic setting, even after controlling for contextual factors, such as case salience, the institutional position of the assigning justice, and time pressures that are likely to influence assignment decisions.

EXPLAINING ASSIGNMENT DECISIONS

If our model of strategic interaction characterizes the opinion assignment process, we expect the chief justice to pursue his policy preferences within the constraints imposed by his colleagues. Returning to the model presented in Chapter 1, the first factor affecting assignments pertains to the chief's efforts to secure policy outcomes consistent with his preferences. Given the disproportionate influence that the opinion writer has in shaping the tenor and scope of the final opinion, we expect that the chief justice will assign majority opinions to those who are ideologically proximate to himself (Murphy 1964; Rohde 1972a; Rohde and Spaeth 1976; Segal and Spaeth 1993; Ulmer 1970a). Such a justice would be most likely to write an opinion that reflects the legal rules preferred by the chief. Consistent with this expectation is our first hypothesis:

> *Opinion Distance Hypothesis:* The chief justice is more likely to assign cases to associates who are ideologically proximate to himself.

Although we expect the chief to favor his ideological allies, a chief justice playing the collegial game would recognize that a strategically proper move involves assigning opinions to ideological moderates when the majority coalition is a minimum winning coalition (Ulmer 1960, 643–644). By assigning a case with a fragile majority to a more moderate justice, the chief justice may discourage justices from defecting and thus preserve his preferred outcome (Danelski 1968; McLauchlan 1972; Murphy 1964; Ulmer 1970a; Rohde 1972a; Rohde and Spaeth 1976; but see Brenner 1982; Brenner and Spaeth 1988a; Rathjen 1974).[4] Whether the chief selects the colleague who is likely to write an opinion consistent with his policy preferences depends on the size of the conference majority in a case. Taking into account the size of the majority coalition at conference is consistent with the second postulate discussed in Chapter 1, which suggested that justices' choices are shaped in part by the choices of their colleagues on the bench. Thus, because Chief Justice Burger occupied a position close to an ideological pole,[5] we expect to see the following hypothesis:

> *Majority Coalition Size Hypothesis:* The chief justice is more likely to assign a case to a justice who is less ideologically proximate, the smaller the initial conference majority.

As discussed in Chapter 1, contextual variables that are independent of the collegial game may affect justices' choices. One important contextual feature of a case is its salience. Chief justices certainly recognize that some cases are more important than others. Rehnquist admitted as much when he described his experience as an associate justice: "My law clerks were always in high

---

[4] This strategy may not work. Brenner and Spaeth (1988a) discovered that during the Warren Court a marginal justice of a minimum winning coalition was no more likely than any other member of the coalition to maintain the original coalition.

[5] Of the justices who served on the Burger Court, only William Rehnquist was more consistently conservative than Burger between the 1969 and 1985 terms. Burger supported the conservative position in 65.6 percent of all cases. This is calculated from Spaeth (1998) by examining each case (with case citation as the unit of analysis) that was fully argued with a signed or per curiam opinion, including judgments of the Court.

hopes that one of the cases . . . [they] regarded as very important would be assigned to me" (Rehnquist 1987, 296). If the chief justice cares about policy outcomes, we expect him to be particularly anxious to assign salient cases to justices who are ideologically proximate (Ulmer 1970a; Rohde 1972a; Slotnick 1979a). Of course, the concept of salience is somewhat ambiguous. Some cases have political overtones that make them particularly salient. Other cases may have a significant subsequent impact on the development of the law but will not necessarily be politically salient. For this reason, Cook (1993) and Brenner (1998) argue that case importance operates on both a political and a legal dimension. Thus, we hypothesize the following:

> *Case Importance Hypothesis 1a:* The chief justice is more likely to assign politically salient cases to associates who are ideologically proximate.

> *Case Importance Hypothesis 1b:* The chief justice is more likely to assign legally salient cases to associates who are ideologically proximate.

Of course, the chief justice can improve the probability that the final opinion will be consistent with his policy preferences by self-assigning cases. Cognizant of the disruption that would occur if the chief assigned every opinion to himself, the chief is particularly likely to self-assign opinions for important cases (Rohde 1972a; Slotnick 1978, 1979a; Davis 1990; Brenner 1982, 1993). Thus, we advance two additional hypotheses:

> *Case Importance Hypothesis 2a:* The chief justice is more likely to assign politically salient cases to himself.

> *Case Importance Hypothesis 2b:* The chief justice is more likely to assign legally salient cases to himself

To protect his relationship with other justices, to promote Court harmony, and to facilitate Court efficiency, the chief inevitably feels constrained to equalize workload across the justices too (Baum 1997; Maltzman and Wahlbeck 1996b; Rehnquist 1987; Spaeth 1984; Slotnick 1979b). Segal and Spaeth (1993, 271) refer to this constraint when they argue that "within the goal of equality of assignment, assignors are free" to make any assignment decision. Chief justices themselves have repeatedly recognized the importance of equalizing the Court's workload. Chief Justice Rehnquist, for instance, claims that he tries "to be as evenhanded as possible as far as numbers of cases assigned to each justice" (1987, 297). Because associate justice assignments are traditionally sent to the chief prior to the chief making his assignments, the chief is likely to take into consideration the number of assignments a justice receives from associate justices during a round of assignments.[6] A memo from Chief Justice Burger (1977) illustrates this idea: "Just as I was about to send the current assignments out, I received Bill Brennan's assignment of cases. This requires me to do a total and complete revision." If the chief is indeed concerned with maintaining his relationship with his colleagues (and in promoting Court collegiality) by ensuring an equitable distribution of the majority opinion assignments, we expect to find the following:

> *Equity Hypothesis:* The chief is less likely to assign cases to justices who, in the current assignment round, have already received assignments from associate justices.

In addition to taking into account the importance of a case and the distribution of opinions across justices, each justice's institutional position is another contextual factor that may influence assignment decisions. Of course, not every justice plays the same role on the Court. Some justices inevitably stake out positions as experts in certain areas of the law. A chief justice likely considers each justice's expertise when assigning cases. Obviously, Justice Marshall (the former counsel for the National Association for the Advancement of Colored People) would have been more grateful if he was given an important civil rights opinion to write than if he was assigned a case involving state-federal relations. In addition to fostering the goodwill of his brethren, a chief who takes his role as the Court's taskmaster seriously may want the Court's opinion written by an expert. By assigning cases to those justices with the relevant substantive expertise, the chief is able to encourage specialization, reduce the research time that the opinion writer needs, and possibly improve the quality of the Court's opinion (Brenner 1984, 1985; Brenner and Spaeth 1986; Brenner and Palmer 1988; Epstein and Knight 1998, 127).[7] Thus,

> *Expertise Hypothesis:* The chief is more likely to assign cases to justices who have substantive expertise in the type of case under consideration.

---

[6] The chief justice assigns opinions by circulating an opinion assignment sheet (approximately every month) after the conclusion of the two-week oral argument session. Burger included associate justice assignments on the same sheet. Thus, the chief usually has access to associate justice assignments prior to circulating his assignment of cases.

[7] Epstein and Knight speculate that assigning opinions to experts is strategically proper because such opinions are likely to be of a higher quality and thus have "a greater chance of being accepted and respected by the external community" (1998, 127).

A second institutional position that may affect the likelihood of gaining assignments is a justice's length of service on the Court. A number of scholars have suggested that new justices on the Court may be assigned relatively easy cases as part of the process of assimilating to their new position. This transition period might be necessary to allow time to acquire experience and become comfortable in their new setting (Brenner and Hagle 1996; Hagle 1993; Howard 1968; Wood et al. 1998). This leads us to expect:

Freshman Hypothesis: Newcomers to the Court will be less likely to be assigned complex cases.

Competing time pressures represent another set of contextual characteristics. One of the most important of these constraints is the Court's workload. By assigning cases to those who currently have lighter workloads, the chief enhances the number of cases the Court can handle and reduces the time pressures that occur toward the end of a term. For this reason, Brenner and Palmer (1988) suggest that the chief's assignments are determined in part by each justice's ability to complete the cases that have been assigned to him or her. Thus, we expect:

Workload Hypothesis: The chief is more likely to assign cases to justices who currently have lighter workloads relative to their colleagues.

The Court's traditional recess at the beginning of July may affect each justice's workload and thus opinion assignments. As a result of this adjournment date, a "June crunch" develops as the Court tries to finish work on the cases on its docket (McGuire and Palmer 1995; Rehnquist 1989). As the Court's taskmaster, the chief attempts to ensure the timely completion of the Court's agenda before the Court's summer recess. Characteristic of the chief's taskmaster role is a memo that Chief Justice Burger circulated to the conference on May 10, 1983, reminding the conference that "This is the time of the year when we remind ourselves of the May 31 'target date' to have all assigned opinions in circulation. Verbum sat sapienti! [A word to the wise is sufficient]" (Burger 1983). Because of the chief's concern with the Court's capacity to finish its work prior to the scheduled recess, we hypothesize the following:

End-of-Term Hypothesis: Toward the end of each term, the chief justice is less likely to assign an opinion to ideological allies.

Finally, although it is common to see the chief justice as the Court's taskmaster, and therefore constrained by factors related to smooth operation of the Court as an organization (Brenner and Hagle 1996; Ulmer 1986; Danelski 1968), one might expect that assignments made by associate justices would not be marked by these same constraints. After all, associate justices occupy a different institutional position than the chief. Unconstrained by the institutional responsibilities that come with the chief justice's position, one might expect that associate justices would be generally more free to assign opinions on policy grounds. If so, this would lead them, for instance, to be more apt to assign opinions to themselves. This does not mean, however, that associate justice assignments are made in a strategic vacuum. To the contrary, we expect associate justices to be just as concerned about maintaining the integrity of the conference coalition as the chief justice, leading them to assign to more moderate justices in cases where they encounter a small conference majority. These expectations generate a number of hypotheses about the assignment choices of associate justices:

Associate Justice Hypothesis 1: Associate justices will be more likely to make assignments to justices who are ideologically aligned than to those who are ideologically distant. The effect of ideology, moreover, will be even more pronounced in legally or politically salient cases.

Associate Justice Hypothesis 2: Associate justices will be more likely to self-assign cases, especially in politically or legally salient cases.

Associate Justice Hypothesis 3: Associate justices will be influenced by the strategic constraint imposed by the size of the conference coalition.

Associate Justice Hypothesis 4: Associate justices are less likely to be influenced by the constraints of equity, expertise, workload, or end of term.

DATA AND METHODS

To explain opinion assignment decisions, we need evidence regarding who voted with the majority at conference, who assigned the majority opinion, and to whom the opinion was assigned. To determine how a justice voted at conference, we used Justice Brennan's docket sheets, which list each justice's vote.[8] To determine who assigned the majority opinion, we relied on Justice

---

[8]   If Brennan's docket sheet was missing or blank, we used the docket sheets found in William Douglas's personal papers.

Brennan's copy of the initial assignment sheets circulated by Chief Justice Burger. As we mentioned in the previous chapter, these sheets detail every majority opinion assignment and who made the assignment. Because we are interested in understanding what criteria assignors use when making assignments, our dependent variable is whether or not a justice who voted with the majority was initially assigned the majority opinion in cases decided between the 1969 and 1985 terms.[9] If a particular justice was assigned an opinion, the justice is given a 1 for that case and all other justices who voted the majority are given a 0.[10] We examine two sets of data for the 1969–1985 terms, one for the 1,891 cases in which Chief Justice Burger assigned the opinion, and one for the 310 assignments made by an associate justice during this same time period.[11] We use a conditional logit model to estimate both models, one each for the likelihood that the chief justice or the associate justice assigns the opinion to each justice in the majority.[12]

---

[9]   Because reassignments may be just a formality and are made to a justice who has written a dissenting or concurring opinion that has gained the support of a Court majority, our dependent variable is based on the initial assignments made by the chief. On occasion, a reassignment is made because the initial assignment was simply a mistake or some new fact (such as a justice's reluctance to write a particular opinion) comes to the chief's attention.

[10] To determine who cast a vote with the majority at conference, we use Brennan's and Douglas's docket books to identify how the members of the Court voted in conference. Because our dependent variable is whether or not a given justice who voted with the majority was assigned the majority opinion, the data set consists of one observation for each majority vote. In eleven cases, the opinion was assigned to a member of the conference minority. Because the assignor apparently believed that this justice was part of the choice set, we included these observations in the data. Similarly, we dropped the observation associated with the chief where the assignment sheet indicates that an associate justice assigned the opinion, even though the docket sheets reveal that Burger was in the conference majority. We included Burger in the choice set, however, when he made the assignment even though he passed or failed to express the majority position at conference.

[11] In this book, we examine the 2,307 cases where an assignment was made or a signed opinion was released during the Burger Court. Of these cases, Spaeth (1994) coded 10 as containing "miscellaneous" values. Because of the ambiguous nature of this value area, we dropped from our analysis these 10 cases. We also dropped 2 cases that are not included in Spaeth's *United States Supreme Court Judicial Database* because, although they were argued and drafts were circulated, the cases were rescheduled for argument the following term and no opinion was released. This leaves us with 2,295 cases. For purposes of the analysis reported in this chapter, we also omitted the 91 per curiam and memorandum assignments. We do not omit formal opinion assignments that resulted in a per curiam opinion. Finally, we deleted from this analysis three additional cases because the assignor was the only member of the conference majority or the identity of the assignor was unknown from the assignment sheets.

[12] Because our unit of analysis is whether a justice in the conference majority is assigned the opinion, measured as a dichotomous variable, one would normally use logistic regression to estimate the likelihood that a specific choice will be made (King 1989; Aldrich and Nelson 1984). Logistic regression, however, is based on the assumption that the observations are in-

Independent Variables

The hypotheses just outlined suggest that a justice's ideology, workload, expertise, and tenure on the Court shape the assignor's likelihood of assigning him or her an opinion. Thus, we need a series of justice-specific independent variables. By interacting these justice-specific variables with a series of case-specific variables (the size of the original coalition, the importance and complexity of the case, and the stage during the term at which a case was assigned), we can determine the conditions shaping assignment choices. Appendix 2 contains summary statistics for our independent variables.

Justice-Specific Attributes

Ideology. To assess each justice's ideological compatibility with the assignor on each case, we calculated an issue-specific (e.g., civil rights, first amendment) compatibility score between the assignor and each justice in the majority conference coalition for every case. This score is determined by using original conference data, Spaeth's (1994) twelve substantive value groups, and the per-

dependent and identically distributed binary outcomes. In these data, of course, the observations are not independent, for the likelihood that the chief will assign the opinion to one justice is dependent on the probability that the chief justice will assign it to another member of the majority. The interdependence of choices suggests that a conditional logit model is the appropriate estimation strategy (Greene 1997; Maddala 1983). In particular, we estimate our model using the "clogit" command in Stata 5.0. Such a model allows us to estimate the likelihood that the chief will assign an opinion to a specific justice, conditioned on the likelihood that the opinion will be assigned to another justice.

Conditional logit makes the independence of irrelevant alternatives assumption (IIA), which essentially means that the probability of choosing any two alternatives is unaffected by all the other alternatives in the choice set. This assumption is often violated, and scholars have therefore developed diagnostics for testing IIA, as well as produced several models that do not carry this assumption. The most commonly employed test is the Hausman test (Hausman and McFadden 1984; Zhang and Hoffman 1993), but it has a weakness and is inestimable when the inverse of the difference between matrices is not positive definite (see Zhang and Hoffman 1993, 200). Unfortunately, this test is not estimable for our data. Yet, even if we detected a problem, there appears to be no solution, given the nature of our data. Three alternative modeling approaches do not make the IIA assumption: nested logit, multinomial probit, and a heteroscedastic extreme value (HEV) model (see Greene 1997, 912–926; Maddala 1983, 59–78; Ginter and Allenby 1995; Bhat 1995; Alvarez and Nagler 1998). The first option, however, is not workable on our data because there is no clear tree-and-branch structure to the assignment decision. The second option is not feasible because it is extremely difficult to estimate such a model with more than four choices, and we have up to nine (see Greene 1998, 543). Finally, our data are inestimable with the HEV model, most likely because we do not have a universal choice set – that is, the same set of justices are not available for assignments across the entire time period due to retirements and new appointments.

centage of cases in which each justice voted for the liberal outcome over his or her career on the Court (Epstein et al. 1994, table 6–1).[13] The score is computed by taking the absolute value of the difference between the justice's issue-specific percent liberalism score and the assignor's score. Thus, if the justice's ideology is identical to the assignor's, ideological distance is zero. The more distant the justice is from the assignor, the higher the score.[14]

Self-Assignment. We used a dichotomous variable that identifies whether a justice is the assignor. This variable is then interacted with the measures of *Legal Salience* and *Political Salience* that we discuss later to test the Case Importance Hypotheses 2a and 2b.

Equity. To test the Equity Hypothesis, we calculated the number of associate justice assignments that each justice received between each set of assignments made by the chief justice. If the assignor is concerned about equalizing the distribution of the Court's workload, we expect this number to be negatively correlated with a justice receiving an assignment.

Expertise. To measure whether a justice has substantive policy expertise, we calculated an issue-specific opinion ratio (OR) for each of the justices.[15] The

---

[13]   For 155 of cases included in our study, Spaeth attributed the case to two of the value categories. In these instances, we assumed that each justice's ideological score was the average of the two value areas.

[14]   We are confident that our measure of justices' ideology is currently the best available. Yet, it is not immune from criticism. First, one might wonder why, given our argument that justices might sometimes vote sophisticatedly, we use a measure of preferences built from their votes. Theoretically, we expect that the level of sophisticated behavior is higher for the choices justices make in the process of writing opinions than for the final vote on the merits. The reason is because justices are most concerned with having legal rules reflect their policy preferences, and thus they are less concerned with whether the lower court is affirmed or reversed. Thus, our expectation is that the overall level of sophisticated voting in final votes is not unusually high, meaning that aggregate voting scores are reasonably representative of a justice's ideological orientation.

     A second issue regards whether justices have stable ideologies over time. Although some research (Epstein et al. 1998) suggests that justices' voting patterns differ over time, it is still not clear to what extent this variance is due to preference change. Moreover, given the small number of cases decided by some justices on some issues in some years, developing a robust measure of ideology that varies across time becomes difficult.

[15]   Each justice is given a unique OR for each of 133 narrow issue areas that Spaeth (1994, 1995b) identified. To identify the 133 issues, we rely upon the 263 issue categories that Spaeth identifies and then group those issues that Spaeth reports as being related. For example, the 5 specific issue areas that Spaeth identified as related to federal transportation regulation (railroad, boat, truck, pipeline, and airline) are grouped together.

OR is the number of cases in which a justice wrote a dissent or concurrence divided by the number of like cases that reached the Court since that justice's appointment and up to the term preceding the case in question.[16] Because this measure is based on information up to the term preceding the case in question, it is updated annually to reflect a justice's learning and the development of expertise over time. We then compared each justice's OR to the OR for other justices serving on the Court when the case was heard. Our measure of *Expertise* is then each justice's z-score, which compares the justice's OR with the mean OR for all justices serving on the Court divided by the standard deviation of OR among that group of justices (see Hays 1994, 191). A high score indicates that a justice has more expertise than the average for all justices on the Court, whereas a low score reflects less expertise than the average justice.[17] A score of zero indicates that the justice has precisely the average amount of expertise. Because we hypothesized that experts disproportionately get opinion assignments, we expect a positive relationship between expertise and receiving an opinion assignment.

Freshman. Any justice who had served less than two full years when the case was assigned was coded as 1, but if otherwise, 0.[18]

---

[16] This approach to measuring expertise is similar to that employed by Brenner and Spaeth (1986) and Brenner (1984) where they compare the author's opinion assignment ratio (OAR) with the OAR of the other justices as a group. Another tack to measuring the role of experience has been to examine the justices' years of experience and age (Slotnick 1979c).

[17] One might suspect that this measure is affected by the justice's ideological position on the Court. We rely upon the OR, rather than the proportion of majority opinions written, because the latter is sensitive to both a justice's ideological position relative to his or her colleagues and the assignment decisions of the chief justice and the senior associate justice (Brenner 1990). Because the OR takes account of dissents and concurrences written by each justice up to the term preceding the case in question, it is not sensitive to a justice's ideological position relative to his or her colleagues and the chief justice's assignment decisions. Moreover, because the correlation between expertise and ideology is .113 (p < .001), we are confident that there is not a collinearity problem.

  Second, one might suspect that, rather than tapping expertise, this measure captures a justice's propensity to write separate opinions. There is some merit to this suggestion. In fact, when we regress the rate at which justices write opinions in each issue area on the proportion of all cases in which the justices write separately, the coefficient is statistically significant (p < .001). However, a justice's general propensity to write separate opinions explains a very small fraction of the variance in the justice's decision to write separately in each of the issue areas ($R^2 = .05$). Thus, we conclude that while our measure taps a justice's general inclination to write a separate opinion, this accounts for a very small proportion of the variance in our measure.

[18] For our purposes, service time began on the day on which the oath of office was administered (Epstein et al. 1994, table 5–2).

Workload. The measure of each justice's workload is based on the number of majority and separate opinions on which he or she was working on the day a case was assigned. To determine the day on which a justice began work on a majority opinion, we used the date on which the case was assigned to the justice as indicated on the original assignment sheets circulated to the Court by the chief justice.[19] To determine when a justice began working on a separate opinion, we used Justice Brennan's circulation sheets, which indicate the date on which a justice announced that he or she would write a separate opinion.[20] If a justice had not yet circulated the final draft of an opinion, we assumed that he or she was working on the opinion.[21] We then calculated a z-score for workload by comparing a justice's workload with the average workload of sitting justices.[22] Larger positive scores therefore indicate that a justice currently has a heavier workload at a particular point in time than the average justice. Because we expect the assignor to assign cases to those justices who are current on their work, we anticipate a negative relationship between current workload and the likelihood of receiving an assignment.

Case-Specific Attributes

Political Salience. As a measure of political salience, we examined the number of amicus briefs, as found in Gibson (1997).[23] Because amicus participation

---

[19] In eight cases during the Burger Court, the original opinion assignment was not noted on the assignment sheet. In these cases, we instead used the date of oral argument, which was identified by Spaeth (1994) or on Lexis. In 131 cases, a justice was assigned the opinion, but the opinion was reassigned before any drafts were circulated or the author lost the opinion in the writing phase. For these cases, we relied on the assignment sheets and memos in William Brennan's case files for indications of a formal reassignment date. If the case was not formally reassigned, we used the date of the subsequent author's first majority draft to identify when the previous author stopped working on a case. In particular, we assumed that the previous author's last day on the case was one day earlier than the day the subsequent author circulated his or her first majority opinion draft.

[20] If no such "will write" memo was circulated, we instead assumed that the justice began working on the opinion on the date on which the first draft of the separate opinion was circulated to the other justices.

[21] We determined the date of the final draft from Justice Brennan's circulation records, which contain, among other information, the dates on which all majority and separate opinion drafts are circulated.

[22] It is necessary to use a z-score since justices' workloads necessarily begin light and become heavier as the term progresses. If we were to use the actual workload number, this would not only measure the justices' work status, but also the point in the term when the assignment was made.

[23] Some suggest that a preferable measure, albeit ex post, is whether the case was the lead case discussed in a front-page story in the *New York Times* (Epstein and Segal, forthcoming). We

has increased over the time period under investigation, we calculated term-specific statistics – that is, mean and standard deviation – and determined whether a case had more amici filings than the average case heard during a term. More specifically, our measure is a term-specific z-score for amicus participation. The interactions between *Political Salience* and the *Ideology* and *Self-Assignment* variables provide a test of these hypotheses.

Legal Salience. As a measure of legal salience, we created a dummy variable to identify any case where the Court, according to Spaeth (1994), either struck a law down as unconstitutional or overturned or altered precedent.[24] With the same interactions we discussed for the *Political Salience* measure, we can test similar hypotheses.[25]

Winning Margin. We identified the conference vote of each justice and calculated the size of the winning conference coalition. Specifically, to measure the conference margin, we subtracted the number of votes needed to form a winning coalition from the number of justices who voted with the assignor.[26] The interaction between this case-specific measure and each justice's ideological distance tests this hypothesis.

Case Complexity. Although one could use numerous indicators of case complexity, none fully captures the concept. Thus, we measured case complexity by combining three indicators, all derived from Spaeth (1994): the number of issues raised by the case, the number of legal provisions relevant to a case, and

should note that our measure and the *New York Times* measure are related. A difference-of-means test reveals that cases reported in the *New York Times* had a significantly higher amicus participation rate, as measured by our amicus z-score (t = -10.0967, p < .001).

[24] Of the 2,201 cases included in our analysis, 224 (10.4 percent) are identified as legally salient.

[25] We should note that both *Political Salience* and *Legal Salience* are conceptualized and measured as general effects flowing from the salience of a case, and not the importance one justice, rather than another, places on a case. Some might argue that this measure underestimates the level of legal importance since a case might be legally salient without striking down a law or overturning precedent. Although this is a plausible concern, a difference-of-means test discloses that the cases we designate as legally important were cited in subsequent cases, according to *Shepard's Citations,* more frequently than cases that did not share that designation (t = -11.7504, p < .001) (see Spriggs and Hansford 1999).

[26] There were several cases in which there was no clear majority supporting one position at conference. For instance, in 108 cases, only a plurality favored the dominant position, the Court was equally divided, or the assigned author was a member of the conference minority. In these cases, the margin variable took on a negative value to reflect the author's need to attract additional votes before gaining a majority.

the number of opinions released in a case. Factor analysis of these three indicators produced a single factor with an eigenvalue greater than one. We adopted each case's factor score as the measure of *Case Complexity*. The interaction between this case-specific measure and *Freshman* tests whether freshmen are assigned less complex cases.

End of Term. We created a variable to identify the number of days from the date an opinion was assigned until July 1, the traditional end of the Court's term. The interaction between this variable and *Ideology* permits us to test the hypothesis that the assignor disproportionately suppresses his ideological preferences near the end of the term.

RESULTS

Table 2.2 presents the estimated coefficients and significance levels for conditional logit models predicting majority opinion assignments made by Chief Justice Burger and the associate justices during the 1969 through 1985 terms. The highly significant chi-square in both models enables us to reject the null hypothesis that each coefficient jointly equals zero. Whereas the average justice who votes with the majority at the initial conference is assigned the majority opinion by Burger 14.7 percent of the time, our multivariate model predicts 359 of the 1,891 assignments made by Chief Justice Burger (19.0 percent).[27] In contrast to a model of random opinion assignment, this is a reduction of error of 4.2 percent. In comparison, the average justice who sides with the conference majority when an associate justice serves as the assignor receives the assignment 18.4 percent of the time. Our model successfully predicts the assignee in 130 out of 310 assignments (41.9 percent). This constitutes a 28.4 percent reduction of error.

Chief Justice Burger's assignments can, first of all, be partially explained by the ideological distance between him and the justices in the conference majority. We cannot directly test the Opinion Distance Hypothesis with our inclusion of interactions with ideological distance. Because the general ideological

[27] The percentage correctly predicted is the ratio of predicted to observed outcomes aggregated across all cases. The justice with the greatest likelihood of being assigned a particular case is determined by applying the coefficients generated by our model to the data. We predict that the chief will assign each case to the justice with the highest predicted value.

Table 2.2. *Conditional Logit Model of Opinion Assignment on the Burger Court*

Variable	Burger Assignments Estimate (Standard Error)	Associate Justice Assignments Estimate (Standard Error)
Policy Preferences		
Ideology	.017 (.006)	.001 (.013)
Self-Assignment	−.167 (.086)	1.166 (.191)***
Strategic Interaction		
Ideology * Winning Margin	−.004 (.001)***	−.014 (.005)**
Contextual Controls		
Ideology * Political Salience	−.003 (.001)***	−.001(.002)
Ideology * Legal Salience	−.006 (.006)	−.001 (.013)
Self-Assignment * Political Salience	−.018 (.021)	.022 (.049)
Self-Assignment * Legal Salience	.287 (.246)	−.076 (.404)
Equity	−.095 (.035)**	−.019 (.096)
Expertise	.066 (.026)**	−.035 (.069)
Freshman	−.072 (.096)	.548 (.308)
Freshman * Case Complexity	−.048 (.097)	−.155 (.282)
Workload	−.107 (.027)***	−.021 (.071)
Ideology * End of Term	−.000 (.000)*	.000 (.000)
Number of Observations	12,874	1,687
−2 X Log-Likelihood	7,088.877	941.424
Chi-Square (13 d.f.)	76.32***	100.97***
Percent Correctly Predicted	19.0	41.9
Percent Reduction of Error	4.2	28.4

* $p < .05$; ** $p < .01$; *** $p < .001$ (one-tail tests).

distance coefficient reported in Table 2.2 taps the effect of ideology under sub-stantively uninteresting constraints, we run a simple difference-of-means test to determine if justices assigned the opinion are ideologically closer to Burger compared with those passed over by the chief. The ideological distance of as-signed authors is 15.1, whereas, in contrast, the ideological difference between Burger and the remaining justices is 16.0. This difference, though small, is in the expected direction and is statistically significant ($p < .05$).[28]

[28] When we run our model, omitting the ideology interactions and the self-assignment inter-actions, ideology fails to attain statistical significance.

The weak substantive effect of ideology, standing by itself, is not as surprising as it may initially appear. First, Maltzman and Wahlbeck (1996b) find that during the 1987–1989 terms Chief Justice Rehnquist did not consistently favor his ideological allies. Second, one should recall that we theoretically expect ideology to operate conditionally through several strategic and contextual constraints. We therefore expect our results to reflect that ideology matters more (or less) depending on the particular situation confronting the chief justice. As we turn to the interactions with *Ideology*, we see that this is precisely the type of influence we find.[29]

The interaction between *Ideology* and *Winning Margin* provides empirical support for the Majority Coalition Size Hypothesis. When the chief is assigning an opinion for a plurality conference coalition, as he did in *James v. Valtierra* (1971), where only Justices Black, Harlan, and White voted with him at conference, justices who are ideologically removed from the chief are more likely to receive the assignment than justices who are ideologically aligned with Burger.[30] In a case like *James*, Burger is more than twice as likely to assign the

[29]   One might also notice that our models in Table 2.2 do not include, as separate variables, several of the component parts of our interaction terms (i.e., *Political Salience, Winning Margin, Case Complexity*, and *End of Term*). In addition to our having no theoretical expectation that these variables would, by themselves, have any influence, a conditional logit model cannot include them because they do not vary across the justices in each case. Such a model requires that each variable actually varies across the alternatives in a choice set.

To ensure that their exclusion did not contaminate the results reported in Table 2.2, we conducted several diagnostics, learning that both the coefficients and standard errors reported in the table for chief justice and associate justice assignments are unaffected. More specifically, we estimated our model with all of the variables in Table 2.2 plus the variables that do not vary across a case (i.e., *Political Salience, Winning Margin, Case Complexity*, and *End of Term*) using two different approaches. First, we ran a logit model with robust standard errors clustered on cases, which should correct somewhat for the nonindependence of the choices in a case. The coefficients and standard errors are nearly identical to those reported in Table 2.2. Second, we ran a random effects cross-sectional time series logit model, grouping on each case. Once again, the results were nearly identical to those from the conditional logit model. We therefore conclude that the omission of these variables is not affecting the coefficients in our conditional logit model. There is, however, one way to include variables that do not differ across the choices in a case in a conditional logit model. One would interact each of the variables with a series of dummy variables representing each alternative in the choice set. This approach, however, would yield a large number of interaction terms – likely leading to collinearity – and would not be very informative for our analysis.

[30]   When interacting two continuous variables, the noninteracted variable is interpreted as the effect of that factor when the interaction term is set at zero (see Friedrich 1982). So, for example, our *Ideology* variable is the effect of ideological distance when each term that is interacted with it equals zero. In other words, the estimated coefficient for *Ideology* measures its effect in cases that are of average political salience, not legally salient; the conference coalition was exactly the size needed to form a majority; and the case was assigned on July 1. Although the *Ideology* estimate, standing alone, is not substantively interesting, in tandem with

opinion to an ideologically distant justice, like Justice Black, than to Burger's allies on the coalition, Justice White here.[31] This preference for ideologically distant justices grows less pronounced with a larger conference coalition. This advantage shrinks to 83.5 percent in minimum winning cases and dwindles to 33.9 percent when the chief's coalition has two more justices than is necessary to form a majority. Indeed, the conditional effect of ideological distance is indistinguishable from zero when Burger's conference coalition is unanimous or

the interaction terms, it allows us to gauge the effect of *Ideology* conditioned on other variables. This assessment is made by multiplying the estimate for the interaction term by the value of interest for the second variable and adding that product to the *Ideology* estimate. For example, if one wants to know the effect of ideological distance for varying sizes of conference majority coalitions, one can multiply the *Ideology* * *Winning Margin* estimate by the *Winning Margin* value of interest. So, if one was interested in the effect of *Ideology* when the assignor was part of a plurality conference coalition consisting of four justices, one would multiply the *Ideology* * *Winning Margin* estimate by -1, resulting in a product of .0043. This number is then added to the *Ideology* estimate of .0170 to reach an estimated effect of ideological distance under this scenario of .0213. It then becomes apparent that ideological distance has a greater effect on the assignment decision when the chief is operating from a plurality than when he was part of a minimum winning conference coalition, where the estimated effect is equal to the *Ideology* estimate of .0170. The question remains, though, whether the effect of ideology under this condition is statistically significant. The comparison of the estimate and its standard error reported in Table 2.2 does not adequately perform the hypothesis test as the effect of the variable may be significant at some levels of the other variable and insignificant at other levels. To determine the answer to this question, one must calculate a standard error with information of the covariance between, and the variances of, these estimates. According to Friedrich (1982, 810), the standard error can be calculated as follows:

$$s(b_1 + b_3 X_2) = \sqrt{\text{var}(b_1) + X_2^2 \, \text{var}(b_3) + 2X_2 \text{cov}(b_1, b_3)},$$

Where b_1 is the estimate for the noninteracted variable, like *Ideology*; b_3 is the estimate for the interaction; and X_2 is the value of the base interaction term, like *Winning Margin*.

In our running example, the standard error for *Ideology* when the conference plurality coalition is short one vote of attaining a majority is .0064. This occurs because the covariance between the estimated coefficients of *Ideology* and the *Winning Margin* interaction term is -.0000041, while the variance of the *Ideology* coefficient is .000031 and the variance of the interaction is .0000018. When we set X_2 at -1, as we do in the preceding example, the resulting standard error equals .0064.

Given an estimated effect in the expected direction and a z-score of 3.328, one can conclude that the effect of *Ideology* under this condition is statistically significant. To calculate the z-score, one divides the estimated standard coefficient (.0213) by its standard error (.0064). Thus, the probability that ideology has no effect on the assignment decision is about .0005.

[31] *James v. Valtierra* (1971) is a civil rights case in which the ideological distance between Burger and the other coalition members is 49.1 for Black, 19.6 for Harlan, and 13.4 for White. In the simulation results for larger coalition sizes, we add the next closest ally of Burger. Thus, for instance, to simulate the effect of *Ideology* where *Winning Margin* equals zero, we add Justice Blackmun. He is followed by Justice Stewart and Justice Brennan.

nearly unanimous as reflected in a margin of three. The chief is clearly responding to this important strategic characteristic of a case.

Our model results further support the claim that ideology's effect is conditioned upon the contextual situation confronting the chief. Consistent with Case Importance Hypothesis 1a, the negative coefficient for *Ideology * Political Salience* indicates the chief is significantly more likely to favor a justice with whom he is ideologically allied when politically salient cases are under review. When political salience is low, by contrast, the effect of ideology is positive and significant, meaning that he is more likely to assign to justices who are ideologically removed from his position.[32] Simulated probabilities show the importance of this dynamic. In a case of average amici participation, a justice who is ideologically distant from the chief, like Douglas in civil rights cases, is more than twice as likely to receive an assignment than John Harlan, the justice whose policy convictions in civil rights were most closely aligned with those of the chief.[33] Contrast that to a similar comparison at varying levels of political salience: the advantage enjoyed by Douglas over Harlan grows by 14.0 percent for a case at the 25th percentile in political salience, but shrinks by 31.5 percent in a case that fell in the 75th percentile of political salience. At higher levels of political salience, as was seen in *United States v. Leon* (1984) with its fifteen amicus briefs, the edge shifts to Burger's ideological friends. Given our hypothetical choice set, Harlan would be 61.0 percent more likely to receive the assignment in such a case than the ideologically distant Douglas. As seen in the statistically insignificant result for the *Ideology * Legal Salience* interaction, a similar pattern does not hold in cases of legal salience. Moreover, contrary to our expectation, Chief Justice Burger does not assign himself cases that are either politically or legally salient.

A justice's institutional position has some influence on assignments, too. The positive and statistically significant estimate for *Expertise* is consistent with the hypothesis that the chief justice makes an effort to assign cases to

[32]   The effect of *Ideology* is statistically indistinguishable from zero when the political salience variable ranges from 2.9 through 13.5.

[33]   We employ a simulation for illustrative purposes using the ideological distance in civil rights cases for justices sitting on the Court during the natural court that began with the appointment of Justice Blackmun. According to Epstein et al. (1994, table 6–1), Burger supported the liberal position in 37.2 percent of all civil rights cases decided during his tenure on the bench. This stands in contrast to Douglas's 92.7 percent support, which represents the strongest support for civil rights on the bench. Harlan's record is most similar to Burger's, with a support level of 44.8 percent. This means that Douglas's ideological distance is 55.5, whereas Harlan's is 7.6.

those justices who have substantive expertise in the case. Take, for example, *Briscoe v. Bell* (1977), a voting rights case. According to our measure, Justice Marshall had the most expertise in voting rights for the 1976 term. In contrast, Justice Stevens, a relative newcomer, had the least expertise in this area of law. Not surprisingly, Marshall was 18.8 percent more likely to gain the assignment in this unanimous case than Justice Stevens. We uncovered, however, no support for the chief assigning noncomplex cases to freshman justices, as the effect of *Freshman* is indistinguishable from zero as the value of case complexity increases.

The effect of ideology also varies by time constraints operating on the Court. Consistent with the End-of-Term Hypothesis, the chief is significantly less likely to assign opinions to ideological allies as the Court's July recess approaches. This difference becomes apparent if we compare the likelihood that an ideologically distant justice, like Douglas, will receive a civil rights case from Chief Justice Burger to the likelihood that an ideological ally, like Justice White, will receive the assignment instead.[34] On February 1, five months from the Court's summer recess, Justice Douglas is 71.6 percent more likely to receive the assignment than Justice White. By May 1, Douglas's advantage over White grows to the point where Douglas is more than twice as likely to win the assignment. We should note that the effect of ideology is statistically insignificant, and thus indistinguishable from zero, before December 1, which is 212 days before July 1.

Although our findings indicate that Burger used the assignment process to further his policy goals, they also support the assertion that the chief's decision is constrained. In addition to the constraint imposed by the approach of the end of the annual term, the chief justice also attempts to distribute the Court's workload equitably. In contrast to a justice who has not received any assignments from an associate justice, a justice with one such assignment is 8.9 percent less likely to gain an assignment from the chief. This disparity grows to 16.8 percent and 24.6 percent when a justice receives two or three associate justice assignments, respectively.[35]

We also hypothesized that the chief's concern with the smooth operation of the Court leads him to favor justices who have kept ahead of their work. The

[34] For purposes of this simulation, we use the nine-justice choice set from the natural court that began with Justice Blackmun's appointment.

[35] For purposes of this simulation, we allow one justice to have the stated number of associate justice assignments, while the remaining eight justices have none.

positive and significant relationship for *Workload* finds support for this proposition. A simulation based on *Weinberger v. Rossi* (1982) illustrates the effect of justices' workloads on the assignment decision. Justice Rehnquist was working on the fewest opinions of the nine sitting justices in this unanimous decision – four when this opinion was assigned on March 8, 1982. In contrast, three justices – Brennan, Powell, and Stevens – were working on twelve opinions. Based on our simulation, it is not surprising then that Rehnquist was assigned this opinion given that the likelihood of that choice was 30.3 percent greater than picking one of the three justices working on twelve opinions.

ASSOCIATE JUSTICE ASSIGNMENTS

The statistical results regarding the determinants of the associate justices' assignments are consistent with our expectation: the associate justice is freed from the contextual constraints to which the chief is subjected and largely assigns opinions to those justices who are ideologically allied. A difference-of-means test that compares the ideological distance of justices who were assigned the opinion with those who were not chosen supports this notion. The justices who were given the majority opinion assignment by an associate justice had an ideological distance, on average, of 12.0. This stands in contrast to the ideological distance of the remaining conference coalition justices who had an average ideological distance of 17.7, which is a statistically significant difference ($p < .001$).

The fully specified multivariate model discloses that the bivariate effect of ideology on the associate justices' assignment is largely an artifact of self-assignment. Associate justices are most likely to assign themselves the opinion. This is true in both salient and nonsalient cases alike. As reported in Table 2.2, the statistically significant coefficient for *Self-Assignment* without any interaction confirms that associate justices assign themselves cases that are not particularly interesting. Indeed, the assigning associate justice is over three times more likely to receive the assignment than the other associate justices in the conference majority. When we examine the effect of self-assignment under varying conditions of salience, though, we still find that associate justices have a proclivity for self-assignment, although the insignificant interaction term indicates that the influence of self-assignment does not change with a one-unit increase in either political or legal salience. The simulation confirms this:

the associate justice is only 5.2 percent more likely to self-assign in cases falling at the 75th percentile of political salience and only 1.4 percent less likely to self-assign in cases at the 25th percentile of political salience. In both of these conditions, the associate justice is significantly more likely to self-assign. The same holds true for cases of legal salience: associate justices are almost three times as likely to self-assign in a legally salient case instead of assigning it to another justice.[36] Again, however, the data do not indicate that associates are more likely to self-assign legally salient than nonsalient cases; they are about equally likely to self-assign either type of case.

Still, these results should not be interpreted to suggest that associate justices fail to play the collegial game. The choices made by associate justices, like those made by the chief, depend on both their policy goals and the collegial nature of the institution. Their strategic behavior is seen in the effect of ideology conditioned upon the size of the initial conference coalition. The effect of ideological distance appears to be conditioned upon the size of their conference coalition as seen in the negative and statistically significant estimate of *Ideology * Winning Margin*. Associate justices are more likely to assign opinions to justices who are ideologically friendly when the conference majority is large. Indeed, this is seen in the estimated effect of *Ideology*, which is negative and significant when the conference majority margin is at least two.[37]

Finally, the constraints on the chief justice as the Court's taskmaster, as seen in the significant influence of *Equity, Expertise, End of Term*, and *Workload*, do not appear to affect assignment choices by associate justices. These variables both individually and as a group fail to shape the associate justices' assignments. Not only are they statistically insignificant under conventional tests, but they bias our hypothesis testing into accepting the null hypothesis, which we expect to find. In order to reduce this bias, we must raise the threshold for accepting the null hypothesis. There is varying opinion on the appropriate level, but it generally falls within a range from .10 to .30 (see Blalock 1979, 161; Hall and Grofman 1990, 1156; Julnes and Mohr 1989). Regardless of the

---

[36] One can see this result by adding the coefficient for *Self-Assignment* with the coefficient for *Self-Assignment * Legal Salience*, which indicates the influence of *Self-Assignment* in legally important cases. The coefficient of approximately 1.09 (p < .001) shows that associates are more likely to self-assign legally important cases.

[37] The estimated effect of *Ideology* is positive and significant when the associate justice is working with a very small conference coalition. More specifically, when the associate justice needs to gain three additional adherents to form a majority, the associate justice is more apt to assign the opinion to an ideologically distant justice. Needless to say, this situation occurs rarely.

level, we are able to accept the null hypothesis. An alternative argument is that these variables serve as a constraint as a group. To test this possibility, we conducted a likelihood ratio test, which reveals that a model with these variables excluded does not perform significantly differently than the fully specified model (chi-square with 3 d.f. $= 0.42$; $p = .94$). Finally, the data do not support the idea that freshman justices are assigned less complex cases.

CONCLUSION

The content of Supreme Court opinions depends in part on who speaks for the Court. For this reason, one of the most important stages in the decision-making process is the selection of the majority opinion writer. In this chapter, we have shown that assignors systematically use their power of assignment to further their policy goals, while simultaneously responding to strategic and contextual constraints engendered by each case. Our analysis therefore highlights the conditional and constrained nature of opinion assignment.

The chief's ability to pursue his policy goals, we find, depends upon the prevailing political and institutional contexts of the Court. Nothing better highlights the constrained nature of the chief's assignment choices than our results for the effect of ideological distance. Although the bivariate support for the Opinion Distance Hypothesis is consistent with expectations that policy preferences matter, we also found clear empirical support for the idea that policy preferences operate conditionally. The interactions between *Ideology* and other factors demonstrate that Chief Justice Burger systematically assigned opinions to less ideologically compatible judges under certain conditions. Importantly, Chief Justice Burger's assignments depended on the actions and decisions of his colleagues. The impact of smaller conference coalitions on Burger's assignments – leading him to favor assignments to ideological moderates – suggests the strategic character of Burger's assignment patterns. Concern about the maintenance of fragile coalitions clearly shaped assignment choices during the Burger Court. This finding is consistent with the central argument in this book: justices' decisions result from the pursuit of their policy preferences within constraints that stem from the collegial nature of the institution.

An additional dimension to the conditional nature of the chief's pursuit of his policy preferences results from the salience of a case. Although Burger tended to favor his ideological allies, he disproportionately favored them on politically salient cases. When it mattered most, conservative justices profited by Burger's control over the assignment process. Even though Burger was on the conservative wing of the bench, he did not consistently favor ideological allies.

Still, the chief's assignment choices are constrained by more than the collegial nature of the institution and case salience. Rather than simply allowing his policy preferences to drive assignments, Burger attempted to facilitate the smooth operation of the Court by ensuring that the Court's workload would be distributed equally and fairly. Furthermore, the chief also favored justices who were experts in the policy area being considered by a case, as well as those with lighter workloads. Perhaps the best illustration of how contextual factors can restrict choices is that Burger appears to have downplayed ideological considerations as the end of the Court's annual term approached.

Finally, the chief justice is not alone in trying to use the assignment process to secure his policy preferences. Associate justices, like chief justices, also pursue their policy preferences by giving desirable assignments to those with whom they agree (frequently themselves). Nevertheless, associate justices are also constrained by the collegial nature of the institution: like the chief, the smaller the initial conference coalition, the more likely associate justices are to assign opinions to ideologically distant justices. Perhaps our most interesting finding about the assignment decisions made by associate justices is that they appear unaffected by many of the contextual factors that shape the chief's assignments. Associate justices during the Burger Court did not favor justices with lighter workloads or justices failing to carry their fair share of the opinion-writing burden. While the chief's institutional responsibilities limited his ability to pursue his preferred legal outcomes, senior associate justices did not experience such a constraint.

Of course, although opinion authors may have a disproportionate ability to shape the final opinion, they do not have a free hand to craft opinions alone. Justices who are not assigned an opinion are not simply passive observers of opinion writing. Instead, they strategically attempt to encourage the opinion authors to craft opinions consistent with their values and goals. Such strategic efforts by justices to secure their own policy goals are the focus of our next chapter.

3

A Strategic Response
to Draft Opinions

On June 25, 1980, Justice Harry Blackmun announced from the bench the Court's opinion that he wrote in *Ohio v. Roberts*. The opinion overturned the Ohio Supreme Court's decision to reverse Herschel Roberts's conviction for possession of heroin, receiving stolen property, and forgery. Although the Supreme Court's opinion had very negative consequences for Roberts, the effect of the opinion extended far beyond him. The Court's opinion helped define the Sixth Amendment's provision that "In all criminal prosecutions, the accused shall enjoy the right . . . to be confronted with the witnesses against him." Most importantly, although Justice Blackmun wrote the opinion, the decision did not completely reflect Blackmun's view of the Constitution. As will become clear in this chapter, *Ohio v. Roberts* nicely illustrates the strategic and collaborative politics of the opinion-writing process on the U.S. Supreme Court.

Roberts was arrested after attempting to buy a piece of jewelry using a check with Bernard Issacs's forged signature. While searching Roberts, the police discovered several pieces of property, including some credit cards, that Issacs subsequently identified as his own. Roberts told the police that his girlfriend, Anita Issacs, the daughter of Bernard Issacs, had given him permission to use the check and was waiting for him in the mall parking lot. Unable to find Ms. Issacs, the police searched Roberts's car and found additional possessions from the Issacs's home, as well as a stash of heroin.

During his trial, Roberts testified that Ms. Issacs had given him her parent's checkbook and credit cards with the understanding that he could use them. At Roberts's preliminary hearing, however, Anita Issacs responded to defense questioning by denying that she gave Roberts permission to take articles from her parents' home or to use her father's checks. By the time of the criminal trial, Anita Issacs had run away from home and thus did not appear in court to testify. The prosecution therefore rebutted Roberts's testimony by reading Ms. Issacs's preliminary hearing testimony into the record. Roberts was convicted, and in his appeal he argued that his inability to cross-examine Ms. Issacs during the trial violated the Sixth Amendment. The Ohio Supreme Court upheld an Ohio appellate court's decision to overturn Roberts's conviction.

After hearing an appeal of the Ohio Supreme Court's decision, the justices met in conference to cast a preliminary vote in the case. Three of the nine justices (Brennan, Marshall, and Stevens) voted to uphold the Ohio Supreme Court. Lewis Powell's conference notes make clear that Brennan and Marshall each thought that the right of defendants to cross-examine needed to be protected. Justice Stevens contended that in this particular case the state had not demonstrated that it had made an adequate effort to find Ms. Issacs. The other six justices (Blackmun, Burger, Powell, Rehnquist, Stewart, and White) thought that the Ohio Supreme Court should be reversed. On December 12, 1979, Chief Justice Burger assigned the opinion to one of the more moderate members of the majority coalition: Justice Blackmun.[1]

Blackmun's first draft of the opinion, which was circulated on May 12, 1980, had the potential to expand the breadth of the confrontation clause while simultaneously overturning the Ohio Supreme Court's decision. In the draft, Blackmun reversed the Ohio court on the grounds that Roberts had the opportunity for "effective" cross-examination during the preliminary hearing. The day after Blackmun circulated his draft, on May 13, Justices Stewart and Rehnquist joined it. On May 15, Justice Powell circulated a memo that would subsequently alter the Court's interpretation of the Sixth Amendment. Powell's memo suggested that Blackmun drop the "effective" cross-examination phrase:

Although I am impressed by the thoroughness of your opinion, I am concerned – if I understand it correctly – by the standard you appear to approve: whether, in addition to the opportunity to cross examine, it must have been "effective" or the *de facto* equivalent of cross examination. . . . I would prefer to hold that the Confrontation Clause is satisfied whenever defense counsel had an unrestricted opportunity to examine the

---

[1]   During his tenure on the Court, Justice Blackmun voted in the liberal direction in criminal procedure cases 40.2 percent of the time. The only majority coalition member who was more moderate was Justice Stewart, who voted in the liberal direction 46.1 percent of the time (Epstein et al. 1994, table 6–1).

witness in any way he chose, and in fact availed himself of that opportunity to some extent. (Powell 1980a)

Powell believed that the "effective" standard contained in the Blackmun opinion would "encourage District Courts to engage in the task of determining whether cross examination in fact had been 'effective'" (Powell 1980b). Instead, Powell wanted the Court to employ a standard that just assessed whether the defendant had the opportunity for cross-examination. The day after receiving Powell's memo, Blackmun politely rejected the standard Powell proposed. Blackmun wrote:

Thank you for your letter of May 15. I took the word "effective" from *Mancusi v. Stubbs*, 408 U.S. 204 (1972). There the Court upheld the admission of prior-trial testimony, observing that the defendant, at the earlier proceeding, "was represented by counsel who could and did effectively cross-examine prosecution witnesses." . . . Given these considerations . . . I felt it better not to decide whether the Confrontation Clause is satisfied regardless of the nature of prior cross-examination. . . . Of course, if you and three others want the more far-reaching approach, I shall be glad to counsider [*sic*] revision (Blackmun 1980a)

Blackmun explained that, although he was not trying to impose a new standard, since he had technically reserved the "effectiveness" question, he was unwilling to commit to Powell's suggested policy.[2] However, Blackmun's note also signaled to Powell that he would take his suggestion seriously if Powell had the votes. Inevitably, Blackmun had some degree of confidence in making this statement since two of the six members of the majority coalition, Stewart and Rehnquist, had already signaled to Blackmun that they approved of his approach by joining his opinion.

While Blackmun may have thought that he had the votes to defeat Powell's efforts to drop the "effectiveness" standard, Justice Stewart immediately signaled that the Powell approach might work. Stewart wrote that "Although I have already joined your proposed opinion for the Court, I would have no objection whatever to modifications along the lines suggested by Lewis" (Stew-

---

[2]   Blackmun indicated to Powell that "I thought I reserved this issue [the effectiveness standard] in the sentence you quote in your letter" (Blackmun 1980a). Powell's clerk pointed out, however, that, "Justice Blackmun is, of course, correct that his draft opinion would not hold that the Constitution requires an 'effective' cross-examination. He expressly reserves the question. Yet, what he has done is to create a 'safe' way for lower courts to resolve these questions by finding that the examination was 'effective'" (Richey 1980a).

art 1980). In response to Blackmun's note, Powell's lead clerk on this case, Mary Ellen Richey, explained to Justice Powell that:

Justice Blackmun's letter of May 16 in effect rejects your suggestion in this case . . . . At present, Justice Stewart and Rehnquist have joined Justice Blackmun. Justice Stewart also has responded affirmatively to your analysis, though without suggesting that he would "jump ship" if it came to that. Justices Stevens, Brennan and Marshall are in dissent to be authored by Justice Brennan. He may criticize the majority by showing the problems with the "effectiveness" standard, as he did in *Green*. . . . The Chief and Justice White have yet to be heard from, although they voted with the majority at Conference.

I suppose the next step is to respond to Justice Blackmun renewing the objection. . . . We could then wait to see whether Justice White or the Chief express any sympathy for your view. Alternatively, we could begin work on a separate concurrence. (Richey 1980a)

On May 21, Powell took an aggressive posture. He circulated a memo to the entire conference announcing that "I would prefer not to encourage District Courts to engage in the task of determining whether cross examination in fact had been 'effective.' Accordingly, I will try to write a brief opinion concurring in the judgment" (Powell 1980c). Whereas Powell's initial suggestion did not provoke Blackmun to make the changes he sought, Powell's threat to write a concurrence, along with Stewart's signal that Powell was taking the right approach and Burger and White's refusal to publicly support Blackmun, provoked Blackmun to retreat. The same day he received Powell's memo, Blackmun circulated the following note: "In view of the position that Lewis has taken in this case, and Potter's acquiescence in it . . . I am willing to attempt a modification of my proposed opinion to accommodate Lewis. I suspect it is better not to have the Court completely fractionalized. I shall get a draft to you as soon as possible" (Blackmun 1980b). In response to the Powell memo, Chief Justice Burger decided to weigh in by telling Blackmun: "I would join your initial circulation but in view of your memo dated May 21, I will await your revised draft" (Burger 1980).

On June 12, Blackmun proposed in a letter to Justice Powell, which was also circulated to the other justices who already signaled their willingness to join him (Burger, Rehnquist, and Stewart), a revision of the eight pages that articulated the effectiveness standard he had originally proposed. Blackmun (1980c) closed his note accompanying the redrafted pages: "Would you please let me know whether this revision meets your concern. . . . If this is not acceptable, then perhaps I should consider adhering to my original writing with which the Chief, Potter, and Bill Rehnquist have shown an inclination to join." Blackmun's closing both signaled his preference for his original version of the "effectiveness standard" and threatened Powell by telling him that if the revision was unacceptable he would likely not get any changes.

According to Powell's clerk,

> Justice Blackmun has given you half of what you requested. He explicitly disavows any effectiveness standard, thus eliminating many of the problems you raised. . . . For two reasons, however, I would recommend joining the latest effort. First, eliminating the apparent "effectiveness" test is a major improvement. Second, this case is probably at best a halfway effort on the way to answering the important question of whether mere opportunity is enough. (Richey 1980b)

Powell followed the tack proposed by his clerk. After receiving her note, Powell informed Blackmun that he would join the opinion if a few minor changes were made to it. Blackmun made the changes and circulated the modified opinion. Within days, Burger, White, and Powell officially joined the Blackmun draft opinion.

Powell's efforts to shape the opinion in *Ohio v. Roberts* (1980) are neither new nor unique. It is clear that justices who vote with the majority at the initial conference on a case's merits do not view such a vote as carte blanche to the majority opinion author to craft the Court's opinion as he or she desires. Justices frequently make concerted efforts to shape the final opinion. For instance, Justice Brennan's circulation records indicate that in 535 of the cases decided during the Burger Court (23.4 percent), a justice tried to change the majority opinion by sending a note to the majority opinion author recommending a specific change in the opinion. In 50.1 percent and 63.2 percent of the cases, a justice respectively circulated a concurring or dissenting opinion draft. The intention of these opinions is frequently to shape the majority opinion. As Justice Scalia stated in a speech delivered at the Supreme Historical Society on June 13, 1994, "the most important internal effect of a system permitting dissents and concurrences is to improve the majority opinion" (Scalia 1994, 41).

Although opinion authors such as Blackmun may have a disproportionate ability to shape the law, it is clear that they cannot act unilaterally. Blackmun's opinion in *Ohio v. Roberts* was shaped in part by what we have termed the collegial game, that is, by the tactics and positions embraced by the other members of the majority coalition, as well as by his own policy and legal preferences. If Powell had merely made a suggestion and not threatened to circulate a concurrence, Blackmun likely would not have dropped the "effectiveness" standard that sparked Powell's objection. Although Powell's declaration that he would write separately and the signals sent by the other justices had no effect on Roberts's future, they altered the Court's interpretation of the Sixth Amendment. In other words, the politics of opinion assignments discussed in the previous chapter are only a portion of the many decisions that shape the law. In this chapter, we systematically explore the tactics that justices use to shape the legal rules articulated in majority opinions. Our goal is to determine whether the model articulated in the first chapter can account for the tactics justices use in efforts to produce majority opinions that as closely as possible match their preferred policy outcomes.

RESPONDING TO THE MAJORITY OPINION

To influence the opinion writer, justices have available a variety of means beyond simple persuasion and personal regard, and they must choose which are most likely to produce the desired effect. As Murphy writes, "a justice must learn not only how to put pressure on his colleagues but how to gauge what amounts of pressure are sufficient to be 'effective' and what amounts will overshoot the mark and alienate another judge" (1964, 57). Justices may choose to appear unsure, make suggestions with or without threats, announce their intention to write separately, circulate a separate opinion draft, or change votes. Each of these tactics has the potential to affect the content of the final opinion. Each justice has to make a decision regarding which tactics he or she seeks to employ, and, in this chapter, we explore such attempts to shape majority opinions.

We first investigate the responses of members of majority conference coalitions and later consider the replies from minority coalition members. We make this distinction because members of the majority are in the best position to influence the legal doctrine being crafted in a majority opinion. Justices commonly note that when writing the majority opinion they are particularly concerned with how majority coalition members react to their draft opinions.[3]

---

[3] Wahlbeck, Spriggs, and Maltzman (1998) also empirically demonstrate that the tactics used by minority coalition members do not lead to greater accommodation by opinion authors in the form of a larger number of opinion drafts.

William Rehnquist, for instance, suggests that "the proof of the pudding will be the reaction of those who voted with the majority at conference when they see the draft opinion" (Rehnquist 1987, 301). William Brennan notes as well that once a justice circulates a majority opinion draft the author is most concerned with "whether those who voted with him are still of his view and what they have to say about his proposed opinion" (Brennan 1960, 405).

Joining the Majority

The first, and most obvious, way a conference majority justice can respond to a majority opinion draft is by joining it. The most common phrasing of a "joinder," as the justices sometimes phrase it, is the following: "Please join me" (O'Connor 1984b). This reply informs the majority opinion author that a justice agrees with both the disposition of the case (i.e., to affirm or reverse the lower court) and the legal rationale supporting that outcome. Such a reply is exactly what the author hopes to receive. As Justice Powell's briefing notes for his law clerks states: "After an opinion is circulated, we anxiously await responses from other Chambers. The happiest response is simply a note saying 'Please join me'" (Powell 1984a). Table 3.1 presents the frequency of justices responding with a joinder. It is apparent that memos declaring that a justice will join the majority are the most common response to drafts that an author receives. Instead of joining, however, justices can employ a series of tactics to influence the majority opinion, to which we now turn.

Appearing Unsure

One tactic justices somewhat regularly employ is to inform the justice who drafted the majority opinion that they are unwilling to join the opinion until subsequent majority or separate opinions are circulated. For example, on April 2, 1973, Justice Blackmun responded to a draft opinion that Justice Marshall circulated in *Wardius v. Oregon* (1973) by writing "I still have trouble with the recirculation of March 27. I, therefore, shall wait for any dissent, in whole or in part, that may be forthcoming" (Blackmun 1973). Because justices who vote with the majority at conference normally "join [the majority opinion] without waiting for circulation of the dissent" (Rehnquist 1987, 303), notifying the opinion author that one is unprepared to join has two effects.

First, it signals the author that the justice might want changes made to the

Table 3.1. *Majority Conference Coalition Justices'*
Responses to Majority Opinion Drafts

Type of Response	Total Frequency of Response (%)	Number of Cases with Response (%)	Justices' First Response (%)
Join Majority	11,409 (66.2)	2,271 (99.2)	10,044 (79.4)
Wait	389 (2.3)	293 (12.8)	343 (2.7)
Suggestion	488 (2.8)	320 (14.0)	349 (2.8)
Threat	383 (2.2)	231 (10.1)	230 (1.8)
Will Write	485 (2.8)	403 (17.6)	304 (2.4)
Circulate/Join Concur	3,164 (18.4)	965 (42.1)	1,006 (8.0)
Circulate/Join Dissent	922 (5.3)	396 (17.3)	375 (3.0)
Total	17,240 (100.0)	2,290	12,651 (100.1)

opinion. As we will see in the next chapter, when a justice informs the majority opinion author that he or she wants to await subsequent developments, the author is likely to accommodate that justice by circulating additional drafts of the majority opinion (see Wahlbeck, Spriggs, and Maltzman 1998). Second, signaling a willingness to wait enhances a justice's subsequent bargaining leverage. As Murphy notes, "an uncommitted justice has great bargaining advantages, advantages which a deeply committed justice might assume by appearing unsure" (1964, 58). Although informing the author that one wants to wait until additional opinions are circulated enhances one's bargaining leverage and can even entice the majority opinion author to revise his or her opinion, it does not provide the opinion author with any substantive recommendation for altering the draft.

Table 3.1 makes clear that the use of "wait statements" by members of the majority coalition is not rare. In 293 of the 2,290 (12.8 percent) cases decided during the Burger Court, at least one member of the majority coalition sent the majority opinion author a letter stating that he or she was waiting for other opinions or subsequent drafts.

Suggestions and Threats

If a justice wants to express particular problems with an opinion, he or she may suggest that the opinion author make substantive changes, such as add or delete a phrase, a sentence, or a paragraph in the opinion. By articulating a specific concern, this response goes beyond the general uncertainty expressed in a wait statement. Justice Powell's May 15 note to Justice Blackmun about his *Ohio v. Roberts* (1980) opinion is only one of many instances in which a justice tries to influence an opinion by circulating a suggestion. For example, in *Ruckelshaus v. Monsanto Company* (1984), Justice Rehnquist noted to the opinion author, Harry Blackmun, that: "I think you have written an excellent opinion in this case, but I am troubled by a couple of points which I want to call to your attention" (Rehnquist 1984a).

In contrast to a suggestion, justices can try to entice majority opinion authors to modify their opinions by threatening not to join the opinion unless specific changes are made. Chief Justice Burger, for instance, sent Justice Marshall, the author of the majority opinion in *Berkemer v. McCarty* (1984), the following comment: "I am unable to join an opinion in this case unless it reflects that a 'car stop' does not invoke Miranda" (Burger 1984a). As well, Justice O'Connor closed a memo to Justice White, the author in *United States v. Karo* (1984), with the following statement: "If you could see your way to incorporating this modification in your circulating draft I would be pleased to join" (O'Connor 1984c).

Chief Justice Burger's memo to Justice Marshall and Justice O'Connor's note to Justice White differ in tone from Rehnquist's memo to Blackmun. Whereas Burger and O'Connor made very explicit their willingness to join the majority opinion if and only if the author made changes they sought, Justice Rehnquist never informed Blackmun what would happen if his suggestion was not accommodated. As Justice Scalia explains, the Court's members take such threats seriously: "nothing causes the writer to be as solicitous of objections on major points as the knowledge that, if he does not accommodate them, he will not have a unanimous court, and will have to confront a separate concurrence" (1994, 41). Scalia's assertion is consistent with Murphy's claim that "threats to change a vote or to write a separate opinion, dissenting or concurring, are the sanctions generally most available to a justice" (Murphy 1964, 57).

Suggestions and threats, like wait statements, are neither rare nor ineffective. During the Burger Court, majority coalition justices sent one or more suggestions to the majority opinion author in 320 of the 2,290 (14.0 percent) cases where an opinion assignment was made or a signed opinion was released during the Burger Court.[4] Suggestions that were coupled with threats were

---

[4] This figure is understated since it is based exclusively on memos that are circulated to every justice. As Epstein and Knight (1995, 29–30) note, scholars cannot obtain all private memoranda that may have been circulated between two justices but not sent to the entire conference. Thus we exclude these memos. For a discussion of private memos, see Appendix 1.

made in 231 (10.1 percent) of these cases. In many cases, more than one justice made a suggestion or threat. According to Brennan's circulation records, 871 suggestions or threats to the majority opinion author were made by majority coalition justices and circulated to all of the justices. As we will see in the next chapter, suggestions and threats usually bring about concessions by majority opinion authors.

Stating an Intention to Write Separately

Another option available to a justice is the declaration that he or she will write a separate opinion. A justice is either explicitly or implicitly declaring that a separate opinion is forthcoming because the majority's legal position is objectionable in some way; consequently, such a response represents a threat to the opinion author. If the author chooses to alter the opinion consistent with the justice's concerns, then that justice is quite likely to join the majority rather than write separately.

A justice's signal that he or she will write a concurrence is cheaper to send than the signal sent by actually circulating a concurrence without any forewarning. Writing a concurrence creates opportunity costs, including the time and energy necessary to write the opinion, as well as placing the justice in a position from which it is more difficult to retreat. Thus, it might be preferable, in some circumstances, to declare that a concurrence is forthcoming in the hopes of encouraging the author to accommodate without actually having to write the separate opinion.

When a justice signals that he or she plans to write separately, the information conveyed is somewhat different from that contained in a suggestion or, as we shall see, the separate opinion itself. Whereas the latter two provide concrete information about a particular justice's problems with the draft opinion, the former sometimes just alerts the author that the justice has unstated problems with the opinion. The announcement that a separate opinion is going to be circulated by a justice also sends an important signal to those justices not authoring the majority opinion. It informs them that one of their brethren disagrees with the draft's legal logic, and it raises the possibility of future accommodation. According to Justice Scalia, "the mere *prospect* of a separate writing renders the writer of the majority opinion more receptive to reasonable suggestions on major points" (Scalia 1994, 41). Other justices are thus likely to view the declaration to write separately as suggesting that future bargaining and accommodation may take place. Justices who voted with the majority coalition signaled their intention to write on a reasonably frequent basis. In 403 (17.6 percent) of the cases decided during the Burger Court, at least one majority coalition justice informed his or her colleagues that a separate opinion was forthcoming.

A signal that a justice will write can also indicate that he or she is dissatisfied with the author's current level of accommodation and thus wishes to make public the disagreement. As you will recall, Powell's statement that he would write a concurrence in *Ohio v. Roberts* resulted from Blackmun's unwillingness to accommodate Powell's suggested changes to the opinion. That threat was sufficient to wrest the requested change. Another example occurs in *Marrese v. American Academy of Orthopaedic Surgeons* (1985). After receiving O'Connor's draft of the majority opinion, Burger indicated that: "I could happily join your opinion if you could add something along these lines" (Burger 1984b). O'Connor, however, responded to Burger by noting: "Your remaining substantive comments would require a major alteration in the present draft. . . . I will circulate some revisions before long in hopes of resolving some of the questions. The revisions may not meet all your concerns" (O'Connor 1985a). After another round of exchanging memos, Burger finally responded with "I fear we are not on the same 'wave length' on this case, and I will have something around as soon as possible" (Burger 1985a). Chief Justice Burger thus signaled his disagreement with the opinion by noting his intention to circulate a concurring opinion. Here, the threat was insufficient, and Burger followed through with his threat and circulated a concurrence.

Concurrences and Dissents

Suggestions, threats, and signals that justices will write separately can sometimes entice an author to alter an opinion, but other times they do not. In such instances, a justice may want to circulate either a concurrence or dissent. There are at least two reasons to write separately. First, a justice may want to circulate a separate opinion as a way of affecting the legal principles sustaining the majority opinion. This outcome can occur because an opinion author may take a separate opinion more seriously than either a threat or a suggestion. According to then Judge Ginsburg, separate opinions "when drafted and circulated among the judges . . . may provoke clarifications, refinements, modifications in the court's opinion" (1990, 143). Murphy (1964, 60), as well, argues the motivation behind the circulation of separate opinions "is essentially an effort to resolve conflict within the Court by persuading, in one fashion or another, other Justices." For instance, after Justice Harlan circulated a concurring opinion draft in *Greenbelt v. Bresler* (1970), Justice Stewart modified his draft opinion for the Court. This prompted Harlan to respond with: "The restructuring reflected in your circulation of today satisfies me, and I am accordingly withdrawing my separate concurring opinion" (Harlan 1970a). In 965 of the 2,290 (42.1 percent) cases decided during the Burger Court, a conference majority justice circulated at least one concurring opinion draft among the justices.[5]

If the majority opinion author does not revise the opinion to reflect a concurring justice's concerns, a concurring opinion can ultimately serve as a sanction by articulating the flaws in the majority opinion. By providing alternative ways to view the legal rule underlying the majority opinion, separate opinions can influence how the majority opinion is perceived, and even implemented, by judges, political decision makers, or private parties. In this sense, separate opinions possibly weaken the precedential basis of an opinion. We know, for example, that opinions accompanied by concurrences are at greater risk of being overruled in the future (Spriggs and Hansford 1998).

Given these possible effects of separate opinions, authors, without unnecessarily abandoning their policy preferences, have incentives to minimize their publication. As Murphy explains, "The two major sanctions which a justice can use against his colleagues are his vote and his willingness to write opinions which will attack a doctrine the minority or majority wishes to see adopted" (1964, 54). Indeed, as Justice Blackmun informed Justice Brennan, the majority opinion author in *Michelin Tire Corp. v. Wages* (1976), "I would be willing to join an opinion that overrules *Low*. Your opinion does not do that. If it remains as it is, the alternatives left to me, therefore, are (1) either to concur separately . . . or (2) to dissent" (Blackmun 1975).

Finally, the most severe sanction a majority coalition justice can employ against a majority opinion author, as the second option in Blackmun's memo

---

5   This figure is derived from Brennan's circulation records. The circulation of a concurrence is not necessarily equivalent to the publication of such an opinion. On occasion, as our example indicates, a justice will circulate a concurrence and later withdraw it and join the majority opinion. Thus, the circulation of a concurrence category in our dependent variable is not identical to the publication of a concurrence, the latter of which is treated by the explanatory model in Wahlbeck, Spriggs, and Maltzman (1999).

in *Michelin Tire* suggests, is to withdraw his or her vote. Justice Brennan explains, "It is a common experience that dissents change votes, even enough votes to become the majority" (Brennan 1960, 405). Justices sometimes find themselves in a position where the dissenting views more closely reflect their position than the majority opinion. In these instances, justices can respond by changing their votes (Hagle and Spaeth 1991; Maltzman and Wahlbeck 1996a). This circumstance is evidently what led Justice Douglas to switch his vote in *Coleman v. Alabama* (1970). As he wrote to Justice Brennan, the majority opinion author, "In No. 72 – *Coleman v. Alabama*, I sent you a return some weeks back joining your opinion. I have been greatly troubled by the right to counsel point and after some indecision, I have finally decided to go with Hugo's views on that question" (Douglas 1970). A justice's most powerful sanction is certainly to switch his or her conference vote to the dissenting position. Still, the frequency of a justice being this assertive is somewhat rare. Of the 12,651 instances where a justice cast a conference coalition vote with the majority during the Burger Court, 616 (4.9 percent) were eventually changed to a dissenting vote. Although on an individual level justices rarely reverse their vote, on a case level such fluidity occurs on a more regular basis. During the Burger Court, a justice voted with the majority at conference but later circulated or joined a dissent in 396 cases (17.3 percent). As we show in the next chapter, majority opinion authors regularly make an effort to accommodate their colleagues. Indeed, such accommodation accounts for one of the reasons why justices tend not to resort to such extreme action.

In summary, there are numerous tactics that majority conference coalition justices can use to respond to a draft opinion. Each of these options is likely to send a different message to the majority opinion author and to other justices on the Court. A justice's decision to simply "join" the majority opinion is, of course, a nonthreatening response that requires no changes on the part of the author. More-assertive responses include justices stating that they will wait until other opinions are circulated, making a suggestion, or threatening the opinion author with withholding one's vote unless changes are made. After these options, three additional choices remain: stating an intention to write separately, circulating (or joining) a concurrence, or switching votes to the dissent, the latter of which is clearly the most aggressive response a justice can make. After briefly describing minority coalition members' responses to majority opinion drafts, we explore the conditions most likely to motivate a majority coalition justice to adopt one of these tactics.

The Responses of Minority Coalition Justices

Minority coalition justices largely have available to them the same set of responses used by majority coalition justices. They thus can send a wait signal, declare that they will write, circulate a dissent, or switch their vote and either circulate a concurrence or join the majority. Of course, the latter two alternatives mean a justice would be switching from the minority to the majority coalition, which most likely indicates some form of accommodation by the author. In this section, we seek to differentiate minority responses from those of the majority and provide a descriptive account of their content and frequency.

The actions of minority justices are not necessarily equivalent to those same actions when adopted by members of the majority. As we discuss, certain responses from the minority represent routine declaration of intent rather than attempts to influence the majority. Wait statements and a statement that a dissent is forthcoming, for example, merely show that a justice will either write the dissent or most likely join one. Further, we expect minority coalition justices to make explicit suggestions or threats to opinion authors much less frequently than justices in the majority. They, first of all, not only disagree with the legal reasoning favored by the majority but also prefer a different disposition. Minority coalition justices are therefore much further away from the position embraced by the majority and thus less likely to be able to make a suggestion to modify the opinion's legal reasoning.

Majority opinion authors also have a much greater incentive to accommodate the desires of the majority coalition, on whose behalf they are writing. This idea follows from the majority opinion author's overriding goal: to produce an opinion that as closely as possible reflects his or her view of the case. Generally, minority members are further removed from the author's preferred legal ruling. Accommodating these justices would thus likely result in fairly substantial changes to the majority position. This, in turn, is likely to be met with resistance by other members of the majority. In fact, such a change to the opinion could alienate a majority coalition justice enough that he or she would refuse to join it.

Turning to the data, we see that minority coalition members more frequently announced their intention to wait than members of the majority did. Over 14.3 percent of minority coalition justices signaled that they would wait for the dissent or further developments prior to making a decision in the case. This compares to just over 2.9 percent of majority coalition justices stating their intention to wait. Also, over 20.9 percent of the justices voting with the minority announced that they would be writing separately. Thus, whereas only 6.4 percent of majority coalition justices stated that they would either await further action or write separately, over 34.4 percent of minority justices so responded.[6]

Wait and write statements by minority coalition members are not necessarily attempts to bargain with the author. Of those justices whose first action was to await developments, 73.8 percent signed a dissenting opinion as their second move. An additional 3.7 percent of those waiting subsequently noted that a dissent was in preparation. It appears that such wait statements mainly notified the author and other justices that a justice would wait for the dissenting opinion to come out before saying he or she would join it. A few justices, it seems, were also deciding whether to write, rather than join, a dissent. Thus, unlike a wait statement by a majority justice, which signals some level of disagreement with the logic of the majority, such a memo from a minority member is more routine. As well, the circulation of a dissent, while at times possibly influencing the majority opinion, has less of a tactical component to it. The circulation of a concurrence tells the majority opinion author what particular problems keep a justice from joining the opinion. If the opinion were changed, then the concurring justice would presumably withdraw his or her opinion and join the majority. Such a result is dramatically less likely to occur if a justice circulates a dissent. Even if changes are made to the majority in response to the dissent, they are probably unlikely to be significant enough to convince many dissenters to join.

As we expected, far fewer minority justices voiced particular concerns with a draft majority opinion in the form of suggestions or threats. Only 82 suggestions and 71 threats were sent by members of the minority coalition during the Burger Court. The frequency of such memos is much smaller than the 488 suggestions and 383 threats delivered by members of the conference majority. This evidence is consistent with our claim that minority coalition justices are far removed from the position of the majority and thus have little incentive to try to modify its legal reasoning. These justices also frequently circulated or joined draft dissents, as 66.4 percent of them did in cases decided during the Burger Court. Finally, at some point during the opinion-writing

---

6 These calculations are based on the 12,651 conference majority justices and the 4,945 minority justices in these 2,290 cases. Thus, these figures are not identical to column 1 of Table 3.1, which displays all actions (n = 17,240) for majority coalition justices.

process, 24.2 percent of minority justices joined a majority opinion draft, while an additional 15.1 percent joined or circulated a concurring opinion draft.

EXPLAINING JUSTICES' RESPONSES
TO MAJORITY OPINION AUTHORS

If the model we articulated in the first chapter accurately characterizes Supreme Court decision making, we expect that two principal factors influence how justices respond to authors: their policy preferences and the strategic interdependencies with their colleagues. These factors should matter even after controlling for contextual variables that may influence a justice's actions. We discuss each in turn.

The first factor is a justice's concern for public policy and the law. The course of action that a justice pursues is therefore likely to depend in part on the implications a particular choice holds for a justice's ability to successfully introduce his or her policy objectives into law. As a result, we expect justices to bargain with opinion authors when opinions do not reflect their views. The extent to which a particular opinion draft reflects a justice's policy preferences depends in turn on several factors. Because authors have a disproportionate influence over the final opinion, one factor that determines whether a draft is acceptable to a justice is his or her ideological proximity to the author. Second, although opinion authors play a significant role in developing the opinion, they cannot act unilaterally. The author's choices regarding the opinion's legal reasoning are in part structured by the choices of other justices. As a result, a justice will find an opinion more acceptable when the coalition supporting it has views similar to those of the justice. Thus, consistent with the outcome postulate articulated in Chapter 1, we anticipate:

> *Opinion Distance Hypothesis 1:* The closer a justice is ideologically to the majority opinion author, the less likely the justice will respond with a wait statement, suggestion, threat, will write signal, concurrence, or dissent.

> *Opinion Distance Hypothesis 2:* The closer a justice is ideologically to the original majority coalition, the less likely the justice will circulate a wait statement, suggestion, threat, will write signal, concurrence, or dissent.

We further anticipate that, while justices pursue their policy preferences, they do so within the strategic constraints resulting from the collegial character of the Court. The first important strategic factor pertains to the size of the majority coalition in each case. A justice's leverage is greatest in a close case. This idea directly follows from the Court's institutional rule that an opinion generally sets precedent only if a majority of the justices on the Court support it. Thus, justices are less likely to accept opinion language with which they disagree when the original coalition is smaller. We therefore expect:

> *Majority Coalition Size Hypothesis 1:* The smaller the majority conference coalition, the more likely the justice will circulate a wait statement, suggestion, threat, or will write signal.

Past research, moreover, demonstrates that, because justices have more leverage over majority opinion authors when the conference coalition is small, authors are more likely to accommodate their colleagues' concerns (Rohde 1972a, 1972b, 1972c; Murphy 1964, 65; Wahlbeck et al. 1998; see Riker 1962; Riker and Niemi 1962). We therefore argue that the conference vote margin affects the circulation of separate opinions differently than it does the other tactics. Although justices who are part of a small majority coalition will be more likely, for example, to propose a suggestion, they will not be as likely to take the effort to draft a separate opinion. The reason is simple: if the coalition is small, then the author is more likely to accommodate a justice's concerns and thus a separate opinion is less necessary. Given the increased likelihood of accommodation with small conference coalitions, we expect the following:

> *Majority Coalition Size Hypothesis 2:* The smaller the majority conference coalition, the less likely a justice will circulate a draft concurrence or dissent.

The second strategic constraint bears on justices' past cooperative relationships with their colleagues. Because justices are engaged in long-term interactions with their colleagues, we expect tit-for-tat relationships to develop. Murphy (1964, 52), for example, argues that a justice can "build up a reservoir of good will for later use" by joining the majority opinion despite having certain reservations about it. This tactic is useful because such a justice "may have put himself in an excellent position to win reluctant votes from colleagues on other issues" (Murphy 1964, 53). Given the fact that justices interact on numerous cases with each other, we expect:

> *Cooperation Hypothesis:* A justice is more likely to circulate a wait statement, suggestion, threat, will write signal, concurrence, or dissent if the author has not cooperated with him or her in the past.

In order to determine if justices attempt to maximize their policy goals while attending to the strategic interdependencies on the Court, we need to control for alternative contextual explanations. One important factor that may influence how a justice responds to a draft opinion is the importance of a case. Justices, like most Court observers, recognize that some Supreme Court cases are more important than others. If a justice views a case as relatively unimportant, he or she is more likely to resist paying the personal and workload costs associated with responding to the author. As we discussed in the previous chapter, case salience consists of both a political and a legal dimension. We therefore hypothesize the following:

> *Case Importance Hypothesis 1:* The more politically salient a case, the more likely a justice will circulate a wait statement, suggestion, threat, will write signal, concurrence, or dissent.

> *Case Importance Hypothesis 2:* The more legally salient a case, the more likely a justice will circulate a wait statement, suggestion, threat, will write signal, concurrence, or dissent.

A second factor pertains to a justice's institutional position, and Chapter 1 suggested that institutional position includes three facets. First, the chief justice has a particular interest in ensuring the smooth operation of the Court. As we discussed in the previous chapter, the chief's role is characterized in part by his persistent efforts to ensure that the Court's work is completed in a timely manner. Because changes in the majority opinion slow down the opinion-writing process, we expect:

> *Chief Justice Hypothesis:* The chief justice will be less likely than other justices to circulate a wait statement, suggestion, threat, will write signal, concurrence, or dissent.

A justice's length of service on the Court is the second aspect of institutional position. Freshman authors, we suggest, are likely to receive different responses from justices than their more senior colleagues. As we discussed earlier, justices may seek to establish a cooperative relationship with a new justice through their responses to the new justice's majority opinion drafts. Deference is one way of accomplishing such a goal. The third component of institutional position is a justice's expertise in the issue being addressed by a case. Experts in a particular area presumably have greater knowledge about and interest in the case, and expertise increases their incentive to modify the majority opinion. These two aspects of institutional position suggest:

Freshman Hypothesis: If the majority opinion author is new to the bench, other justices are less likely to issue a wait statement, suggestion, threat, will write signal, concurrence, or dissent.

Expertise Hypothesis: Justices with greater expertise in the issue area of a case are more likely to respond with a wait statement, suggestion, threat, will write signal, concurrence, or dissent.

Another contextual factor taps the influence of the competing demands justices encounter. Although the chief's institutional position may bestow extra institutional pressures, all justices encounter time constraints. These demands are likely to be greatest when workload pressures are higher. As a result, the amount of outstanding work a justice has is likely to affect his or her responses to the majority opinion author. As we learned in the previous chapter, the chief justice takes a justice's workload into consideration when making opinion assignments. Given this relationship, justices themselves likely do not consider workload considerations to be trivial. The manual Justice Powell prepared for his law clerks is instructive. Powell wrote: "As we move deeper into the Term, say from and after February, the number of opinions circulated by each Chamber multiplies, and the problem of keeping abreast is a serious one" (1984a, 19).

Workload Hypothesis: A justice with a heavy workload is more likely to simply join an opinion and less likely to circulate a wait statement, suggestion, threat, will write signal, concurrence, or dissent.

Of course, as Powell noted, workload pressures are exacerbated as the end of a term approaches. It seems reasonable to expect that the time available to complete work on a case might affect the willingness of a justice to challenge the opinion author. Taking an aggressive stance, such as making a threat or writing a concurrence, forces a justice to incur extra work and slows down the opinion-writing process. Toward the end of a term, justices recognize that workload demands are accentuated, which may discourage them from taking aggressive stances. A memo from Justice John Harlan to Chief Justice Burger in June 1971 illustrates this point: "I am glad to join your opinion in each case. If end-of-Term pressures permit, I may write something in addition" (Harlan 1971a). Such pressures suggest the following relationship:

End-of-Term Hypothesis: The closer the end of the Court's annual term, the less likely a justice will issue a wait statement, suggestion, threat, will write signal, concurrence, or dissent.

Finally, the capacity of a majority opinion author to write an opinion that satisfies a majority of the Court is also a function of case complexity, which relates to the quantity and difficulty of legal issues and problems raised in a case. If a case is especially complex, we expect the majority opinion author to be less likely to have crafted a draft opinion that successfully addresses all pertinent concerns of a justice. Consistent with this expectation is the finding of Wahlbeck et al. (1998) that opinion authors circulate a greater number of drafts in complex cases. Thus, we expect:

Case Complexity Hypothesis: The more complex a case, the more likely a justice will circulate a wait statement, suggestion, threat, will write signal, concurrence, or dissent.

According to our model, justices make choices designed to shape the law in a manner consistent with their policy goals. In some instances, we expect a strategic justice to pursue aggressively changes in a draft opinion. In other instances, a justice will be more reluctant to pursue modifications. Justices, in short, pursue their policy preferences within constraints. It is our expectation that each of these hypotheses characterizes meaningful influences on justices' decisions about how aggressively to pursue challenges to majority draft opinions.

DATA AND METHODS

It is exceedingly difficult to capture the richness and complexity of justices' responses to majority opinion authors in any single model. We therefore present several different ways of examining the foregoing hypotheses, each aimed at tapping the underlying causal forces leading a justice to reply in specific ways to majority opinion drafts. We first examine a simple dichotomous dependent variable: did each majority coalition justice either join the majority opinion outright or alternatively criticize it in some way? This particular cut on the data sheds light on why justices choose to respond negatively to majority opinion drafts.

This approach, however, does not distinguish between the alternative tactics available to justices, and, thus, our second model disaggregates justices' first reactions to authors into the different tactics outlined in the prior section.[7] More specifically, we examine majority conference coalition justices' initial responses to the majority opinion author. We explain the first response of each majority coalition justice because this initial response clearly articulates a justice's attempt to shape the draft opinion.[8] Most justices (79.8 percent) only adopt one response, and thus their initial position in a case represents their only interaction with the author. Column three of Table 3.1 reports the frequency of the various first responses that occur.[9]

Because the dependent variable in the first model is dichotomous, indicating whether a justice bargains, we employ logit to estimate it.[10] Our dependent variable for the second model, justices' first responses to authors, contains seven categories: justice joins majority opinion; justice issues a wait statement; justice makes a suggestion; justice articulates a threat; justice signals that he or she intends to circulate a separate opinion; justice circulates or joins a draft

[7] Thus, our dichotomous dependent variable equals 1 if a justice, at any point during the writing of a case, adopted one of these tactics (e.g., will write signal). The polychotomous dependent variable, by contrast, only examines a justice's first reaction to the opinion author.

[8] More specifically, we examined the first response that each majority conference coalition justice made to the majority opinion author in 2,290 cases. We exclude from the analysis in this chapter four cases where the majority opinion author was the only justice who supported a particular disposition. For example, in *Regents of the University of California v. Bakke* (1978), Justice Powell was assigned the opinion but was the only justice who favored partial affirmance and partial reversal. We also deleted a case where no opinion drafts or memorandums were circulated.

Because the options available to the majority opinion author differ systematically from those of other justices, we excluded the justice who was assigned the majority opinion from the analysis. This approach produced 12,651 observations.

If more than one justice circulated a majority opinion, we treated the final opinion author as the majority opinion author. In 51 of the 2,290 cases (2.2 percent) included in our analysis, more than one justice circulated a majority opinion draft. In most of these cases, this occurred because of a shift in the majority. This means that for these cases the justices agreeing with the final author's position at conference are treated as majority coalition justices. Also, if a per curiam opinion or memorandum is assigned and ultimately a signed opinion is released, we included the case in our study.

[9] The number of Supreme Court cases in this chapter does not equal the number reported in Spriggs, Maltzman, and Wahlbeck (1999). The reason is that here we examine justices' responses in every case where an opinion assignment was made or a signed opinion was released, whereas in the earlier article we only looked at cases in which a signed opinion was released. Thus, we here include an additional twenty-four cases to the data, where an opinion assignment was made but no signed opinion was released.

[10] We estimate the two models reported in this chapter with the "logit" and "mlogit" commands in Stata 5.0.

concurring opinion; justice circulates or joins a draft dissenting opinion.[11] Because our dependent variable is nominal with multiple categories, we employ multinomial logit, an estimator that is very similar to the one we used in the previous chapter (conditional logit).[12] Since this technique estimates the likelihood that a response will be chosen compared with another alternative, which serves as a base, it yields six sets of estimates. We use "join majority" as the model's baseline, and thus the estimates for each tactic capture a justice's tendency to adapt that response to the majority opinion rather than join it.[13] As a result, we can uncover the causal mechanisms leading to the use of each tactic available to majority coalition justices.

[11] To determine whether a justice informed the majority opinion author that he or she intended to wait, made a suggestion, made a threat, stated that he or she would write separately, or circulated or joined a concurrence, we used the detailed circulation records that Justice Brennan maintained, which are discussed in Appendix 1.

We coded majority coalition justices as waiting if they sent the majority opinion author a letter stating that they were waiting for other opinions, subsequent drafts, and the like. If a majority conference coalition justice sent a letter that contained a suggestion about how to change the majority opinion, we coded that justice as having made a suggestion. If the letter explicitly made a suggestion a condition for joining the opinion or threatened to join another opinion if a suggestion was not followed, we coded the justice as having made a threat. If justices specifically stated they intended to write a separate opinion, then we coded them as signaling they would write. Majority coalition justices' actions were coded as concurrence if they did not announce that they were dissenting and circulated or joined a concurrence, an opinion concurring in part or dissenting in part, or an opinion simply labeled a separate opinion. We coded majority coalition justices as dissenting if, according to Brennan's circulation records, they circulated or joined a draft dissent.

[12] Although one might consider this dependent variable to be ordered, and thus use ordered probit to estimate the model, we think multinomial logit (MNL) is the more appropriate technique for two reasons. First, the ordering of the tactics is not entirely clear. Whereas joining the majority is an unaggressive response and the tactic of changing votes and circulating a dissent is the most aggressive, the options in between are more ambiguous. For instance, is a wait statement more or less aggressive than a will write signal or a suggestion? Although a wait statement is less substantive than a suggestion, our data (see "The Sequencing of Justices' Responses" later in this chapter) suggest the former may signal greater disagreement. Second, ordered probit assumes that the effect of a variable remains constant across the categories of the dependent variable. If the data violate this assumption, then the appropriate estimator is MNL. We tested this assumption using a likelihood ratio test and rejected the null hypothesis ($p \leq .001$) of proportionality of odds across the categories. Thus, because our data violate this assumption, we are more confident in the MNL results. Nevertheless, the ordered probit results are basically consistent with those of MNL: all coefficients appear in the expected direction and are statistically significant except for *Legal Salience, Workload,* and *Winning Margin.*

[13] As each of the justices in these data appears repeatedly over time, it is therefore possible that the residual for a particular justice's decision in one case is correlated with the residual for that justice in another case (see Stimson 1985). We control for the possibility of correlated errors within justices by using the robust variance estimator. By clustering on justices, we control for any within-justice error correlation across cases (White 1980; Kennedy 1992, 278–289).

Independent Variables

Author Distance. We calculated an issue-specific compatibility score between the author and each justice in the majority conference coalition for every case.[14] This score is determined by using original conference data, Spaeth's (1994) twelve substantive value groups (e.g., civil rights), and the percentage of cases in which each justice voted for the liberal outcome while on the Court (Epstein et al. 1994, table 6–1). The score is computed by taking the absolute value of the difference between the justice's value-specific liberalism (i.e., percentage of the time a justice voted liberally over his or her career on the Court) and the majority opinion author's liberalism.[15] Thus, if the justice's ideology is identical to the author's, the author distance is zero. The more distant the justice is from the majority opinion author, the higher the score.

Coalition Distance. We calculated the absolute difference between the justice's issue-specific ideology and the conference coalition's mean ideology, excluding the author. This score is based on the twelve substantive value groups identified by Spaeth (1994). For each of these twelve areas, we calculated the percentage of cases in which each justice voted for the liberal outcome (Epstein et al. 1994, table 6–1). Greater ideological distance between the justice and the conference coalition's ideology produces a larger positive score.

Winning Margin. As in the previous chapter, we measured the conference margin by subtracting the number of votes needed to form a winning coalition from the number of justices who voted with the author.

Cooperation. To measure the degree of previous cooperation between a justice and the author, we calculated the percentage of time that the author joined a separate opinion written by the justice in the previous term. The number of separate opinions written by each justice and the number of those separate

---

[14] See Appendix 2 for descriptive statistics for all of our independent variables.

[15] Thus, this measure is constructed from the same data as the ideology measure in Chapter 2. The only difference is that in the previous chapter we cared about the distance between the assignor and each justice, whereas here the relevant comparison is the distance between the majority opinion author and each justice.

See Chapter 2 for more-specific details on the calculation of this variable. In four cases, the opinion was written by a three-justice team. In these cases, we used the median justice's ideology for the author. We also used this corrective in creating our *Cooperation* score for these four cases.

opinions that the author joined are drawn from Spaeth (1994). To purge our measure of cooperation of ideological compatibility between justices, we developed a quasi-instrumental variable. We regressed the percentage of time the author joined another justice's separate opinions on their ideological distance, using the residual from this regression as our measure of *Cooperation*.[16]

Chief Justice. A dummy variable is used to signify Chief Justice Burger.

Freshman Author. Any author who had served less than two full years when the first majority opinion draft was circulated was coded as 1, otherwise 0, consistent with Chapter 2.

Workload. The measure of each justice's workload is the number of majority and separate opinions on which he or she was working on the day the first draft of the majority opinion was circulated to the conference. We used the decision rules articulated in Chapter 2 to determine when a justice began and completed work on an opinion.

End of Term. This variable is the number of days from the date the first draft of the majority opinion was released until July 1, the traditional end of the Court's term.[17]

Case Complexity. We measured this variable by combining two indicators, both of which were derived from Spaeth (1994): the number of issues raised by the case and the number of legal provisions relevant to a case. We then factor-analyzed these two indicators and adopted each case's factor score as the measure of complexity.[18]

---

[16] We use separate opinions, rather than majority opinions, because joining a separate opinion is a better indicator of cooperative behavior. Justices who plan to concur or dissent can write their own opinion, rather than joining a colleague's dissent or concurrence. Such a decision enables one to avoid the costs associated with coordinating one's efforts. In contrast, a justice does not have an option to publish his or her own majority opinion.

[17] The measures of *Workload* and *End of Term* slightly differ from those employed in Chapter 2 in that here we calculate both from the release of the first majority opinion draft rather than the opinion assignment date. We do so because a justice is deciding how to respond after the draft is released, which obviously occurs sometime after the opinion is assigned.

[18] This measure differs from the one employed in Chapter 2 in that here we exclude the number of separate opinions as one of the indicators of *Case Complexity*. We do so to avoid the endogeneity that could possibly result from including the number of separate opinions as one

To capture each justice's *Expertise* and the *Legal* and the *Political Salience* of each case, we employed measures identical to those used in Chapter 2.[19]

RESULTS

Majority opinion authors frequently received responses to their majority opinion drafts expressing some level of uncertainty or disagreement. In 60.4 percent of cases, the author received at least one response from a majority member other than a simple join of the opinion. In 20.4 percent of the cases, moreover, the author confronted a suggestion or a threat from some member of the conference majority. Of course, in many cases more than one justice tries to shape the final majority opinion, and in some cases, a single justice will embrace more than one tactic. For example, in 3.5 percent of the instances in which a justice first sent a "wait" statement, his or her next action was to circulate a suggestion.

The Decision to Respond to the Author

The results in Table 3.2 demonstrate that justices' responses to majority opinion authors' draft opinions result from their policy preferences as well as from constraints imposed by the collegial game. Importantly, these results appear compelling even after we control for a variety of contextual features relating to cases and justices. Of the 12,651 justices voting with the majority in the 2,290 cases decided during the Burger Court years, 2,998 (23.7 percent) of them responded to the author with other than just a "join" memo. That is, they bargained with the majority opinion author at some point during deliberations in the case.

As becomes apparent from Table 3.2, justices are more likely to respond negatively, that is, to bargain, if they are either ideologically removed from the author or the supporting coalition. When a justice is in ideological harmony

part of the independent variable explaining whether a justice may have circulated a concurrence or dissent.

[19] One concern with the *Expertise* measure may be that it introduces circularity into the model since one alternative that a justice might choose to pursue is to write a concurrence, and concurrences are incorporated into the expertise measure. This concern is somewhat alleviated given that the *Expertise* measure does not include cases decided in the current term, including the case at issue.

Table 3.2. *Logit Model of Coalition Justices' Decisions
to Engage Majority Opinion Authors*

Variable	Estimate	Robust Standard Error
Constant	−2.023***	.180
Policy Preferences		
Author Distance	.026***	.003
Coalition Distance	.013***	.003
Strategic Interaction		
Winning Margin	−.055*	.029
Cooperation	−2.526***	.385
Contextual Controls		
Political Salience	.043***	.005
Legal Salience	.201	.123
Case Complexity	.088***	.016
End of Term	.002***	.000
Workload	.008	.008
Chief Justice	−.432***	.066
Freshman Author	−.133*	.070
Expertise	.078**	.033
Number of Observations	12,651	
Log-Likelihood	−6,546.588	
Chi-Square	8,739.75***	
Percent Correctly Predicted	77.0	
Percent Reduction of Error	3.1	

*p ≤ .05; **p ≤ .01; ***p ≤ .001 (one-tail tests).

with the author, he or she submits a bargaining memo only 15.0 percent of the time, whereas this number swells to 56.7 percent when a justice is in ideological conflict with the author.[20] Similarly, if a justice embraces an ideological viewpoint that is at odds with the majority conference coalition, the chance he

[20] We calculated the relative impact of each statistically significant variable while holding constant for all other factors at their means. The *Author Distance* value for a justice who is in "ideological harmony" (or "aligned") with the author equals 0. This would occur if the author and the justice were perfectly aligned. To ascertain the substantive impact of a justice being "ideologically distant" from (or "in conflict with") the opinion author, we set the author distance score at 78.1. This is the largest score that exists. The figures for the "aligned"

or she will not simply join the majority rises. The probability a justice will bargain with the author is 19.6 percent when ideologically aligned with the majority conference coalition. When a justice is ideologically opposed to the majority, his or her tendency to bargain increases to 32.7 percent.

According to the collegial game, a justice's decision whether and how to bargain with the author depends on the strategic context, not just policy preferences. Our results support the claim that judicial behavior is interdependent. The statistically significant *Cooperation* variable indicates that justices adopt tit-for-tat strategies with one another. For example, if the author had previously been extremely uncooperative with a justice, our simulation reveals, the justice was likely to respond negatively to draft opinions 30.1 percent of the time. In contrast, a justice has only a slim 3.3 percent chance of bargaining with the author if the author had been very cooperative in the past.

The result for *Winning Margin* supports our argument that smaller conference coalitions encourage justices to bargain. The simulation indicates that when a justice is a member of a minimum winning conference coalition, he or she is assertive toward the majority author 24.1 percent of the time. This tendency decreases slightly, to 20.3 percent, when a justice is part of a unanimous conference coalition. Although justices are motivated by their policy preferences, they also consider the strategic landscape on the Court when deciding how to respond to drafts of the majority opinion.

The contextual control variables that we include in our model also affect whether justices bargain with opinion authors. Political salience leads to a greater inclination for justices to respond negatively to an author's draft opinion for the Court. When deciding a highly politically salient case, rather than a nonsalient one, the tendency to bargain moves substantially, from 20.6 percent to 57.4 percent. While the coefficient for *Legal Salience* appears in the appropriate direction, it is just below conventional levels of statistical significance.

In addition, we suggested that justices' institutional positions condition their choices. The chief justice, as we expected, was less likely to take an as-

---

and "distant" *Coalition Distance* measures were set at 0 and 52.02, respectively. These are the largest and smallest observed coalition distance scores. The values for *Cooperation* were set at the highest and lowest observed values of −.16 and .84. The values for *Political Salience* were set at 37.27 and −.92 for, respectively, high- and low-salience cases. For *Case Complexity*, the complexity score was alternatively set at the highest complexity score for any of the 2,290 cases in our data set (factor value of 6.89). This is compared with the "easy" case simulation where we set the complexity score at −.53, the minimum observed factor value. We set *Expertise* at the highest and lowest values, 2.67 and −2.11, respectively.

sertive position than his colleagues. Based on our simulation, Chief Justice Burger was likely to react critically to draft opinions 16.3 percent of the time, while the likelihood his colleagues would do so was 23.1 percent. Freshman authors, contrary to Murphy's assertion, were not less likely to receive entreaties from their colleagues. A justice's expertise, though, does appear to matter, with more expertise leading to a greater tendency to bargain. A justice who possesses significantly more expertise than his colleagues has a 26.0 percent chance of negatively responding to an opinion. Justices with considerably less than average expertise bargain a bit less often, doing so 19.5 percent of the time.

One of the two time constraints also affected the way justices reacted to authors. First, justices making decisions further away from the end of the Court's annual term were more likely to bargain with an opinion author. If there were two hundred days left in the term when the first draft was released, then the probability a justice would bargain was 24.5 percent, whereas this number dropped to 20.0 percent if there were only thirty days left in the term. A justice's workload, however, had no influence on this decision. Finally, justices bargained more frequently in more complex cases: if a case was not complex, a justice bargained 21.4 percent of the time, whereas this tendency increased to 34.3 percent in very complex cases.

Justices' First Responses to Authors

Although justices sometimes embrace multiple tactics in a single case, it is their initial response that frequently sets the stage for future negotiations. Conference majority justices' initial responses to majority opinion authors ranged from joining the majority opinion to circulating a draft dissent. Most (79.4 percent) justices' first action, as Table 3.1 displays, was to join the majority opinion. Only 2.7 percent of justices announced their intention to wait as their first action, a signal to the author that a draft opinion might be unsatisfactory. Justices also made suggestions or threats to the opinion author in, respectively, 2.8 percent and 1.8 percent of their initial replies. An additional 2.4 percent of these justices' first actions signaled that a separate opinion would be forthcoming. Finally, 8.0 percent and 3.0 percent of justices circulated (or joined) draft concurrences or dissents, respectively, as their first response to the author's draft opinion.

Table 3.3 reports the results of a multinomial logit model of each majority

Table 3.3. *Multinomial Logit Model of Majority Coalition Members'*
Initial Responses to Majority Opinion Authors

Variable	Wait Estimate (SE)	Suggestion Estimate (SE)	Threat Estimate (SE)	Will Write Estimate (SE)	Concur Estimate (SE)	Dissent Estimate (SE)
Constant	−4.158*** (.434)	-4.167*** (.265)	−4.913*** (.367)	−5.024*** (.468)	−3.178*** (.290)	−3.754*** (.257)
Policy Preferences						
Author Distance	.020*** (.004)	.025*** (.003)	.037*** (.005)	.026*** (.005)	.029*** (.003)	.021*** (.004)
Coalition Distance	.004 (.013)	−.014 (.010)	−.023 (.013)	.016** (.006)	.015** (.005)	.057*** (.003)
Strategic Interaction						
Winning Margin	−.133*** (.040)	.056 (.035)	.214 (.048)	−.038 (.054)	−.006 (.043)	-.233 (.027)
Cooperation	−2.738*** (.860)	−1.861*** (.564)	−2.517* (1.475)	−2.456*** (.793)	−2.553*** (.689)	−2.627*** (.584)
Contextual Controls						
Political Salience	.065*** (.012)	.059*** (.014)	.038* (.021)	.042** (.016)	.025** (.010)	.024 (.015)
Legal Salience	−.071 (.231)	.060 (.151)	−.484 (.312)	.060 (.210)	.469** (.151)	.016 (.225)
Case Complexity	−.065 (.034)	.114* (.058)	−.005 (.075)	−.031 (.060)	.079*** (.015)	.203*** (.032)
End of Term	.003** (.001)	.002** (.001)	.001* (.001)	.005*** (.001)	.000 (.001)	−.001 (.001)
Workload	.022 (.018)	.010 (.022)	.004 (.019)	.031 (.020)	−.005 (.016)	−.024 (.016)
Chief Justice	−.681*** (.168)	−.797*** (.150)	−.576*** (.151)	−.447*** (.133)	−.115 (.115)	−.664*** (.117)
Freshman Author	-.585** (.207)	.107 (.228)	−.001 (.195)	−.352 (.310)	−.002 (.091)	−.193 (.167)
Expertise	−.032 (.085)	−.080 (.068)	.118* (.064)	.100 (.076)	.161** (.057)	−.010 (.063)

Number of Observations	12,651
Chi-Square	112.61***
Percent Correctly Predicted	79.4
Percent Reduction of Error	42.8

Note: SE = standard error.
*p ≤ .05; **p ≤ .01; ***p ≤ .001 (one-tail tests).

conference coalition justice's initial response to the majority opinion author. The statistically significant chi-squared test statistic indicates that we can reject the null hypothesis that all of the independent variables jointly have no effect. The model also correctly predicts 79.4 percent of justices' tactics, for a 42.8 percent reduction of error over a null model of random assignment of the justices to each of the response categories.[21] The statistical analysis strongly supports our contention that justices' tactics to influence the majority opinion result from the pursuit of policy preferences within the strategic interdependencies of the collegial game.

The Opinion Distance Hypotheses 1 and 2 pertain to the extent to which a draft opinion comports with a justice's policy preferences. The positive and statistically significant coefficients for *Author Distance* and *Coalition Distance* confirm that justices are more likely to bargain with the author if they disagree with an opinion draft (as measured by ideological distance). The probability a justice will adopt any type of response, rather than simply join the opinion, rises if he or she is more ideologically distant from the opinion author. A justice is 4.8 percent likely to wait if she is ideologically incompatible with the author, but such a justice has only a 1.8 percent probability of submitting a wait statement when ideologically compatible with the author.[22] Consider a case like *Heffron v. International Society for Krishna Consciousness* (1981), in which Justice White was writing this First Amendment opinion. We would predict that justices ideologically removed from White, such as Justice Stevens, would be more likely to wait, whereas a justice with more compati-

---

[21]   We use tau, rather than lambda, as our proportional-reduction-of-error statistic. Goodman and Kruskal's tau is preferable to lambda, which simply compares the number of prediction errors from the model with the number of errors that would result from always predicting the modal category. Goodman and Kruskal's tau accounts for the distribution of cases across categories by computing expected errors that would result from randomly assigning cases to the different categories (Sigelman 1984, 78–79).

[22]   We calculate these predicted probabilities using the same independent-variable values listed in note 16 of this chapter. These probabilities indicate our model's prediction of the likelihood a justice will adopt one of the tactics, as compared with joining the majority opinion.

We want to emphasize that, while the percentages appear small, the effects of the independent variables are not therefore trivial. First, one can clearly see in our first model that the independent variables generally exert quite substantial influences on whether a justice will bargain at all. One reason the numbers appear somewhat small when looking at each individual tactic is that the baseline probability that a justice will adopt a particular tactic is itself very small. This fact is immediately evident in the proportion of the time a justice adopts any particular position, as identified in Table 3.1. Our model, for instance, predicts that the average justice (i.e., with all variables at their means) only waits 2.5 percent of the time. Thus a change from a low of 1.8 percent to a high of 4.8 represents a reasonably large change of about 167 percent.

ble views in First Amendment cases, like Chief Justice Burger or Justice Powell, would be less likely to wait.[23] It is not surprising that in *Heffron* both Burger and Powell joined the majority opinion outright, while Stevens signaled his intention to wait.

Likewise, our model predicts justices choose to make a suggestion or a threat in 1.7 percent and .8 percent of their first tactics when ideologically aligned with the author, and these numbers rise to 6.6 percent and 8.0 percent when they are ideologically opposed to the author. The effect of ideology clearly presents itself in *Roberts v. United States Jaycees* (1984), a case in which Justice Brennan was authoring a majority opinion regarding the relationship between freedom of association and expression and an organization's exclusionary membership rules. Several justices not sharing Brennan's ideological leanings either made a suggestion or threat as their first response: Justices Powell and O'Connor both proposed suggestions to Brennan's opinion, while Justice White delivered a threat. Those justices sharing Brennan's policy views, such as Justices Marshall and Stevens, joined the majority opinion outright.[24]

As the *Coalition Distance* coefficients show, justices are more likely to state they will write separately or to circulate (or join) a concurrence or dissent as they become further ideologically removed from the majority coalition. Yet, contrary to our hypotheses, justices who were distant from the coalition were not uniformly more likely to use one of the other tactics available to them. For example, in *Welsh v. United States* (1970), a conscientious objector case, a justice such as Harlan, who was ideologically detached from the coalition comprised of Justices Douglas, Brennan, and Marshall, circulated a draft concurrence. Brennan, who was much more ideologically allied with the other justices in the majority conference coalition, joined the majority opinion.[25] More precisely, a justice has a probability of circulating or joining a concurrence or dissent of, respectively, 6.1 and 1.2 percent when aligned with the majority coalition. When distant from the coalition, a justice is much more

---

[23] In *Heffron*, Justices Burger and Powell had an *Author Distance* score of, respectively, 6.4 and 9.5. This compares with an *Author Distance* value of 26.3 for Stevens.

[24] The ideological distance between Brennan and the two justices making suggestions, Powell and O'Connor, in this case was respectively 39.1 and 40.7; this figure is 36.3 for White. The most ideologically similar justices to Brennan in *Roberts* were Marshall, at .6, and Stevens, at 20.6.

[25] The *Coalition Distance* value for Harlan in *Welsh v. U.S.* was 32.7, whereas it was only 6.5 for Brennan.

likely to adopt either response, as these numbers increase respectively to 10.4 and 18.2 percent.

Once again, we see that justices make decisions in part based on the choices of their colleagues. According to the Majority Coalition Size Hypothesis 1, the tendency of majority coalition members to issue a wait statement, announce either a suggestion or threat, or signal they will write varies inversely with the size of the conference coalition. The *Winning Margin* coefficient is significant for only one type of tactic, wait statements, and thus we find minimal support for this hypothesis. The simulation shows that when the majority coalition is minimum winning, a justice tends to wait 3.2 percent of the time. If we compare this case with those with unanimous conference votes, a justice only waits with a probability of 1.9 percent. In *Paris Adult Theater I v. Slaton* (1973), with its minimum winning conference coalition, two of the justices in the majority coalition (Blackmun and Powell) decided to wait for further developments. The winning conference coalition in *Eastland v. United States Servicemen's Fund* (1975) was unanimous, and none of the justices chose to wait. The Majority Coalition Size Hypothesis 2 suggests that justices are less likely to concur or dissent when the conference majority is small. This idea is not supported by the data.

The Cooperation Hypothesis, which like the Coalition Size Hypothesis derives from our Collective Decision-Making Postulate, argues that justices engage in tit-for-tat behavior. In other words, justices reward authors who have cooperated with them in the past and sanction others. The negative coefficients for *Cooperation* show that justices are less likely to express any type of disagreement, rather than join the majority, the more cooperative the author had previously been with them. The likelihood that a justice issues either a suggestion or a threat, for instance, is .6 and .2 percent if an author had been entirely cooperative. These probabilities substantially increase to 3.2 percent and 2.1 percent if the author was uniformly uncooperative in the past. In *Logue v. United States* (1973), for instance, the majority opinion was authored by Justice Rehnquist, who in the past had been reasonably cooperative with Justice Powell and Chief Justice Burger but not so cooperative with Justice Brennan and Justice Stewart.[26] In this case, we thus witness Justices Powell and Burger join the majority opinion, while Justice Brennan threatened to withhold his support unless changes were made to the opinion, and Justice Stewart proposed a suggestion.

[26]   Our measure of *Cooperation* equals .07 for Powell, .08 for Burger, −.02 for Brennan, and −.07 for Stewart in *Logue v. United States* (1973).

Turning to the effect of our contextual variables, we find support for the hypothesis that justices will more aggressively pursue their policy preferences when cases are salient. First, the results bore out this hypothesis for cases that manifested political salience. Justices in such cases were more likely to use any tactic (rather than join the majority) except for one, circulating (or joining) a draft dissent. For instance, when a case is highly politically salient, the probability a justice will wait, articulate a threat, or signal he or she will write equals 15.5, 3.6, and 5.8 percent, respectively. A completely nonpolitically salient case prompts justices to respectively adopt one of these tactics in only 2.2, 1.4, and 2.3 percent of their initial tactics. Consider two cases, *Richmond Newspapers v. Virginia* (1980) and *United States v. Albertini* (1985). In the former, five amici briefs were filed, resulting in a higher than average *Political Salience* score, whereas no briefs were filed in the latter and thus it assumes a lower than average value on this variable.[27] In *Richmond Newspapers* we see that, consistent with our expectations, five justices either circulated or joined a concurrence and one justice issued a threat, while in *Albertini,* by contrast, every member of the conference majority merely joined the majority opinion. Second, *Legal Salience* leads to an increase in concurrences but has no influence on other types of responses. In legally salient cases, a justice is 10.6 percent likely to circulate or join a draft concurrence, and this figure lowers to 6.9 percent in nonlegally salient cases. The cases that attract the most attention from those outside of the Court also attract the most attention from the justices themselves.

Justices' institutional positions may also affect their willingness to be assertive. First, we hypothesized that the chief justice would be less likely than his colleagues to pursue his policy goals aggressively. Chief Justice Burger was less likely to wait, suggest, threaten, signal he would write, or dissent than his colleagues. The likelihood of the chief waiting, making a suggestion, or saying he would write separately, rather than joining the majority opinion, respectively equals 1.4 percent (waits), 1.4 percent (suggestions), and 1.5 percent (will writes), as compared with 2.7, 2.8, and 2.3 percent for other justices. Although it is difficult to make generalizations with an "N" of one, it is clear that Chief Justice Burger was not as aggressive as his colleagues. We suspect that this largely stems from his institutional position. As Chief Justice, Burger

---

[27] *Richmond Newspapers v. Virginia* (1980) had five amici briefs filed in it, for a *Political Salience* score of 4.35, meaning that this case had 4.35 standard deviations more briefs filed in it than the average case in the 1979 term, which triggered 1.88 briefs. In *United States v. Albertini* (1985), by contrast, no amici briefs were filed, resulting in a *Political Salience* score of −.89.

had a particular interest in the Court appearing unified and in releasing its opinions in a timely manner.

According to the Freshmen Hypothesis, a justice is less likely to respond in an aggressive fashion when freshman justices are writing the Court's opinion. The results for *Freshman Author* provide minimal support for this hypothesis. Although the likelihood of a justice sending a wait statement diminishes when a freshman was authoring the majority opinion, we find no indication that other justices are less likely to, say, make a suggestion, issue a threat, or circulate a separate opinion when the majority opinion author is new to the bench. A justice was 1.5 percent likely to wait when a freshman was authoring the opinion, as opposed to 2.6 percent when other justices were the majority author. The final institutional position hypothesis suggests that expert justices are more willing to be assertive than their less experienced colleagues. Our analysis indicates that a justice's relative expertise affects his or her decision to either threaten the author or circulate a concurrence, but has no influence on any other tactic. Justices who lack experience in a case, as compared with their colleagues, are only 1.2 percent likely to issue a threat and only 5.2 percent likely to concur. Justices with considerable expertise, however, make a threat 2.0 percent of the time and concur in 10.6 percent of their first replies.

We also expect justices to take into consideration other contextual factors that place demands on their time. First, contrary to our expectation, the size of a justice's workload, our data suggest, has no influence on the decision about how to respond to majority opinion drafts. Second, in the preceding chapter, we learned that the opinion assignment strategy employed by the chief varies as the Court's term approaches its conclusion. Here we learn that as the end of the term approaches, a justice's tendency to wait, make suggestions, or state he or she will write drops. If the end of the term is two hundred days away, a justice states he or she will write separately in 3.2 percent of his or her first actions. As the end approaches, with only thirty days left, the likelihood a justice will announce a separate opinion is forthcoming decreases to 1.5 percent. However, *End of Term* exerts no appreciable influence on the other tactics available to justices.

The results for the *Case Complexity* variable confirm a portion of our expectations. Justices were much more likely to either make suggestions, circulate concurrences, or circulate dissents as their initial action in complex cases, though the other tactics were not influenced by this factor. For example, if a case was extremely complex, a justice tended to respond with a suggestion, a concurrence, or a dissent, respectively, 5.0, 10.8, and 8.3 percent of the time. In a noncomplex case, by contrast, these percentages respectively drop to only 2.5, 6.9, and 2.1 percent. For instance, *Mulloy v. United States* (1970) was, according to our measure, a noncomplex case, and every member of the conference majority merely joined the majority opinion. This result compares with the tactics used by justices in *Larson v. Valente* (1982), a more complex case, in which O'Connor joined a draft concurrence and Stevens circulated a draft dissent.[28] Such a finding likely reflects the multidimensional character of complex cases, which makes it particularly difficult to assemble and hold a stable majority (Arrow 1951).

THE SEQUENCING OF JUSTICES' RESPONSES

The preceding models explain two facets of a justice's choice of tactics in a case, whether to bargain with the author of the majority opinion and which tactic to adopt as the initial position in a case. While relatively infrequent, justices occasionally adopt more than one response to the author. In this period, justices chose to employ multiple tactics in a single case 20.2 percent of the time. Over 86.8 percent of justices' subsequent responses took one of two forms: they either circulated or joined concurring or dissenting opinion drafts or they joined a subsequent draft of the majority opinion. In addition, very few justices articulated more than two responses to the author in a single case, and most of these actions were multiple drafts of separate opinions – 8.3, 4.0, and 1.9 percent of justices, respectively, made three, four, or five responses to the author. Thus, we will briefly describe the sequencing of justices' tactics to get additional leverage on why justices choose the tactics they do.

We first explore the patterns in the data with regard to staking out an initial position and then joining the majority opinion. Of the 2,560 occasions when justices made a second response to the author, 38.3 percent of the justices joined the majority opinion. Justices whose first action was either a suggestion or a threat, for instance, joined the majority opinion in 58.2 and 41.8 percent of their second actions. Justices who first announced that they were awaiting subsequent developments joined less often, doing so in 33.8 percent of their second responses. In addition, 19.8 percent of justices who initially

---

[28] *Mulloy*, which involved one legal issue and one legal provision, has a *Case Complexity* score of −.53, whereas *Larson*, with one legal issue and two legal provisions, achieves a score of .57.

indicated they would write a separate opinion instead joined the majority as their second reply. Of those justices who concurred in the first round and then articulated a subsequent response, 18.7 percent actually joined the majority opinion. From these data, we infer that justices' decisions to adopt some tactic and then later join the majority reflect the process of authors' accommodating their colleagues. As we will see in the next chapter, opinion authors frequently accommodate their colleagues' concerns.

The other dominant pattern in the data regards the movement from a first response that expressed some level of disagreement with the majority opinion to circulating (or joining) a concurring or dissenting opinion draft. Justices whose first response was to wait concurred as their second action 32.4 percent of the time. Of those justices who proposed a suggestion or articulated a threat, 16.8 and 16.5 percent respectively concurred in their second reaction to the author. Those justices signaling that a separate opinion was in the works afterward signed a draft concurrence 49.2 percent of the time.

Though a less frequent occurrence, justices occasionally switched their conference votes and circulated or joined a draft dissent. Of the justices who waited in their first response, 21.5 percent dissented in their second one. Only 4.1 percent of justices making a suggestion or a threat as their first tactic then dissented as their second action. When majority justices first stated they would write separately, they circulated or joined a draft dissent in 21.5 percent of their second actions. As one would expect, justices also circulated second drafts of separate opinions as their second response: of those justices making a second response, those who either concurred or dissented in their first response also concurred or dissented in their second one 69.1 percent of the time.

These data therefore suggest that justices who decided to wait as their initial response tended to have more far-reaching concerns than those who made suggestions or threats, given that the latter justices subsequently joined the majority opinion more frequently. It also seems likely that those justices who circulated a separate opinion were accommodated less often by the author since their incidence of joining the majority was lower than for other justices.

CONCLUSION

The strategic model is based upon two postulates. First, legal opinions, rather than just votes, are important; and justices therefore prefer legal rules that reflect their policy preferences. Second, Supreme Court opinions are crafted in a collaborative environment among the justices, and thus justices act strategically in order to get opinions that as closely as possible mirror their policy orientations. Our finding that justices spend the time and energy trying to influence the shape of the final opinion is consistent with these postulates. Justices care about more than just the disposition of a particular case. Although case outcomes are important, the strategic model also suggests that justices – as rational actors – put considerable care into their choice of tactics for shaping the Court's final opinions. Moreover, the model expects to find that justices' choice of tactics will vary in a systematic and predictable way. Indeed, as the politics of opinion writing during the Burger Court show, justices' responses to the majority opinion author reflected a number of ideological, strategic, and contextual forces. We infer, therefore, that justices choose tactics in a case based on the relative costs or benefits to their policy goals of alternative choices.

The course of action Burger Court justices pursued was influenced, first, by the extent to which an opinion was acceptable, as measured by a justice's ideological distance from the author and the majority conference coalition. The collaborative nature of decision making on the Court also affected justices' decisions, and thus justices' responses were affected by the choices made by other justices. Thus, it is not surprising that the size of the initial coalition and the past level of cooperation between each justice and the author influenced how a justice responded to draft opinions.

Although policy objectives clearly have an effect on a justice's behavior, it is also evident that these factors alone cannot explain the opinion-writing process. Our analysis shows that justices do indeed pursue their policy preferences within strategic constraints on the Court. This finding is robust even after controlling for such contextual constraints as the complexity and salience of a case, each justice's institutional position and workload, and the Court's calendar. Our results suggest that justices are indeed rational actors – systematically making judgments about the most efficacious tactic to secure favored outcomes. Of course, whether these tactics result in the outcomes they are intended to secure raises an interesting theoretical and empirical question. If justices are indeed rational, when do opinion authors accommodate their colleagues and when do they ignore their colleagues? We consider this question in the next chapter.

4

The Decision to Accommodate

Neither the *Pennsylvania v. Muniz* (1990) nor the *Ohio v. Roberts* (1980) opinions discussed earlier reflect their author's sincere preferences. In his letter to Marshall, Brennan, the author of the majority opinion in *Pennsylvania v. Muniz,* admitted that his "hand was forced by Sandra" and that the result was a more restrictive view of *Miranda* than he preferred (Brennan 1990a). Likewise, in *Ohio v. Roberts,* Blackmun, the majority opinion author, initially responded to Powell's suggestion that the "effective" cross-examination standard be dropped by stating that he would consider the change "if you and three others want the more far-reaching approach" (Blackmun 1980a). Although Blackmun, like Brennan, altered his opinion to accommodate a colleague, both clearly preferred an alternative approach.

Brennan's and Blackmun's willingness to accommodate O'Connor and Powell stands in stark contrast to Justice Marshall's refusal to accommodate Chief Justice Burger in the opinion he wrote in *Ake v. Oklahoma* (1985). This case has its origins in Glen Burton Ake's murder of a couple and the attempted murder of their two children. At trial, Ake was found guilty of first-degree murder and shooting with intent to kill and was sentenced to death. At a pretrial conference, Ake's counsel had informed the court that his client would raise an insanity defense. Given Ake's indigent status, his attorney asked the court either to arrange for a psychiatrist to examine the defendant and assess his mental state at the time of the crime or to provide funds to allow the defense to arrange for one. The trial judge refused the request and, after being convicted and sentenced to death, Ake appealed, claiming that without a psychiatric evaluation he was unable to present a viable defense. In the Court's opinion, Justice Marshall wrote: "We hold that when a defendant has made a preliminary showing that his sanity at the time of the offense is likely to be a significant factor at trial, the Constitution requires that a State provide access to a psychiatrist's assistance on this issue if the defendant cannot otherwise afford one" (*Ake v. Oklahoma* 1985, 74). On December 13, 1984, Justice Marshall circulated a draft of this opinion. All of his brethren except Justices Rehnquist and Burger joined this draft. On December 27, Chief Justice Burger sent Marshall a note informing him that he would join the opinion if "at page 13 second full paragraph, you will insert after 'that' four words 'in a capital case'" (Burger 1984b).

Although Burger may have portrayed his suggestion as merely adding four words, his suggestion was intended to narrow the scope of the Court's ruling so that defendants would not necessarily be entitled to state-funded psychological expertise in noncapital cases. Preferring a broader interpretation of the Court's ruling, Marshall responded to Burger's suggestion with a January 3 memorandum that stated: "Since seven of us agree, my current plan is not to make the change suggested in the Chief's ultimatum" (Marshall 1985).

Marshall's decision to rebuff Burger's effort to limit the ruling to capital cases was buttressed by more than his personal policy preferences. Although he may have suspected that the conservative members of his seven-justice opinion coalition might prefer limiting the ruling to capital cases, he had ample reason to believe that his coalition would hold. Justice Stevens, for example, commented on Burger's suggestion by saying: "My joinder is unconditional and you have my proxy either way. To be perfectly frank, however, I would rather have you accommodate the Chief's suggestion" (Stevens 1985). O'Connor, as well, told Marshall that "I am still with you if you decide to accommodate the Chief's request" (O'Connor 1985b). While O'Connor's memo may have signaled to Marshall that she preferred Burger's language, it also made clear that if he did not accommodate Burger she would not abandon his opinion. Justice White, like Justices Stevens and O'Connor, signaled to Powell that he did not need to accommodate Burger to retain his support. White wrote: "Either way is all right with me" (White 1985). Even though Justice Powell did not directly respond to Burger's "ultimatum," a memo that Powell sent Marshall in mid-December must have been reassuring. In this memo, Powell wrote: "As the only case before us is a capital one, we properly could limit our decision to such cases – though I would not insist on this" (Powell 1984a).[1]

---

[1] When Burger subsequently circulated a concurrence that tried to limit the Court's ruling to capital cases, Powell asked his clerk, A. Lee Bentley, for advice. Bentley wrote a memo back to Powell that concluded, "You told Justice Marshall that you would not insist that the holding

In the previous chapter, we determined that justices' responses to opinion drafts circulated by majority opinion authors are shaped in part by strategic calculation. By expressing uncertainty, making suggestions, issuing threats, or even circulating separate opinions, justices seek to influence the actions of the majority opinion writer and thus shape the content of the majority opinion. In this chapter, we explore the tactics of opinion writers themselves. Indeed, we show that opinion writers are just as strategic as their colleagues. Marshall's rejection of Burger's "ultimatum" in *Ake v. Oklahoma* and Brennan's and Blackmun's accommodation of their colleagues in *Pennsylvania v. Muniz* and *Ohio v. Roberts* were shaped by the strategic context of each case. In other words, these opinion authors were influenced by the collegial game being played in each of these cases. As we argue in this chapter, opinion authors must pursue their preferred policy outcomes constrained by the political contours of each case. The result, we reveal, is highly patterned and predictable behavior of opinion authors in deciding whether, when, and how to respond to pressures from colleagues on the bench.

RESPONDING TO THEIR BRETHREN

Authors respond to the constraints imposed by their colleagues in two ways. First, if opinion authors know that their colleagues are unlikely to sign an opinion that does not reflect their preferences, authors may try to write an opinion comporting with the discussion of the case at conference and thus satisfy their brethren with the first draft of an opinion. We term this type of behavior *preemptive accommodation*. A cover letter circulated by Brennan along with the first draft of his opinion in *Frontiero v. Richardson* (1973) illustrates the concept of preemptive accommodation.[2] As Brennan noted to his colleagues: "I have structured this opinion along lines which reflect what I understood was our agreement at conference. That is, without reaching the question whether sex constitutes a 'suspect criterion' calling for 'strict scrutiny,'

---

be limited to capital cases. Therefore, I do not believe you will want to join the Chief's opinion" (Bentley 1985). Lee's memo and Powell's subsequent decision to continue supporting the majority opinion illustrates the importance of being assigned the majority opinion. Because Marshall was assigned the opinion, he had an opportunity to secure commitments prior to Burger's circulation of his concurrence.

[2] For a more detailed discussion of the strategic bargaining that occurred on the subject of sex discrimination, see Epstein and Knight (1998).

the challenged provisions must fall for the reasons stated in Reed" (1973a).
When it became clear to Brennan, however, that despite his efforts at preemptive accommodation he had failed to garner a majority, Brennan informed
his colleagues in a subsequent memo that he would write an opinion that made
clear that sex is a "suspect criterion." That, said Brennan, is "my own preference" (Brennan 1973b). Brennan's second note underscores that his first draft
was indeed an attempt to accommodate preemptively his colleagues.

Additional anecdotal evidence of preemptive accommodation abounds. According to Chief Justice Rehnquist, the purpose of the conference discussion
is to determine the view of the majority of the Court, thus allowing the author to write an opinion reflecting the majority's view: "The law clerk is given,
as best I can, a summary of the conference discussion, a description of the result reached by the majority in that discussion, and my views as to how a written opinion can best be prepared embodying that reasoning" (Rehnquist
1987, 300). Justice Lewis Powell, moreover, instructed his new clerks: "When
I am writing in a case . . . the Conference views of other Justices on the issue
presented . . . must be taken into account" (Powell 1984a, 2). The constraint
imposed by the conference discussion led Justice Rehnquist, in *Logue v.
United States* (1973), to state the following in a memorandum accompanying
his first draft of the majority opinion: "Though the result reached is in ac-
cordance with my notes of the Conference discussion, I have devoted more
space than many thought at Conference would be necessary to the 'contrac-
tor with the United States' question. . . . Herewith are my reasons for doing
so" (Rehnquist 1973). Opinion authors, in short, realize that, in developing
the first draft of an opinion, they are constrained by their colleagues' preferences as stated at conference.

There is, of course, a strong incentive to practice preemptive accommodation. After all, justices who fail to address the conference majority's view in
the first draft may alienate their colleagues with the first draft. Consider, for
example, *Wardius v. Oregon* (1973), a case in which Justice Powell thought that
the opinion author, Justice Marshall, had not written the majority opinion in
accord with his understanding of the conference vote: "My conference notes
still persuade me that a majority of the Court was willing to address, and decide, all three points along the lines of my prior memoranda to you" (Powell
1973). Subsequently, Powell circulated a concurrence that was only with-
drawn after Marshall made further efforts at accommodation. The failure to
accommodate preemptively may make it harder to eventually win over col-

leagues and may lead them to draft concurring or dissenting opinions. This increases, of course, the likelihood of either a fractionalized majority or, even worse, losing the majority.

Of course, opinion authors are unlikely, and possibly unwise, to incorporate fully the preferences of their colleagues in the first draft. Indeed, there are reasons to expect authors to be very reluctant to accommodate fully their colleagues in the initial draft. Accommodating colleagues immediately may deplete an author's subsequent bargaining leverage. If Murphy is correct when he asserts that "to bargain effectively, one must have something to trade" (1964, 57), we would not expect an author to make so many concessions in the first draft that all future leverage is lost. This result is particularly likely given the bargaining advantages afforded the author by the structure of the opinion-writing process. Because one justice is assigned the task of drafting an opinion for the Court, and given the time and effort associated with drafting competing opinions, the final opinion likely will favor the author's preferred positions, rather than converging on the views of the median justice (see Strøm and Leipart 1993).

Even if opinion authors want to attract the support of their brethren with the first draft, justices, like most political decision makers, do not have perfect information and may not know exactly which positions will attract the support of which colleagues. Although the justices transmit information about their positions at conference, the conference discussion is not intended as a full airing of the justices' positions (Rehnquist 1987, 290–295).[3] Furthermore, if the comments made at conference are "nonbinding," or "cheap" to make, they may not be an accurate predictor of how a justice will respond to the initial draft if his or her views are not preemptively accommodated. Authors who write an initial opinion draft that conforms with the views other justices expressed at conference may sacrifice their policy goals to accommodate their colleagues, but without assurances that such concessions are necessary to win their support. Opinion authors, like all strategic decision makers, thus may frequently discount cheap talk.

The inability or reluctance of opinion authors to address fully their colleagues' views in the first draft creates the opportunity for what we term *responsive accommodation*. This occurs when the majority opinion author modi-

---

[3] Rohde argues that because "the opinion writer may be uncertain about the behavior of other members," he regularly makes "policy broader than was necessary" (1972b, 218).

fies the opinion and circulates subsequent drafts in response to signals from his or her colleagues. For example, in a memorandum accompanying the second draft opinion in *Griggs v. Duke Power Company* (1971), Chief Justice Burger wrote: "I enclose revised draft with areas of change, omission and additions marginally marked. I believe it takes into account some problems raised by memos" (Burger 1971a). Justice Potter Stewart, as well, stated in a memorandum accompanying a draft opinion in *Greenbelt v. Bresler* (1970) that "I have restructured this opinion somewhat, in an effort to meet the difficulties expressed respectively by John Harlan and Bill Brennan" (Stewart 1970).

As we saw in the preceding chapter, after the opinion author circulates a first draft, other justices frequently suggest that the majority opinion author alter the draft, threaten to sign a different opinion if their views are not addressed, signal they will write separately, or circulate a concurring or dissenting opinion as a means of shaping the majority opinion.[4] In this chapter, we explore the conditions that increase the likelihood of preemptive and responsive accommodation. As we explain later, we use the amount of time an author needs to circulate his or her first draft and the likelihood of an author circulating subsequent drafts as measures of preemptive and responsive accommodation. We predict and demonstrate that both types of accommodation are shaped in part by the strategic context framing each case.

THE CONDITIONS OF ACCOMMODATION

According to the collegial game, justices choose how vigorously to pursue their policy preferences within the strategic constraints imposed by their colleagues. We expect the factors identified in the first chapter to influence an opinion author's willingness to accommodate his or her colleagues both preemptively and responsively. Although we predict that both preemptive and responsive accommodation are driven by strategic considerations, preemptive accommodation occurs in a different strategic context than responsive accommodation. An author's willingness to accommodate preemptively a colleague depends primarily on information gleaned during the initial confer-

---

[4] Prior to Chief Justice Fuller's tenure on the Court (1888–1910), opinion authors on the Supreme Court apparently did not generally circulate draft opinions to their colleagues (Ginsburg 1995, 2126). The author thus, in these early years, may have had a "free hand" to write the opinion "his own way" (Ginsburg 1994, 887).

ence, rather than information obtained from justices' responses to draft opinions.

Accommodation is shaped by several factors. Paramount is the ideological distance between the author and the other justices at the initial conference who expressed support for the majority position. For example, if an author holds extreme views and is writing for a coalition that is composed of moderates, he or she will be required to make a greater effort to accommodate his or her colleagues in the first draft than a moderate justice writing on behalf of a moderate coalition. According to Murphy, a strategic justice's "initial step would be to examine the situation on the Court. . . . Where the opposition was intense a Justice might still be able to lessen its impact on his policy aims by decreasing its intensity. Where the opposition was mild, a Justice might conceivably convince his associates that they were mistaken" (1964, 37–38). If justices have different interests than an opinion author, Murphy suggests, the opinion author can decrease the intensity of other justices' opposition by addressing their concerns in the first draft. This leads us to expect:

> *Opinion Distance Hypothesis 1:* Opinion authors who are ideologically distant from the majority coalition on whose behalf they are writing will be more likely to accommodate their colleagues in the first opinion draft.

The ideological composition of the supporting coalition, in contrast to the ideological distance between the author and the majority coalition, also affects the willingness of opinion authors to adjust their opinions. If the majority is particularly heterogeneous, the opinion author will probably have greater difficulty persuading the coalition members to adopt his or her legal reasoning (Axelrod 1970; De Swann 1970; Rohde 1972b, 210; Strøm and Leipart 1993). We therefore predict:

> *Opinion Distance Hypothesis 2:* Opinion authors writing on behalf of an ideologically heterogeneous majority coalition will make a greater effort to accommodate their colleagues than authors writing on behalf of a homogenous coalition.

Given the collegial nature of the Court, justices must respond to the strategic context of a case in order to advance their policy goals. One relevant strategic factor pertains to the size of the majority conference coalition. The preliminary vote, like the conference discussion, provides an opinion author with valuable information about the difficulty that he or she is likely to encounter in building a majority coalition. A strategic opinion author who has votes to spare is less likely to be concerned about accommodating each justice than a justice who needs every vote (Rohde 1972b, 214). This hypothesis follows from the Court's informal rule that the majority opinion usually sets precedent only if a majority of the justices agree with its legal rationale. Chief Justice Hughes put it nicely when remarking that he attempted to write his opinions logically and clearly, "but if he needed a fifth vote of a colleague who insisted on putting in a paragraph that did not 'belong,' in it went and let the law reviews figure out what it meant" (Rehnquist 1987, 302). As others have found, the Court takes longer to process cases when it is fractionalized (Rathjen 1980; Palmer and Brenner 1990). Thus, we hypothesize:

> *Majority Coalition Size Hypothesis:* Opinion authors writing on behalf of small majority coalitions will make a greater effort to accommodate their colleagues than authors writing on behalf of large coalitions.

An additional strategic factor recognizes that justices are involved in long-term relationships with their colleagues and thus are likely to engage in tit-for-tat behavior. In the preceding chapter, for example, we empirically demonstrated that justices more frequently responded critically to opinion drafts if the author had previously been uncooperative with them. Likewise, we expect authors to be constrained by the anticipated level of cooperative behavior of those for whom they are writing. If an author is crafting a draft opinion for a coalition comprising previously cooperative justices, he or she will try to accommodate the concerns of the coalition. If, by contrast, the author is trying to entice a coalition composed of previously less cooperative justices, then she will most likely understand that efforts at accommodation are unlikely to win the coalition over. In other words, there is no reason to preemptively accommodate justices who are historically uncooperative. Based on the strategic constraint created by the likely cooperative nature of the majority coalition, we hypothesize the following:

> *Cooperation Hypothesis:* Opinion authors will make greater efforts at accommodation if the justices whom they anticipate supporting the majority opinion consist of more cooperative justices.

Of course, strategic factors alone do not determine how much effort an author will make to accommodate his or her colleagues. Contextual features of individual cases and justices are likely to influence the amount of effort an author exerts to accommodate his or her colleagues. These factors will also affect the effort justices expend in opinion writing beyond their effect on the authors' willingness to accommodate. Consequently, by including in our model contextual factors that are likely to influence the process of writing opinions, we have more confidence in the findings that flow from the previous hypotheses.

As we saw in the last chapter, justices make a greater effort to shape majority opinions in politically and legally salient cases because of the enhanced importance that they place on the legal doctrine being developed in them. We therefore expect opinion authors to exert more effort to accommodate the concerns expressed by their colleagues in a case that is salient than in a case that is relatively unimportant. Even beyond their attempts at accommodation, opinion authors will make a greater effort to produce a well-crafted opinion in light of their perceived importance. Thus, we expect:

> *Case Importance Hypothesis 1:* Opinion authors will exert more effort in writing a politically salient opinion than a relatively unimportant case's opinion.

> *Case Importance Hypothesis 2:* Opinion authors will exert more effort in writing a legally salient opinion than a relatively unimportant case's opinion.

Consistent with this hypothesis is Rathjen's finding that important cases take twenty-five days longer for the Supreme Court to adjudicate than normal cases (1980, 246; but see Palmer and Brenner 1990).

Another contextual feature pertains to the institutional position of the justices. One type of institutional position often discussed by judicial scholars is that of a "freshman" justice (Hagle 1993; Howard 1968; Wood et al. 1998). Since a freshman justice has not benefited from the interaction with his or her colleagues, he or she may have to exert more effort than other justices in order to craft an opinion that will satisfy the majority of the bench. At the same time, new justices may have to exert more effort simply because they are more likely to be inexperienced opinion writers. Freshman justices are not the only members of the Court to occupy a unique institutional position. In the introduction, we suggested that chief justices feel more pressure to produce a unified Court than their brethren. Moreover, the additional administrative responsibilities facing chief justices may divert their attention and thus influence the amount of effort they put into crafting the Court's opinions. The final component of institutional position is policy expertise. Opinion authors with substantive expertise in the issue area of an opinion may be more resistant to accommodate their less experienced colleagues, and, simultaneously, they simply may be able to work more efficiently than their inexperienced colleagues. Thus we predict:

> *Freshman Hypothesis:* If majority opinion authors are new to the bench, they are likely to exert more effort in writing opinions than more experienced justices.

> *Chief Justice Hypothesis:* Chief justices will make a greater effort at writing opinions than their colleagues.

> *Expertise Hypothesis:* If opinion authors have a great deal of expertise, they are likely to exert less effort in writing opinions than their less experienced brethren.

Time constraints encountered by the opinion author present another contextual feature of the decision-making environment. As we discussed in the previous chapter, these demands are determined in large part by a justice's workload, the Court's calendar, and case complexity. Because the crafting of an opinion and accommodating a colleague require time and effort, we expect:

> *Workload Hypothesis:* The amount of effort an opinion author is likely to exert will depend upon his or her workload.[5]

As we saw in the previous two chapters, another important time constraint concerns the Court's calendar. When the costs associated with delay are steep, the individual who controls the agenda has more power (see Rubinstein 1982; Binmore 1986). In the opinion-writing process, the opinion author helps frame the agenda. The costs of delay are shaped in large part by the amount of time available for negotiation. In the context of the Court's term, time available is influenced by the Court's calendar. Toward the end of the Court's term,

---

[5] As discussed later, as a measure of "preemptive accommodation," we calculate how long it takes an opinion author to circulate the first draft of an opinion. Presumably, justices who have a great deal of work will be distracted from this task and thus will take longer to circulate. As a measure of "responsive accommodation," we look at the tendency of the author to circulate subsequent opinions. Presumably, an author with a large workload will resist having to put together another draft opinion.

the author is less likely to accommodate colleagues' signals, as the Court clock advantages the opinion author. As the Court approaches its traditional July 1 recess, the incentive (and time available) for the author to accommodate his or her colleagues diminishes rapidly. Thus we have:

> *End-of-Term Hypothesis:* The closer the end of the Court's annual term, the less effort an opinion author is likely to expend writing the majority opinion.

The likelihood that an opinion author will write an opinion that satisfies a majority of the Court is also a function of another important contextual factor: case complexity. As we saw in the previous chapter, in cases that are especially complex, members of the Court are likely to be dissatisfied with the majority opinion and thus to seek additional concessions. Furthermore, complex cases are by their nature likely to require greater research than simple cases. As a result, we predict:

> *Case Complexity Hypothesis:* The more complex a case, the more effort an opinion author will be spend in writing the majority opinion.

THE DISTINCTIVENESS OF RESPONSIVE ACCOMMODATION

Each of the preceding hypotheses potentially explains both preemptive and responsive accommodation. For example, the size of the initial coalition will affect justices' willingness to accommodate preemptively because it shapes the calculations that they are likely to make regarding their capacity to hold the majority coalition together. Failure to accommodate preemptively a minimum winning coalition may result in a dissenting opinion gaining a majority vote. But the size of the initial coalition also matters after the first draft has been circulated. If the conference vote was overwhelming, the opinion author has a fair amount of discretion and thus will likely not feel the need to respond to each justice's concerns in subsequent drafts. In other words, the size of the initial conference coalition is likely to affect accommodation at both the preemptive and responsive stages.

The ideological proximity of the author to the other justices is also likely to influence the content of subsequent opinion drafts. Although when preparing the first draft, the author will consider the ideological agreement between herself and members of the conference majority, an opinion author does not need to make an effort in subsequent drafts to accommodate each justice who voted with the majority coalition. Instead, he or she is likely to appease only those justices who voted with the majority and have not yet joined the majority opinion. Thus, the greater the ideological distance between the author and nonjoining majority coalition justices and the more ideologically heterogeneous these nonjoining justices, the more difficult it will be for the author to complete the final opinion.

Still, the responsive accommodation stage is distinctive because of the additional information the opinion author gleans from the signals sent by other justices in response to draft opinions. Indeed, it is this additional information that makes the opinion-writing process and the decisions made by each justice so dynamic. Opinion authors' choices are dynamic because they are driven in part by the concurrent choices made by their colleagues. As these choices are made, opinion authors update their information about the preferences of their colleagues and the feasibility of alternative case outcomes, and they adjust their drafts accordingly. Justices, in short, act strategically.

The most crucial piece of information an author possesses in deciding whether and how to alter a draft opinion is knowledge about the number of justices who have already joined the majority opinion (Rohde 1972b; Murphy 1964). Although the initial conference vote provides the author with an indication of how many justices support a particular disposition, the vote does not clearly reveal whether they will support the legal rules and policy contained in the draft opinion. Once justices react to a draft and make known their views regarding its content, an author will consider whether he or she already has a majority opinion coalition prior to deciding how to respond to a justice who seeks further changes in the majority opinion. Opinion authors who have already secured a winning coalition have little incentive to make additional changes to the opinion (Riker 1962; Rohde 1972b, 1972c). Indeed, such changes may even offend some of the justices who have already joined. The importance of this consideration was illustrated by Marshall's response to Chief Justice Burger's "ultimatum" in *Ake v. Oklahoma* (1985). Justice Rehnquist also recognized this in a letter to Justice Brennan, the majority opinion author in *Trans Alaska Pipeline Cases* (1978). Rehnquist wrote: "If you can accommodate these several concerns, I will be glad to join your opinion for the

Court. Because you already have a Court, however, you may not wish to make any changes at this late date" (Rehnquist 1978). Thus, we make the following strategic hypothesis:

> *Majority Status Hypothesis:* An opinion author who has already secured a majority will be reluctant to engage in further accommodation.

Of course, whether an author already has the support of a majority of the justices evolves over the course of drafting an opinion, as justices decide whether to join draft opinions.

Similarly, the anticipated level of cooperative behavior of those justices who are expected to sign the majority opinion is also likely to influence the content of subsequent drafts. However, once again, authors can update their calculus regarding the anticipated level of cooperation. When deciding whether to accommodate preemptively their colleagues, they are likely to think about how cooperative all members of the majority coalition are. In contrast, when deciding whether to accommodate their brethren in subsequent drafts, strategic authors would only take into consideration those members of the majority coalition who had not already joined the majority opinion.

> *Cooperation Hypothesis:* An opinion author is more likely to accommodate if the nonjoining majority coalition justices have been more cooperative with the author in the past.

As we saw in the previous chapter, justices frequently signal to the majority opinion author and other justices with their responses to particular draft opinions. These signals usually convey either the changes sought by a justice or the justice's commitment to securing those changes. Given the interdependent nature of the opinion-writing process, the majority opinion author will be influenced by the responses of other justices to particular draft opinions. As justices provide additional information to the author, the author is able to modify the opinion draft to make it acceptable to a majority of the justices. One common tactic of the justices is to propose changes to the majority opinion, sometimes explicitly making their incorporation into the majority opinion a precondition for their joining. For example, in *Griggs v. Duke Power Co.* (1971), Justice Stewart informed Chief Justice Burger, who was writing the opinion, that: "I would hope that you might consider the elimination of these two paragraphs. I think they are not necessary in reaching our decision in the case before us" (Stewart 1971). Thus, we predict:

Signaling Hypothesis 1: The greater the number of letters from justices that make suggestions or voice concerns about an opinion, the greater the level of responsive accommodation.

Suggestions and threats are not the only way that justices try to extract concessions from opinion authors. The circulation of a separate opinion may on occasion entice the majority opinion author to alter an opinion (Murphy 1964, 54, 57; Ginsburg 1990; B. Schwartz 1996, 30). According to Justice Scalia, "the first draft of a dissent often causes the majority to refine its opinion, eliminating the more vulnerable assertions and narrowing the announced legal rule" (Scalia 1994, 41). Separate opinions have such effects because they point out the defects in the majority opinion's legal ruling and thus possibly decrease the opinion's impact, influence the development of future law, or impact the legitimacy of the Court (Scalia 1994; Brennan 1986; Johnson 1987a; Segal and Spaeth 1993, 261; Powell 1984a, 17). The effect of separate opinions is further illustrated in a note that Justice Harlan sent to the entire conference on March 16, 1970: "Having considered the separate opinion of Brother Douglas and the return of Brother Marshall to my original circulation in this case, respecting the contemplated Special Master procedure, I am satisfied that their objections to this course are well taken. Accordingly, I am recirculating my opinion, eliminating that feature" (Harlan 1970b). Given the strategic value of separate opinions, we expect:

Signaling Hypothesis 2: The first circulation of a separate opinion will result in a greater level of responsive accommodation.

An opinion author may be provoked to circulate additional drafts by less than a specific suggestion, threat, or even a separate opinion. A declaration that a justice will await further writing or separate opinion drafts may send the message that there is something wrong with the majority opinion. This was made clear in the briefing memorandum Justice Powell prepared for his new clerks. Powell wrote: "After an opinion is circulated, we anxiously await responses from other Chambers. The happiest response is simply a note saying 'Please join me.' Less welcome communications include advice that 'I will await circulation of a dissent'" (Powell 1984a, 13). As we saw in the previous chapter, another way justices signal their displeasure with an opinion is merely to state their intention to write separately. Such a statement represents an implicit threat to the opinion author that if changes are not made a separate opinion may be published that casts doubt on the majority's logic. Thus, we suggest:

Signaling Hypothesis 3: Wait statements by justices will result in a greater level of responsive accommodation.

Signaling Hypothesis 4: Justices stating they will write separately will result in a greater level of responsive accommodation.

DATA AND METHODS

How does one go about measuring preemptive and responsive accommodation? Obviously, there is no perfect measure of an author's willingness either preemptively or responsively to accommodate a colleague. Preemptive accommodation is especially difficult to measure as it is virtually unobservable. Unfortunately, we cannot observe the counterfactual to preemptive accommodation – that an author would have written a different opinion absent preemptive accommodation. Given this measurement difficulty, we use a proxy for preemptive accommodation. Specifically, we look at the amount of time (in days) that elapse between the assignment of an opinion and the circulation of the first draft. We do not argue that the number of days until the author circulates the first draft is solely a function of preemptive accommodation. Rather, so long as we control for contextual factors that may influence the amount of time needed to put together the initial draft of an opinion (e.g., the complexity of a case), the amount of time elapsed is a reasonable indicator of the effort made by an author to accommodate preemptively. This measure is based on the assumption that authors who take the views of other justices into account in crafting the original version of the opinion will take longer than authors who simply express their own policy preferences.[6]

To model the authors' efforts at coalition formation in the responsive accommodation stage, we examine authors' decisions to continue work on an opinion as reflected by the choice to circulate additional opinion drafts. So

---

[6] Admittedly, this is not self-evident. Perhaps, the amount of time needed to circulate the first draft of an opinion stems from purely random factors that have little to do with the strategic environment. To establish the validity of our measure, we demonstrate in Appendix 3 that authors who take longer to circulate the first draft are more likely to have crafted an opinion that is acceptable to a larger number of their colleagues.

long as the proper controls are instituted, additional drafts indicate further effort at accommodation (Wahlbeck et al. 1998; Epstein and Knight 1998; Rohde and Spaeth 1976, 62). To test our hypotheses about responsive accommodation, our data include an observation corresponding to each opinion draft circulation. The dependent variable is coded 1 if that draft is the final version circulated before the decision is announced, 0 otherwise.[7]

Given our dynamic theory of coalition formation, event history analysis is ideally suited for testing our hypotheses (Allison 1984; Greene 1997, 984–999; Yamaguchi 1991; Parmar and Machin 1995; Fleming and Harrington 1991), as it is used when a researcher wishes to explain the timing and sequence of events.[8] Its principal concern is estimation of the hazard rate, which is the "risk" that an event will occur at a particular time, given that it did not occur before then (Allison 1984, 16–17).[9] In this chapter, we estimate the "risk" that: (1) the author will circulate the first opinion draft given that he or she had not already done so; and (2) the author will circulate the final opinion draft given that he or she had previously not completed it.

Because the dependent variable in the preemptive accommodation model is measured as the number of days that transpires between opinion assignment and the circulation of the first opinion draft, we estimate a Cox proportional hazards model.[10] The dependent variable in the responsive accommodation model is dichotomous, taking on the value of 1 for the final draft released in a case. For this latter model, we therefore use a discrete-time duration model in the form of a random effects cross-sectional time series probit model.[11]

---

[7] Information on the date on which drafts were circulated was collected from Brennan's circulation sheets (see Appendix 1).

[8] For duration data, ordinary least squares (OLS) is inappropriate because, among other things, it can produce negative predictions, the error term would not be normally distributed, and coefficients might be biased (see King 1989).

[9] A hazard rate is roughly analogous to a probability, but one significant difference is that a hazard rate does not have an upper bound of 1. If the hazard rate of an event (e.g., the first draft being released) decreases given some change in an independent variable, then this indicates that the instantaneous chance of the event occurring goes down, meaning that the time it takes for the event to occur is longer under that condition.

[10] We estimated the model using the "stcox" command in Stata 5. As each of the justices appears repeatedly in our data over time, it is possible that the residual for a particular justice is correlated across cases. To control for this possibility, we use Stata's robust variance estimator, clustering on opinion authors, which controls for any within-justice correlation across cases.

[11] This data configuration is comparable to event history models used to study policy innovation where there are observations over time for each policy-making unit, for example, a state, until a policy is adopted (Berry and Berry 1990, 1992, 1994; Mintrom 1997). We alternatively

Once again, we limit our analysis to the set of cases decided during the Burger Court (1969–1985 terms). To control for duration dependence in the cross-sectional time series probit model, we include a cubic spline function (containing five knots) for the number of days that elapsed between the first draft's circulation until the circulation of each subsequent opinion draft in each case (see Beck, Katz, and Tucker 1998; Singer and Willett 1993).[12] This approach controls for the possibility that with the passage of time the author becomes more likely to finish work on the case, even after taking into consideration the influence of our independent variables.

We employ event history analysis in part because it possesses a key advantage over other estimating techniques: it can include time-varying covariates, or independent variables whose values vary over the course of a single case. These time-varying covariates are essential for testing our dynamic theory of decision making and thus directly capturing how opinion authors respond to the changing strategic interdependencies across the deliberative process in a case. Because our data for responsive accommodation include an observation for each draft opinion circulated in each case, the hazard rate is determined at each point in time (i.e., after each draft opinion is circulated) by the values of the explanatory variables at that time. We can therefore directly test whether and how choices made by the justices over the course of considering an opinion affect an opinion author's decision to circulate an additional draft. Thus, this modeling procedure allows us to capture changes in the strategic context over time in a single case and truly model the dynamic nature of the decision-making environment.[13]

used a discrete time logit model (with robust standard errors) for responsive accommodation, and the results are approximately equivalent to those reported in Table 4.4. We chose the cross-sectional time series probit ("xtprobit" command in Stata 5) because of its enhanced ability to control for possible correlated errors both across different cases and within one case over time.

To account for the correlation in errors attributable to multiple entries for each case and from one draft to the next, we utilize a cross-sectional time series probit model and robust standard errors, clustering on each case (which controls for correlation of errors across draft opinions within a case).

[12] A cubic spline function is a piecewise cubic polynomial that is everywhere twice continuously differentiable. We alternatively parameterized duration dependence with a variety of other cubic spline functions and linear spline functions, both with a varying number of knots. The substantive results are unaffected by these changes.

[13] Of our two models, the preemptive accommodation model only includes time-invariant independent variables, whereas the responsive accommodation model incorporates both time-varying and time-invariant covariates. The first model does not contain any time-varying covariates because none of our independent variables vary over time across the first stage of the

Independent Variables for Preemptive Accommodation Model

Conference Coalition Distance. We calculated an issue-specific compatibility score between the author and the majority conference coalition for every case. The score is calculated by taking the absolute difference between the author's value-specific liberalism (i.e., the percent of the time the author voted liberally in a particular issue area across his or her tenure on the Court) and the average of the majority conference coalition's liberalism (excluding the author). The further the author is from the coalition, the higher the score.

Conference Coalition Heterogeneity. Based upon the value-specific ideological scores used to calculate the coalition distance measure, we calculated the standard deviation for the majority conference coalition's issue-specific ideology in a case.[14]

Cooperation. Using the measure of cooperation for each justice and the author discussed in the previous chapter, this variable is the mean cooperation score of the majority conference coalition in each case.[15]

Our indicators for *Author Expertise* and *Author Workload* use the same measurement strategy as our measures of *Expertise* and *Workload* in Chapter 3. The only difference is that in this chapter we measure these factors for majority opinion authors, whereas in the past chapter we measured them for justices not

process, the time until the first draft is released. In the second model, all of our variables vary except for *Winning Margin, Political Salience, Legal Salience, Author Expertise, Freshman Author, Chief Justice Author,* and *Case Complexity.*

To use time-varying parameters, our model for responsive accommodation includes an observation for each draft majority opinion in each case decided during the Burger Court. Thus, the number of observations equals the number of majority opinion drafts in a case. To illustrate, the first entry corresponds with the period of time between the circulation of the first majority opinion draft and the second draft. The second observation pertains to the period between the second and third drafts. The values of the time-varying covariates can vary across the observations for draft opinion circulations. For example, if no justice circulates a suggestion between the first and second majority opinion draft, then the value of *Number of Suggestions* (which tests Signaling Hypothesis 1) for this observation equals 0. If, however, a justice circulates a suggestion after the second draft but before the third, this variable would assume the value of 1. It would then return to 0 if no suggestions were made following a subsequent draft.

14   We excluded the author from the majority coalition for the purpose of calculating this score. We identified the majority coalition from Justice Brennan's docket books.

15   In the four cases in which the author was the sole member of the conference coalition, we assigned this variable a value of 0.

authoring the majority opinion. Our measure of *Case Complexity* is identical to that used in Chapter 2. The other case- and author-specific independent variables included in our model of preemptive accommodation (*Political Salience, Legal Salience, Freshman Author, Chief Justice Author, Winning Margin, End of Term*) are identical to the measures used in the previous chapter.[16]

Independent Variables for Responsive Accommodation Model

For the responsive accommodation model, we employed the same static measures for *Political Salience, Legal Salience, Chief Justice Author, Author Expertise, Freshman Author, Case Complexity,* and *Winning Margin* as described earlier. Each of these variables is time-invariant and thus does not change while an opinion is being crafted. However, we also include a number of dynamic variables that change during the writing of an opinion. These are as follows.

Distance from Nonjoiners. Using the data described for *Conference Coalition Distance,* we took the absolute value of the difference between the author's value-specific liberalism and the average liberalism of the majority coalition justices who had not yet joined the majority opinion. Because justices who join the majority opinion are removed from the group of nonjoiners, the nonjoiners' mean ideology is recalculated for every draft, and this measure can thus vary from draft to draft.

Heterogeneity of Nonjoiners. This time-varying variable is calculated using the data described for *Conference Coalition Heterogeneity.* More specifically, we calculated the issue-specific ideological standard deviation of the majority coalition justices who had not yet joined a draft opinion.

Have Majority. We used Brennan's circulation records to calculate the number of justices who had previously joined the majority opinion. We then subtracted the number of justices who had joined from the number of justices needed to form a winning coalition. *Have Majority* is a dummy variable that takes on a value of 1 once the author has the minimum number of justices required to form a majority opinion coalition.

---

[16] Summary statistics for our independent variables for both the preemptive and responsive models appear in Appendix 2.

Cooperation of Nonjoiners. This time-varying variable is calculated using the data described for the *Cooperation* score. We used the same cooperation score described in the previous chapter to calculate the average cooperation score for all justices (regardless of whether they initially voted with the majority coalition) with the opinion author. We then subtracted this average score from the average cooperation score of the conference majority justices who had not yet joined the majority opinion.[17] Larger values indicate that those members of the majority coalition who had not yet joined the opinion are more cooperative than the average justice on the Court. This variable can vary from draft to draft.

Number of Suggestions. For each majority opinion draft circulation, we calculated the number of suggestions sent to the majority opinion author since the prior draft. The value of this variable is subject to change from draft to draft.[18] As with the next five independent variables, we collected these data from Justice Brennan's circulation records (see Appendix 1.)

Number of Waits. This variable is a count of justices who, since the prior draft, had circulated a "wait" statement, which says they would await further writing, other opinions, or subsequent drafts. This variable can vary with the release of each majority opinion draft.

Number of Will Writes. This variable is a count of justices who, since the prior draft, had circulated a "will write" statement, which says they would await further writing, other opinions, or subsequent drafts. This variable can vary with the release of each majority opinion draft.

First Drafts of Separate Opinions. We determined the date on which the first draft of each concurring or dissenting opinion in a case was released, and we

[17] We use this calculation, rather than the raw average cooperation score for nonjoiners, because otherwise we will have missing values in those instances where all justices have joined and the opinion author continues to circulate new drafts. With this calculation, the cooperation for nonjoiners' score is the average cooperation in these instances. In the preemptive accommodation model, we were able to use the raw average cooperation score for the majority coalition (which at this stage is identical to the nonjoiners'), because there are almost always no conference coalitions comprising only the author (see note 15).

[18] This variable also includes memos that we labeled in the previous chapter as threats, or memos containing a suggestion that either makes a justice's joining conditional on the suggestion's incorporation into the majority opinion or threatens to join a separate opinion if not accommodated.

created a variable counting the number of such first drafts that justices circulated after a majority opinion draft was released. The value of this variable will vary from draft to draft.

Workload. We employed a modified version of the same workload measure used in both the preemptive model and the previous chapter. In particular, we measure it as the number of majority and separate opinions on which the majority opinion author was working on the day each opinion draft was circulated.

End of Term. This variable is time-varying and equals the number of days between July 1st and each opinion draft's circulation date. When the draft is circulated at the beginning of the term, the end-of-term value is high. The value decreases as drafts are circulated closer to July 1.

RESULTS

We examined the sequence and timing of majority opinion authors' circulation of draft opinions to capture what we have termed preemptive and responsive accommodation. Table 4.1 provides an overview of our preemptive dependent variable.[19] In the table, we see that the amount of time needed to write the first draft varies considerably. On average, opinion authors take almost forty-eight days to craft the first draft of a majority opinion. Although the dependent variable in our responsive accommodation model captures when an author stops circulating additional draft opinions (not the number of draft opinions), Table 4.2 provides some insight into this variable by showing the number of draft opinions circulated in the cases. During the Burger Court, the average majority opinion author circulated 2.8 drafts prior to publication. Although multiple circulations were common, there was considerable variability. Of the 2,293 cases, 255 (11.1 percent) had only one draft circulated,

---

[19]   While Table 4.1 presents the data in terms of the number of weeks from assignment until the circulation of the first draft, our dependent variable in the preemptive accommodation model of Table 4.3 is measured as the number of days from assignment until the release of the first draft. Table 4.1 displays the data in terms of the number of weeks to make its presentation more manageable.

Table 4.1. *Frequency Distribution of the Time Duration until the Circulation of the First Draft of Majority Opinions*

Number of Weeks	Number of Cases	Percentage of Total
1	68	3.0
2	122	5.3
3	217	9.5
4	328	14.3
5	260	11.3
6	258	11.3
7	190	8.3
8	170	7.4
9	149	6.5
10 or more	531	23.2
Total	2,293	100.1

779 (34.0 percent) had two drafts circulated, and 1,259 (54.9 percent) had three or more drafts circulated.[20]

Tables 4.3 and 4.4 report the results of duration models for both dependent variables.[21] The chi-squared statistic is highly significant in both models, and we can therefore reject the null hypotheses that all of our covariates jointly have no effect. The statistical analyses, moreover, support our theoretical argument that opinion authors pursue their policy preferences within the constraints imposed by the collegial game. Most importantly, our data demonstrate that opinion authors are strategic actors, making decisions based in part on the changing choices made by other justices during deliberations in a case.

Timing of Preemptive Accommodation

Our first set of hypotheses dealt with the ideological nature of majority conference coalitions, tapping both their distance from the author and their ideological diversity. We argued that coalitions more ideologically distant from

---

[20] We dropped two cases from our data in this chapter because, although opinion assignments were made, no draft opinions were ever released. This occurred in *United States v. Koecher* (1986) and *Dewey v. Reynolds Metals* (1971). The former case was rendered moot prior to the first draft being released. In the latter, the Court was initially divided 5–3, but Justice Marshall switched his vote. Thus, an equally divided Court affirmed the case.

[21] The Cox model reported in Table 4.3 does not contain a constant, as it is absorbed into the baseline hazard.

Table 4.2. *Number of Majority Opinion Drafts Circulated in Cases*

Number of Drafts	Frequency	Percentage
1	255	11.1
2	779	34.0
3	687	30.0
4	336	14.7
5	146	6.4
6	57	2.5
7	22	1.0
8	10	0.4
14	1	0.0
Total	2,293	100.1

Table 4.3. *Cox Regression of Preemptive Accommodation
(Timing of the Release of First Drafts of Majority Opinions)*

Variable	Estimate	Robust Standard Error
Policy Preferences		
Conference Coalition Distance	.013	.005
Conference Coalition Heterogeneity	−.013**	.005
Strategic Interaction		
Winning Margin	.058***	.013
Cooperation	.324	.956
Contextual Controls		
Political Salience	−.014	.009
Legal Salience	−.173**	.062
Case Complexity	−.021	.026
End of Term	−.004***	.001
Workload	−.089	.008
Chief Justice Author	−.510***	.122
Freshman Author	−.228	.167
Author Expertise	.018	.051
Number of Observations	2,293	
Log-Likelihood	−15,249.55	
Chi-Square	14,505.01***	

$*p \leq .05; **p \leq .01; ***p \leq .001$ (one-tail tests).

Table 4.4. *Discrete Time Duration Model of Responsive Accommodation (Timing of Release of the Final Draft of Majority Opinions)*

Variable	Estimate	Robust Standard Error
Policy Preferences		
Distance from Nonjoiners	−.011***	.001
Heterogeneity of Nonjoiners	−.020***	.003
Strategic Interaction		
Winning Margin	.176***	.014
Cooperation of Nonjoiners	.098	.388
Have Majority	.802***	.054
Number of Suggestions	−.477***	.110
Number of Waits	−.472**	.108
Number of Will Writes	−.415***	.055
First Drafts of Separate Opinions	−.143***	.028
Contextual Controls		
Political Salience	−.015**	.006
Legal Salience	−.026	.062
Case Complexity	−.052**	.019
End of Term	−.004***	.000
Workload	−.096	.005
Chief Justice Author	−.061	.057
Freshman Author	.066	.071
Author Expertise	.039*	.021
Number of Observations	6,476	
Chi-Square	1,596.57**	
Percent Correctly Predicted	78.8	
Percent Reduction of Error	40.2	

Note: Five coefficients for cubic spline segments are not shown. See note 12 for their discussion.

* $p \leq .05$; ** $p \leq .01$; *** $p \leq .001$ (one-tail tests).

the author and coalitions manifesting greater ideological heterogeneity result in more preemptive accommodation. Thus, we expect that under either of these conditions the risk of a first draft being released will decrease, or, in other words, that it will take the author longer to craft the first draft. The data support the latter but not the former hypothesis. The negative and statistically secure coefficient for *Conference Coalition Heterogeneity* demonstrates that ideologically more heterogeneous majority conference coalitions lead to greater efforts by authors to build coalitions. Specifically, the hazard of the first draft being circulated decreases 35.4 percent when the heterogeneity of the conference coalition changes from being homogeneous to heterogeneous.[22] In other words, at any one point in time, the risk that the author will release the first draft drops over 35 percent when the majority coalition is uncharacteristically heterogeneous.[23]

Turning to our strategic variables, we suggested that small conference coalitions increase justices' leverage over authors and thus compel authors to engage in greater coalition-building efforts. Consistent with this hypothesis, the size of the majority coalition affects an author's choice about when to circulate a first draft. The risk of the first draft being circulated increased by 26.0 percent if the author had a unanimous coalition, as opposed to a minimum winning coalition, at conference. This result indicates that the author spends less time crafting the first draft when writing on behalf of larger conference majorities. Figure 4.1 displays the instantaneous probability that the first draft will *not* come out, given these two conditions on *Winning Margin*. The survival curves show that when the conference majority is minimum winning that the author practices preemptive accommodation. That is, under that scenario the author has a higher probability of not releasing the first draft. We further argued that authors' perceptions of the cooperative nature of conference coalitions place a strategic constraint on their behavior. The data, however, do not provide empirical validation of this idea.

Of course, strategic explanations alone do not fully explain the strategy an opinion author pursues. Frequently, the contextual control variables that we include in our model influence an author's tendency to circulate. Our findings for *Legal Salience* support the contention that in legally salient cases authors take additional measures to secure a coalition. The data show that the

---

22   To calculate the impact of the covariates for this model, we vary one variable at a time based on a specific change in its value. This produces the percentage change in the relative "risk" that the first draft is released given some change in the independent variable. For the formula we used to calculate this estimate, see Box-Steffensmeier (1996, 367). The values of *Conference Coalition Heterogeneity* were set at 0 and 34.56 for ideologically homogeneous and heterogeneous coalitions, respectively. All other variables are either dichotomous (and thus change from 0 to 1) or the relevant values are specified in the text.

23   We also estimated the model using a Weibull, and the results were nearly identical to those from the Cox. Our analysis also indicates that, after controlling for our independent variables, there is some duration dependence in that the more time that has transpired since the opinion was assigned the higher the risk the first draft will be released.

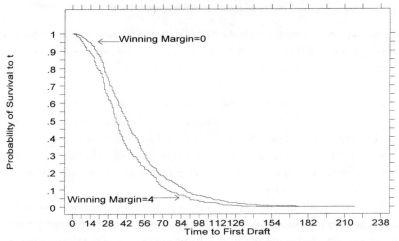

Figure 4.1. Influence of Winning Margin on Preemptive Accommodation.

hazard of an author circulating the first draft decreased by 15.9 percent in legally salient cases. Although the coefficient for *Political Salience* suggests that first drafts in such cases take longer to craft, it is slightly above a conventional level of statistical significance.

We also examined the influence of opinion authors' institutional positions. The data show, first of all, that institutional position exerts a limited influence on the effort a justice puts into the first draft. Chief Justice Burger was, as we anticipated, more likely to take a longer amount of time to generate first drafts of opinions, and the hazard rate decreases by 40.0 percent when the chief was authoring the opinion. Freshman authors, as well as those with greater expertise, do not systematically vary in their efforts before circulating first drafts, contrary to our expectations.

Contextual factors affecting time constraints further influence an author's effort on the first draft. When a case was assigned toward the end of the Court's term, the risk of the first draft being circulated went up. The hazard rate decreased by 45.4 percent if the author was assigned the case with 228 days left in the term rather than 93 days. We also found that a justice's effort in crafting the first draft varied with the author's workload. Not surprisingly, authors who have a lot of work take longer to circulate their assigned opinions. Finally, despite our expectation, we did not find that authors expend significantly greater efforts due to the complexity of the case.

Timing of Responsive Accommodation

Recall that responsive accommodation is a dynamic process by which authors alter opinion drafts in reaction to the information and signals sent by colleagues. As already noted, the core of the opinion-writing process – and thus authors' efforts to build majority opinion coalitions – consists of the exchange among justices over the content of opinion drafts. This interdependent relationship is quite evident in the timing and sequencing of authors' decisions to circulate additional opinion drafts. It is to these empirical results that we now turn, which indicate that responsive accommodation – the decision to circulate additional draft opinions – results in part from the changing strategic context of a case over time.[24]

Consistent with our hypotheses, justices engage in greater effort to build a majority opinion coalition if they are either ideologically further away from those majority conference coalition justices not having joined the opinion or if the nonjoiners are ideologically heterogeneous. Obviously, under either situation an author is going to have a more difficult time persuading his or her colleagues to agree with a draft opinion's legal logic. If, for example, the opinion author encounters a set of nonjoining justices who are ideologically compatible with him or her, then the probability of responsive accommodation (i.e., another draft coming out) is 72.7 percent.[25] If the set of nonjoining justices is ideologically incompatible with the author, the likelihood of additional drafts increases to over 92.0 percent. Additionally, *Heterogeneity of Nonjoiners* indicates that the likelihood of further responsive accommodation is 73.4 percent when the author enjoys a very homogeneous coalition of nonjoiners. The

[24] Table 4.4 does not report the coefficients for the cubic spline variables. They, however, indicate that after parsing out the influence of our independent variables the probability of the author releasing the final draft (i.e., the baseline survival function) climbs quickly in approximately the first month of work on the case but thereafter flattens out. Again, this result is based on the use of a cubic spline function with five knots, though these results are approximately equivalent using other parameterizations for duration dependence.

[25] We estimated the responsive accommodation model using a cross-sectional time series probit model, and thus it is technically appropriate to discuss the results in terms of the probability of another draft being circulated. We calculated predicted probabilities by holding all variables constant at their means and then varying the variable of interest. *Distance from Nonjoiners* was set at 0 (the smallest value in the data) for "compatible" nonjoining justices and 74.0, the largest value of this variable, for "incompatible" justices. *Heterogeneity of Nonjoiners* assumes the values of 0 and 52.33 for, respectively, homogeneous and heterogeneous coalitions. These values are the minimum and maximum for this variable. *Political Salience* is set at −.92 and 52.54 for nonsalient and salient cases. *Legal Complexity* takes on its minimum value of −.92 for "easy" cases and 7.26 for "hard" ones. *Author Expertise* is −1.96 for nonexperts and 2.67 for experts. All other variable values are discussed in the text.

probability of an additional draft rises to 95.3 percent when the nonjoiners are ideologically heterogeneous. Like most of the covariates in this model, these relationships are dynamic because the composition of nonjoiners can change from draft to draft as justices join the opinion. Thus, these results indicate that authors' choices in building coalitions evolve as the ideological makeup of their supporting coalition changes over time.

We further argued that due to the collaborative decision-making setting on the Court, opinion authors make decisions in part based on the concurrent choices made by their colleagues. The data confirm our hypotheses, showing that opinion writing is a strategic, interdependent process, with responsive accommodation resulting in part from the signals sent by other justices. Consistent with the Majority Coalition Size Hypothesis, we find that the size of the winning conference margin influences responsive accommodation. The positive and statistically significant coefficient for *Winning Margin* demonstrates that the likelihood of the author circulating an additional draft opinion decreases for larger conference majorities. If the majority conference coalition is unanimous in size, an author is 61.8 percent likely to accommodate responsively. When the author has only the support of a minimum winning coalition, however, the probability of an additional draft being circulated increases to 84.2 percent.

We also find empirical support for our Majority Status Hypothesis. Once at least a majority of justices have joined the majority opinion, authors are less likely to accommodate responsively. Before the author receives majority support for an opinion, he or she has a 90.1 percent chance of circulating an additional draft. After receiving enough support to set binding precedent, the author is only 68.6 percent likely to continue his or her coalition-building efforts. Additionally, we contended that the greater the level of past cooperation between the nonjoining majority coalition justices and the author, the more the author would continue with responsive accommodation. Our data, however, do not provide empirical support for this hypothesis.

The presence of explicit signals about the acceptability of a draft also tremendously matter. Responsive accommodation occurs much more frequently, first of all, if suggestions are circulated in response to a draft opinion. For example, if no suggestions are submitted in response to an opinion draft, then the chance of additional drafts is 75.5 percent. Yet, if one, two, or three suggestions are made to a draft opinion, then the probability of the author responsively accommodating increases to, respectively, 87.8, 95.0, and

98.3 percent. Suggestions, like our other signaling variables, can vary from draft to draft and thus tap the dynamic nature of Court decision making.

The circulation of the first draft of separate opinions or the presence of either wait statements or will write signals produce a similar influence. If no first drafts of a separate opinion appear in response to a draft majority opinion, the author has a 74.7 percent chance of circulating additional drafts. This probability edges up to 79.0 and 82.9 percent for the presence of either one or two initial drafts of a separate opinion. As well, if no justices respond to a draft opinion with a wait signal, then the author is likely to circulate additional drafts about 76.5 percent of the time. When receiving a wait statement from one justice, the chance of the author furthering his or her coalition-building efforts jumps to 88.3 percent, and two such signals raise it even further to 95.2 percent. In addition, if no justice states that he or she will be writing separately after a draft opinion, it is 74.3 percent likely that another draft will appear. Yet, when one or two justices state such an intention, the likelihood of responsive accommodation enlarges to 85.7 percent and 93.1 percent. In short, the probability of responsive accommodation – of the author circulating additional draft opinions – increases substantially if other justices have negatively responded to it.

We finally turn to the results for our variables that control for case- and justice-level contextual variables. The coefficient for *Political Salience* supports the hypothesis that authors will expend greater effort in writing the opinion if a case is salient. In nonpolitically salient cases, there is a 76.0 percent chance that the author will circulate subsequent drafts. In extremely politically salient cases, by contrast, this likelihood jumps to 93.6 percent. Although the *Legal Salience* coefficient appears in the anticipated direction, it is not statistically significant, meaning we cannot conclude that it has any systematic influence.

We also argued that institutional position influences authors' decisions to circulate additional drafts. Whether the author was a freshman justice has no influence on his or her behavior. Even though the data fail to support the chief justice hypothesis, policy expertise does matter. Nonexperts are more likely to circulate additional draft opinions. The probability that a nonexpert author circulates an additional draft opinion is 79.5 percent. Policy experts are somewhat less likely to continue their efforts in that the probability of additional drafts is a modestly lower 74.1 percent.

Finally, we consider the remaining contextual variables. Consistent with our argument, legally complex cases require extra attention and thus expand the probability that additional opinion drafts will be released. If a case is legally noncomplex, then the likelihood of responsive accommodation is 75.7 percent. In a legally complex case, by contrast, this probability goes up to 86.9 percent. We also discovered that opinion authors are less likely to continue work on an opinion at the end of the term. For example, if July 1 was 173 days away (January 9) then the probability of other drafts coming out is 85.4 percent, whereas if July 1 was 33 days away (May 29) then this probability lowers to 67.2 percent. Contrary to expectations, we did not find support for the hypothesis that justices with heavier workloads are less likely to circulate an additional draft opinion.

CONCLUSION

In the previous chapter, we saw that the interaction of justices' policy preferences with the strategic environment shaped justices' responses to the draft opinions circulated on the Court. In this chapter, we have focused on the behavior of the opinion authors themselves and found them to be strategic in the crafting of both initial drafts and final majority opinions. The collegial game thus proves to be an important component in opinion authors' decisions regarding the writing of majority opinions.

As we argued at the outset of this book, rational actors rarely act on preferences alone. Instead, their choices depend on the implications of such decisions for the pursuit of their goals. In other words, choices made by rational actors are shaped in part by the consequences of their decisions, not simply by their goals. Because opinions of the Court require the support of a majority of the justices and the content of final opinions have legal and political import, a rational justice writing the Court's opinion should be influenced by the collaborative environment in which he or she works. Indeed, this is precisely what we find – both at the initial release of a draft opinion and at each point at which additional drafts are released.

We hypothesized and empirically demonstrated that opinion authors preemptively and responsively accommodate colleagues in predictable patterns. These patterns depend, to varying degrees, on ideological agreement among the justices, the amount of support authors have from their colleagues, the signals sent by those colleagues, and the nature of the cooperative relationship with their brethren. These results therefore offer widespread support for the two postulates that form the basis of the collegial game: opinion authors pursue their policy preferences, but they do so within the strategic constraints imposed by their colleagues on the bench. Opinion authors appear to size up the strategic environment as it evolves for each case across the Court's term, and they respond to their colleagues accordingly. It is the willingness of justices to repeatedly update their choices based on the signals from their colleagues that gives the opinion-writing process its dynamic, strategic, and political nature. Even after controlling for contextual factors such as a case's salience and complexity, how much effort an author exerts in writing an opinion depends upon the strategic context.

If Court opinions are constantly evolving and if justices care about the development of the law, rather than merely a case's disposition, it is reasonable to expect that a justice's willingness to join the final majority opinion coalition depends on what occurs during the opinion-writing process. In other words, one should not expect justices' final votes to reflect only their policy preferences. In the next chapter, we change our focus from how opinions are crafted to how coalitions come together. In other words, do justices' final votes result in part from strategic calculations? And, if so, what consequence does the collegial game have for the formation of opinion coalitions?

5

The Politics of Coalition Formation

In the previous chapter, we saw that Justice Thurgood Marshall refused to accept what he viewed as Chief Justice Warren Burger's "ultimatum" to restrict the Court's ruling in *Ake v. Oklahoma* (1985) to capital cases. In response to Marshall's refusal to add the four words he sought, Chief Justice Burger told Marshall, "I did not know I sent you an 'ultimatum.' I rarely start a new year with such! . . . I will try my hand at a separate opinion" (Burger 1985b). In the end, Burger wrote an opinion concurring in the Court's judgment in favor of Ake, but he refused to join the Court's opinion. Instead, Burger's opinion stated that he interpreted the Court's ruling to only apply to capital cases. Although Marshall was still able to give his opinion the imprint of the Court majority, Burger's decision to concur, rather than join the majority, did influence the development of the law. Since the Court released its ruling in *Ake v. Oklahoma*, Burger's concurrence has been cited in several state cases as justification for restricting *Ake's* scope to capital cases (Medine 1990; Giannelli 1993). As one legal scholar put it, "as a result [of Burger's concurrence], there has been some uncertainty as to whether *Ake* applies to noncapital cases" (Medine 1990, 312).

Although Burger agreed with the final outcome favoring Ake supported by Marshall and the six justices who signed the majority opinion in *Ake v. Oklahoma*, Burger cared about more than just the disposition of the case and its effect on Glen Burton Ake's life. Burger's preference for the way the law was written, rather than the case disposition, affected his final vote. By publishing a concurring opinion, Burger somewhat influenced the development of the law. In contrast, Sandra Day O'Connor's efforts to accommodate her colleagues in *United States v. Hensley* (1985) prompted William Brennan to reverse the position he took at conference and to join the majority coalition.

On January 8, 1985, the Supreme Court announced its ruling in *United States v. Hensley*. The government, in this case, was attempting to reinstate the firearm possession conviction, overturned by the U.S. Court of Appeals for the Sixth Circuit, against Thomas Hensley. At issue was whether the police stop of Hensley's car was lawful under *Terry v. Ohio* (1968). A unanimous Supreme Court ruled that the investigatory stop was permissible even though the basis for the stop was a "wanted flyer" issued by another police department in the Cincinnati metropolitan area, rather than an ongoing investigation.

Police officers in Covington, Kentucky, pulled over Hensley's car after receiving the flyer from the St. Bernard, Ohio, police department. An informant, Janie Hansford, had told the St. Bernard police that Hensley drove the getaway car for an armed robbery in which she participated. Even though St. Bernard police did not believe they had the necessary probable cause for obtaining an arrest warrant, they prepared a wanted flyer that was distributed to other police departments in the area. This flyer informed other departments that Hensley was wanted for investigation and should be picked up and held. Information from the flyer was read aloud at each shift change in Covington, and some officers, who were familiar with Hensley, actively sought him. When he was spotted driving his car, a police officer called his dispatcher to determine if there was an outstanding warrant for Hensley's arrest. While the dispatcher sought that information, the officer stopped Hensley and, with gun drawn, directed him and his passenger to get out of the car. A second police officer arrived on the scene and saw a handgun protruding from under the passenger seat when he approached the car. A subsequent search of the car uncovered two more handguns.

When the Supreme Court discussed this case in conference, William Brennan and Thurgood Marshall maintained that the appellate ruling should be affirmed. Brennan's conference memo indicates that his view stemmed from his objection to using the officer's subjective intent, that is, the officer's reason for stopping Hensley, to determine the validity of the stop. According to Brennan, the stop would have been permissible if the officer merely wanted to question Hensley about the robbery. The officer, however, stopped Hensley to determine if a warrant had been issued for his arrest. In Brennan's view, the Covington police department could not stop Hensley to check for a warrant since police in St. Bernard, who distributed the flyer, could not have stopped Hensley for this reason. In addition to Marshall's support for the

Brennan position, John Paul Stevens implicitly agreed with Brennan's concern with the role of subjective intent, maintaining at conference that "objective standards [are] required."

On November 29, 1984, O'Connor circulated the first draft of her majority opinion, holding that *Terry* stops can be used to investigate past crimes on the basis of flyers distributed by other police departments. Justices Byron White and William Rehnquist joined this draft almost immediately. It received a less welcoming, albeit private, response from Stevens in an exchange that was later made known to the conference. Stevens objected to the test articulated in O'Connor's opinion. Instead of relying on an objective reading of the flyer by an experienced police officer, as the draft opinion stated, Stevens argued that "the validity of the stop . . . should depend on the information that was available to the entire police establishment" (Stevens 1984). That is to say, as he suggested the opinion be changed to read, reliance on a flyer justifies a stop only if the originating department has "articulable facts supporting a reasonable suspicion that the wanted person has committed an offense" (Stevens 1984). Otherwise, Stevens feared, the Court would endorse stops that are "based on totally unsupported flyers or bulletins simply because they appear to be facially valid" (Stevens 1984). Stevens concluded his memo by telling O'Connor that he would join her opinion if she "could see [her] way clear to recasting" the opinion (Stevens 1984).

The following day, O'Connor responded to Stevens by agreeing to the principle that evidence "is admissible if the officers issuing the flyer had specific articulable facts giving them reasonable suspicion justifying the stop" (O'Connor 1984d). When they made this private exchange of notes known to the conference, Blackmun wrote that he would join if O'Connor adopted Stevens's suggestion (Blackmun 1984). A memo from Brennan's clerk suggests this was Brennan's view as well. He prepared a letter to O'Connor to tell her that he would join her opinion if she made the change proposed by Stevens, but he apparently never sent the memo. Instead, even though she subsequently circulated a draft that made the changes suggested by Stevens, Brennan asked O'Connor to address "two relatively minor points" on the standards she articulated (Brennan 1984a). O'Connor responded by noting that the language that Brennan questioned resulted from her exchange with Stevens. Although she was "reluctant to make additional major changes," she proposed language that might accommodate Brennan's concern (O'Connor

1984e). Brennan wrote the next day to thank her "for trying to accommodate me" (Brennan 1984b). After O'Connor circulated the draft reflecting these changes, Brennan quickly joined O'Connor's majority opinion.[1]

As we have seen in the previous chapters, the choices justices make depend in large part on interaction among the justices during the crafting of Court opinions. The deliberations in *United States v. Hensley* highlight the importance of the collegial game in building coalitions on the Supreme Court. The changes O'Connor made to her opinion in response to her exchange with Stevens were important to Brennan's decision to join O'Connor's coalition.[2] As Jim Feldman, Brennan's clerk, put it, the first draft of O'Connor's opinion was "incoherent" (Feldman 1984). The problems, as Brennan saw them, were resolved by the changes made in response to Stevens's suggestions. In this chapter, we demonstrate that Brennan's stance in *United States v. Hensley* was not unique: the willingness of a justice to join the majority opinion coalition routinely depends upon strategic calculations. Justices understand the rules and politics of the collegial game, and they adjust their choices accordingly.

COALITION BUILDING ON THE COURT

In Chapter 4, we learned that opinion authors often struggle to build a majority coalition of (in most cases) at least five justices (Rohde 1972b, 214; Rohde and Spaeth 1976, 193–210). The importance of the coalition-building process has led students of the Court to articulate and test theories to account for the size or composition of final coalitions (see Schubert 1959, 173–210; Ulmer 1965; Rohde 1972b, 1972c; Rohde and Spaeth 1976; Brenner and Spaeth 1988a; Brenner, Hagle, and Spaeth 1990). These studies offer important insights into the makeup of final coalitions, showing, for example, that the importance of a case affects the size of the ultimate majority coalition (Brenner et al. 1990).

---

[1] Brennan also filed a one-paragraph concurring opinion to explain his reasoning.

[2] Equally telling, perhaps, is that Marshall's joinder of O'Connor's opinion was profoundly affected by the choices and suggestions of Justice Brennan. Marshall wrote on the front of O'Connor's first draft, "??? WJB – ." When Brennan wrote Marshall to tell him that he thought O'Connor's opinion obviated his concerns, Marshall wrote "OK" on his copy of the letter. Finally, Marshall put the single word, "Hold," on his copy of Brennan's note to O'Connor requesting further changes in the opinion. Ultimately, Marshall joined O'Connor's opinion on December 18, 1984.

Our focus here moves beyond a study of the size and makeup of Court coalitions. Although these earlier studies tell us much about the impact of justices' legal and policy views on decisional outcomes, left unexplained are the individual choices of the justices as opinion coalitions form. We lack, in short, a comprehensive explanation of what factors lead justices to embrace particular opinions and thus how and why the majority opinion coalition develops. Such outcome-oriented studies, moreover, provide a static portrait of the decision process. But coalition building under the collegial game is a dynamic process. Indeed, coalition formation is best thought of as the final stage in the collegial game. At each stage, justices' choices evolve with the actions and decisions of their peers. An opinion author's concession to one justice, for example, may discourage another justice from joining the majority. To understand fully the coalition-building process, we need to explain which factors influence each justice's decision to sign the majority opinion, recognizing that justices' decisions are made in concert with the choices of their colleagues.

Legal and judicial scholars certainly recognize the importance of the process of building majority coalitions. Nevertheless, we know far more about the politics of case dispositions than about the decisions that result in the formation of majority coalitions. If the collegial game can account for the decisions justices make in shaping the majority opinion, we also expect it to account for justices' willingness to join majority opinions. In short, we expect a justice's decision to join the majority opinion to result from the pursuit of his or her policy goals within the constraints of the collegial game. Although attitudinalists have demonstrated that policy preferences can generally account for the disposition favored by each justice, we argue that preferences alone cannot account for a justice's decision to join a particular Court opinion.

At first glance, studying coalition formation on the Court is quite difficult. All deliberations are veiled in secrecy. But once the cloak of secrecy is lifted – by examining the personal papers of the justices – the process of crafting opinion coalitions becomes transparent. Ironically, it is easier to study the dynamic character of judicial decision making than the dynamic nature of legislative voting, since legislative voting occurs simultaneously for all members.[3] In contrast, Supreme Court justices do not simultaneously decide which opinion they will sign. During the opinion-writing process, drafts of the majority

---

[3] On the difficulty of modeling the dynamics of legislative decision making, see Box-Steffensmeier, Arnold, and Zorn (1997); Binder, Lawrence, and Maltzman (1999).

opinion are circulated, as well as dissenting and concurring opinion drafts. At any time, a justice can circulate a "joinder" announcing his or her intention to sign a particular draft opinion. These "joinders" constitute the final votes cast by a justice.

In this chapter, we show that a justice's decision to join a particular draft of the majority opinion results from the pursuit of his or her policy preferences within constraints imposed by, among other things, the collegial game. These collegial constraints can differ during the deliberations in a case as, for instance, justices decide to join the majority opinion, offer suggestions to the majority, or circulate separate opinions. To capture these dynamics, we focus on the *timing* of justices' decisions to join majority opinions. The central question is whether and when a justice chooses to join a draft of the majority opinion. Such a focus will allow us to test whether the decision to join the majority evolves along with the actions and choices of a justice's colleagues on the bench. As Richard Fenno (1986, 9) put it, "If we are to explain outcomes, *who* decides *when* may be as important to know as who decides what." For instance, while some justices will join the first draft of the majority opinion, other justices will join literally months later, after subsequent drafts have been circulated. Specifically, we model the timing of the 12,119 "joinders" sent during the Burger Court. Table 5.1 shows which draft opinion justices joined, while Table 5.2 indicates how long it took justices to join those opinion drafts. Our examination of the timing of justices' joining of majority coalitions indicates that this decision systematically varies with the politics of the collegial game. The dynamic interactions among the justices shape the makeup of final coalitions.

BUILDING COALITIONS

Justices' decisions to support what becomes the majority coalition are shaped by the pursuit of their policy preferences within strategic and contextual constraints. The factors we expected to shape justices' willingness to accommodate their colleagues and their tactics in shaping opinions should also influence their decisions on whether and when to join the majority opinion. As seen in previous chapters, justices' bargaining tactics are in part shaped by ideological considerations. Thus, the decision to join the majority opinion reflects the extent to which a draft opinion is consistent with a justice's policy pref-

Table 5.1. *Timing of Justices' Decisions to Join Majority Opinion Drafts*

Sequence of Draft Opinions	Number of Justices Joining Draft (%)
First Draft	8,513 (70.2)
Second Draft	2,426 (20.0)
Third Draft	829 (6.8)
Fourth Draft	246 (2.0)
Fifth or Later Draft	105 (0.9)
Total	12,119 (99.9)

Table 5.2. *Length of Time until Justices Join Majority Opinion Drafts*

Number of Weeks	Number of Justices Joining Draft Opinion	Percentage
1	7,343	60.6
2	1,948	16.1
3	963	7.9
4	589	4.9
5	361	3.0
6	269	2.2
7	153	1.3
8	91	.8
9 or more	402	3.3
Total	12,119	100.1

erences. If an opinion seems compatible with a justice's policy preferences, that justice is likely to join as soon as the first draft is circulated. On the other hand, a justice who finds the draft opinion incompatible with his or her preferred policy outcome is likely to hold out for new drafts.

Whether a draft opinion is acceptable to a justice will depend first on his or her ideological proximity to its author. As we have seen, opinion authors attempt to craft opinions that will produce policy outcomes consistent with their policy preferences. Thus, justices are more likely to find an opinion acceptable the closer its author is ideologically to them. As Murphy explains, "It would be much easier for a Justice to vote and join in opinions with a judge whose policy goals were identical or very similar to his own" (Murphy 1964, 73).

The acceptability of a draft will depend, second, on the justice's ideological proximity to the emerging majority opinion coalition. Although opinion authors play a significant role in the development of an opinion, they cannot act unilaterally. The previous chapter demonstrated that, as each new draft is circulated, the majority opinion changes to accommodate various justices. For this reason, it is not surprising that justices occasionally use their colleagues' decision to join as a signal of an opinion's acceptability. The effect of such changes on each justice is not necessarily uniform. Efforts to accommodate one justice may make an opinion even less acceptable to another justice. As much was recognized by Rehnquist in a letter to Justice Thurgood Marshall, the author of the majority opinion in *Alexander v. Choate* (1985): "I realize that these suggestions, if adopted, would entail a major change in your discussion of the 'reasonable accommodation' requirement of the statute, and might even, if acceptable to you, be unacceptable to one or more of those who have 'joined' you" (Rehnquist 1984b).

Policy preferences shape the politics of coalition formation in two additional ways. First, a justice's ideological proximity to dissenting opinions is likely to be important. The power of such alternative opinions is illustrated in a memo from Justice Thurgood Marshall to Justice Potter Stewart in *Rosenberg v. Yee Chien Woo* (1971). Marshall wrote, "I voted the other way and originally joined Hugo's opinion in this case. I have been worried ever since. Your dissenting opinion has finally convinced me that I was wrong. Therefore, please join me in your dissent" (Marshall 1971). Likewise, in *United States v. Johnson*, John Harlan reported to Chief Justice Warren Burger, "I had been awaiting Bill Brennan's dissent before making my final return on your opinion. As I find myself unpersuaded by Bill's dissent, I now write to say that I am ready to join you" (Harlan 1971b).[4] Harlan only joined Burger's majority opinion after discovering that he was closer to the majority than to Brennan's dissent.

Second, a justice will be more likely to agree with the opinion, and thus join it, if he or she voted with the majority coalition at conference. A vote with the majority coalition signals agreement with the disposition of the case and indicates a justice's policy preferences (Segal and Spaeth 1993; Rohde and Spaeth 1976). Justices who favored the majority at conference may also be more likely to join the majority since majority opinion authors take more seriously the suggestions that are made by justices who support the disposition favored by the majority (Wahlbeck et al. 1998).

---

[4] While opinion drafts were circulated and correspondence exchanged among the justices, this case was held over for reargument in *United States v. Johnson* (1971a) and then certiorari was dismissed in *United States v. Johnson* (1971b).

The importance of relative ideological placement suggests the timing of justices' decisions to join the majority opinion will vary in the following ways:

Opinion Distance Hypothesis 1: A justice will be more willing to join the majority opinion if he or she is ideologically closer to the majority opinion author.

Opinion Distance Hypothesis 2: A justice will be more willing to join the majority opinion the closer he or she is ideologically to the existing majority opinion coalition.

Opinion Distance Hypothesis 3: A justice will be more willing to join the majority opinion the further he or she is ideologically from dissenting opinion authors.

Opinion Distance Hypothesis 4: A justice will be more willing to join the majority opinion if he or she voted with the majority coalition at conference.

Because the majority opinion changes along with each new draft and draft dissents are circulated weeks or months after the initial majority opinion draft, the second and third opinion distance hypotheses tap the dynamic nature of the opinion-writing process. As a justice's ideological allies make suggestions and extract concessions from the majority opinion author, for instance, the likelihood of an opinion becoming acceptable and thus the justice joining increases. In contrast, the Opinion Distance Hypotheses 1 and 4 can account only for variation across justices and between cases: because preferences tend to be stable in the short term, a justice who is ideologically distant from the author after one draft will be equally distant from the author after another.

An important collegial constraint that may influence a justice's willingness to join the majority opinion is the number of justices who have already joined the majority opinion. As justices decide to join the majority opinion, the leverage of other justices over the opinion author changes. The more votes needed to secure a majority, the greater the leverage of a potential joiner. Justice Thurgood Marshall recognized as much when he informed Chief Justice Burger that he would not limit his *Ake v. Oklahoma* ruling to capital cases "since seven of us already agree." Although we know that a majority of the justices would have accepted limiting *Ake v. Oklahoma* to capital cases, Marshall had no incentive to back away from a position that he favored and a majority of the bench found acceptable. Likewise, Justice Lewis Powell recognized this dynamic when he wrote to Justice Rehnquist, "In sum, we need your vote, and if my suggested changes are not satisfactory, I will certainly consider any further thoughts of yours" (Powell 1986). Justices are more likely to hold out for changes in draft opinions – and thus join later drafts of the majority – when relatively few justices have joined the opinion. In contrast, once the majority opinion author achieves a majority, a justice's bargaining leverage diminishes drastically (Murphy 1964, 65; Rohde 1972b, 214; see Riker 1962; Riker and Niemi 1962). The timing of a justice's decision to join will thus vary with the size of the apparent majority coalition, leading us to expect:

> *Majority Status Hypothesis:* Once a majority of the Court joins an opinion, the remaining justices will be more likely to join.

This hypothesis, like the Opinion Distance Hypotheses 2 and 3, captures the dynamic character of the collegial game: it suggests that the timing of justices' decisions will vary with the concurrent choices of their colleagues.

Another collegial constraint is imposed by the bargaining tactics of other justices. In the previous chapter, we demonstrated that these tactics send an important signal to the majority opinion author. Frequently, wait statements, suggestions, will write signals, or separate opinion drafts induce an opinion author to alter the content of the majority opinion. Of course, the public nature of the memorandums and opinions that constitute the bargaining tactics discussed in Chapter 3 also signal to the other justices that there is something wrong with the majority opinion and that subsequent drafts may be forthcoming. Because authors often accommodate justices' concerns, justices are likely to wait to see whether and how the author responds to such requests. This dynamic, strategic element of the opinion-drafting process suggests:

> *Signaling Hypothesis 1:* The number of letters from justices that make suggestions or voice concerns about a draft opinion is inversely correlated with other justices' willingness to join the majority opinion.

> *Signaling Hypothesis 2:* The number of first drafts of separate opinions circulated in response to a draft opinion is inversely correlated with other justices' willingness to join the majority opinion.

Signaling Hypothesis 3: The number of wait statements by justices in re-action to a draft opinion is inversely correlated with other justices' will-ingness to join the majority opinion.

Signaling Hypothesis 4: The number of will write statements by justices sent in response to a draft opinion is inversely correlated with other jus-tices' willingness to join the majority opinion.

Each of these signaling hypotheses incorporates the dynamic nature of Court decision making because the making of suggestions, the publicizing of one's intentions, and the drafting of separate opinions can be spread throughout the duration of the coalition formation process.

Because justices are involved in a repeated game with each other, the na-ture of the cooperative relationship between pairs of justices is also likely to influence a justice's willingness to join an opinion being authored by another justice. Patterns of past cooperative behavior between two justices may lead one to join the opinions of the other, even if it falls short of his or her most preferred language for the legal rule being articulated. Conversely, justices might punish colleagues who fail to cooperate with them. For example, Court observers have recently suggested that Justice Antonin Scalia's unwillingness to compromise and his acerbic opinions have offended his colleagues. One for-mer Scalia clerk has noted that Scalia has "completely alienated" Sandra Day O'Connor and "lost her forever" (Garrow 1996, 69). Given the possibility of tit-for-tat relationships, we expect the following strategic relationship:

Cooperation Hypothesis: If the majority opinion author has cooperated with a justice in the past, that justice is likely to be more willing to sign the majority opinion than if there is a history of noncooperation.

Once again, to test the hypotheses that are derived from the collegial game requires one to control for contextual factors that, independent of the inter-action among the justices, may also affect judicial behavior. As we have seen in the previous chapters, justices do not view every case equally. Instead, jus-tices make a more concerted effort to shape the final opinion if they view the opinion as important. Thus, we expect a justice to be less willing to defer to the author and join an opinion draft when the case is important. A memo from Justice Hugo Black to Justice Brennan, who was authoring the majority opin-ion, illustrates the role of case importance: "As you will recall, I voted to reverse these cases. . . . I am still of that opinion but in view of the comparative unimportance of the cases in our whole field of jurisprudence, I have decided to acquiesce in your opinion" (Black 1970). Thus,

> *Case Importance Hypothesis 1:* Justices will be less willing to join the majority opinion if a case is politically salient.

> *Case Importance Hypothesis 2:* Justices will be less willing to join the majority opinion if a case is legally salient.

A justice's institutional position may also influence his or her willingness to join a particular opinion. First, as we hypothesize in Chapter 3, justices may be less likely to bargain with freshman authors (see Murphy 1964, 49). If so, justices should be more willing to join draft opinions if the author is new to the bench. Second, the chief justice inevitably feels more pressure to produce a unified Court than his brethren. Thus, the chief should be more willing to join opinions than his colleagues, all else being equal. Third, if an experienced justice is authoring the majority opinion, other justices might view this as a signal that the legal reasoning contained in an opinion is sound. Therefore, we expect justices to be more willing to join an opinion being crafted by an expert. As Murphy notes, "An actor might conclude that 'A is an expert in this field, and I am not. The cost of becoming an expert is so high that I find it more efficient to follow A than to become an expert myself'" (1964, 39). We hypothesize the following:

> *Freshman Hypothesis:* If the majority opinion author is new to the bench, other justices will be more willing to join the majority opinion than if a more senior justice is authoring the majority opinion.

> *Chief Justice Hypothesis:* Chief Justices will be more willing to join the majority opinion than their colleagues.

> *Expertise Hypothesis:* If an opinion author has a great deal of expertise, other justices will be more willing to join the majority opinion.

Competing time pressures that justices encounter constitute the third contextual feature of decision-making settings. Extracting concessions from the opinion writer prior to joining the majority opinion requires an investment of time and energy that justices frequently do not have. The time pressures a justice feels depend on two factors – the justice's workload and the amount of time she or he has to complete the work. Workload pressures are likely to be exacerbated at the end of a term. For this reason, McGuire and Palmer note, "the point in the term at which a case receives formal treatment on the merits could well have implications for the outcome" (1995, 694). In particular, end-of-term pressures may compel justices to join an opinion, rather than hold out for subsequent drafts, as the Court reaches its traditional July recess. This was suggested by Justice Harlan in a memo to Chief Justice Burger, "I am glad to join your opinion in each case. If end-of-Term pressures permit, I may write something in addition" (Harlan 1971c). We expect:

Workload Hypothesis: The heavier a justice's workload, the more willing he or she will be to join a majority opinion.

End-of-Term Hypothesis: As the end of the Court's annual term approaches, justices will be more willing to join the majority opinion being circulated.

These two factors also capture the dynamics of the Court's decision-making context. A justice's workload and the length of time till the end of the annual term vary over the course of deciding a particular case.

The likelihood that a justice will find an opinion acceptable is a function of another contextual factor: case complexity. In the previous chapter we learned that, when a case is complex, the opinion author will make additional efforts at accommodation. According to Chief Justice Rehnquist, "many of the cases that we decide are complex ones, with several interrelated issues, and it is simply not possible in the format of the conference to have nine people answering either yes or no to a series of difficult questions" (Rehnquist 1987, 293). As a result, it should be harder for a justice to come to a decision and for an author to build a winning coalition for cases that address numerous, difficult legal issues. This suggests:

Case Complexity Hypothesis: The more complex a case, the more reluctant a justice will be to join the majority opinion.

DATA AND METHODS

To uncover the politics of opinion coalition formation, we model the timing of justices' decisions to join each majority opinion released during the Burger Court. Specifically, we examine the number of days from the circulation of the first-draft majority opinion until each justice joined the majority opinion in each case decided during the Burger Court.[5] These data capture the dynamic process of majority opinion coalition formation by focusing on each justice's decision about *when* to join the majority opinion.

As in the previous chapter, a duration model is the appropriate estimation strategy. Such an estimating technique has two distinct advantages for modeling this dependent variable. First, duration models are capable of dealing with events that may never occur.[6] Second, such a statistical model is well suited for testing our dynamic conception of coalition formation. Because a duration model can include time-varying covariates, we can incorporate independent variables that reflect the changing posture of justices during the deliberative process in a case and thus show how a justice's decision to join the majority opinion is affected by the concurrent choices of the other justices.

[5]   The calculation of the number of days it takes a justice to join begins with the date on which the first majority opinion was circulated. This means that justices who joined the same day as the first majority opinion draft was circulated take on the value of 1, justices who joined the day after the first majority opinion was circulated are assigned a 2, and so on. We obviously exclude the majority opinion author from this analysis.

      Information on the date on which each justice joined the majority opinion was largely collected from Brennan's circulation sheets (see Appendix 1). If we could not locate the information on the circulation sheet, we consulted Brennan's, Marshall's, and Douglas's case files. Of the 12,213 majority opinion signatures that occurred during the Burger Court, 12,119 were noted on Brennan's circulation sheets or in the case files. We therefore excluded the 94 missing joinder memos from our analysis because we could not locate a date for that action in either Brennan's circulation sheets or Brennan's, Douglas's, or Marshall's case files.

[6]   A duration model is appropriate for handling data that are right censored, that is, data for which an event never occurs. In the context of our data, justices who never join the majority opinion – they dissent from it or author a concurring opinion that joins no part of the majority – represent censored data. Excluding these justices could result in selection bias, and a duration model includes the information by treating justices who did not join the majority opinion as censored data. The data therefore contain a variable for whether the justice was censored (i.e., never joined the majority) or not censored (i.e., joined the majority), and the model is estimated using both types of observations. The censored observations contribute to the likelihood through the survivor function, which indicates the probability of not having an event at time t, and the noncensored observations through the probability density function, which is the instantaneous probability of having the event at time t (Greene 1997, 986–987: Yamaguchi 1991, 11). Examples of the use of censored data in duration models abound in the literature. Yamaguchi, for example, uses a Cox model in exploring the length of time until a student drops out of college, and he censors students who did not drop out of college (Yamaguchi 1991, 139). In an examination of campaign war chests and challenger entry into congressional races, Box-Steffensmeier (1996) and Box-Steffensmeier and Jones (1997) censor observations in which a challenger never entered. In a study of race rioting in the 1960s, Myers (1997) censors cities in which a riot never occurred. We, however, also estimated our model on only those justices who actually joined the majority opinion, finding that the results were largely compatible. The results for three variables did change, though: *Dissent Distance* and *Workload* dropped out of statistical significance, while *Legal Salience* became statistically significant.

By focusing on the timing of this decision and by using a duration model, we can explicitly test how the changing decision context in a case affects a justice's decision to join the majority.

Our dependent variable is the hazard rate (or instantaneous "risk") that a justice will join the majority at time t, conditional on him or her not already having done so (Yamaguchi 1991, 9). We can therefore estimate the risk of justices joining each draft of the majority opinion circulated for each case. To do so, our data set includes an observation for each justice and every circulation of a new majority opinion draft in each case decided during the Burger Court.[7] The hazard rate is therefore determined at each point in time (i.e., after each draft opinion is circulated) by the values of the explanatory variables at that time.[8] This strategy follows directly from the decision-making process on the Court, in which each justice must decide whether to join an opinion draft after it is circulated. Our duration model, which takes the form of a Cox proportional-hazards model, therefore directly captures the decision-making context each justice faces.[9]

Independent Variables

Coalition Distance. This is a modified version of the coalition distance measure used in Chapter 3 and in the preemptive accommodation model of Chapter 4. Whereas the *Coalition Distance* measures employed in Chapters 3 and 4 were static in nature (they were used in models where time-varying covariates would be inappropriate), in this chapter we create a dynamic coalition distance

---

[7] Because each of the justices in our data appears repeatedly over time, it is possible that the residual for a particular justice's time until joining the majority opinion in one case is correlated with the residual for that justice in another case (see Segal, Cameron, and Cover 1992; Stimson 1985). We control for correlated errors by using the robust variance estimator (Lin and Wei 1989). More specifically, we used Stata's robust command, clustering on the thirteen justices in our study. The procedure controls for "within-justice" correlation over time.

[8] Thus, the data may contain multiple entries for a justice in a particular case. To illustrate, the first entry for each justice corresponds with the period of time between the circulation of the first majority opinion draft and the second draft, if any is circulated. The second observation for a justice pertains to the period between the second and third drafts. The number of days that have passed since the first draft has been circulated reflects the number of days until the circulation of the next draft, if the justice did not join the earlier draft, or the number of days from the first circulation until the justice told the author that she would join the draft opinion. In addition, we include a censoring variable that indicates whether the justice joins that draft of the majority opinion. Once the justice joins the majority opinion, we do not add further observations for the justice in subsequent circulations.

[9] We used the "stcox" command in Stata 5.0 to estimate this model.

measure. This measure, like the one in the previous chapters, is determined by calculating the absolute ideological difference between the justice and the coalition that has formed supporting the opinion. The ideological difference is based on the same issue-specific compatibility scores used in Chapters 3 and 4. Unlike the coalition score we calculated in the previous chapters, the coalition's mean ideology is subject to change from draft to draft as new justices enter the coalition. A larger positive score on this variable indicates that the opinion coalition is further from the justice than from the majority opinion author.[10]

Dissent Distance. The ideological distance between the justice and the closest dissenting opinion author, compared with the majority opinion author, parallels the *Coalition Distance* measure. First, we calculate the absolute difference between the justice and the ideologically closest justice who had circulated a dissenting opinion in the case. Second, we subtract the ideological distance between the justice and the closest dissenter from the *Author Distance* measure used in Chapter 3.[11] If the dissenters are closer to the justice than the author, the *Dissent Distance* variable receives a positive value; it is scored negative if the author is ideologically closer than the dissenters. This variable may change with each draft.

Conference Majority. We use a dichotomous variable for whether each justice voted with the conference majority, as gleaned from Justice Brennan's docket

[10]   Because there would be missing data in those instances where no justices had joined the majority coalition, we employed a two-step procedure for calculating the coalition distance measure. First, we calculated the absolute difference between a justice's issue-specific ideology and the forming majority coalition's mean ideology (excluding the justice and the author) using the liberal voting record in Spaeth's value groups (see Spaeth 1994; Epstein et al. 1994, table 6–1). The identity of the justices who had joined the majority is taken from Brennan's circulation records of justices' actions. If no justices had joined the majority, the justice's difference between the forming majority coalition and the author is equal to 0. Second, we subtracted the *Author Distance* measure from the ideological distance between the justice and the opinion coalition. If the forming majority coalition is further from the justice than from the majority opinion author, the coalition ideology variable receives a positive value, while it receives a negative value when the forming coalition is closer to the justice than to the author. In effect, this measure taps whether the coalition that has joined the opinion is likely to have pulled the opinion toward or away from the justice.

[11]   The identity of justices who had circulated a dissenting opinion was taken from Brennan's circulation records. If no justices had circulated a dissenting opinion, the justice's difference between the dissenters and the majority opinion author is equal to 0.

books. If a justice voted with the majority at conference, we code him or her as 1, 0 otherwise.

Workload. This is a slightly modified version of the workload measure used in the previous chapter to determine whether opinion authors engaged in responsive accommodation. In the previous chapter, we measured the workload of each opinion author as the number of majority and separate opinions on which he or she was working on the day each opinion draft was circulated. The measure in this chapter differs in only one respect; instead of looking at an opinion author's workload, we examine the workload of each justice who is deciding whether to join the majority, updating the workload score as each draft is circulated.

The measures for *Number of Suggestions, Number of Waits, Number of Will Writes,* and *First Drafts of Separate Opinions* are nearly identical to those in Chapter 4. There is only one difference in their measurement from Chapter 4: because here we expect that one justice's decision depends on the tactics embraced by other justices, we exclude a justice's own tactics from his or her measure. Thus, each of these measures is a count of the number of such responses to a draft opinion coming from justices other than the one being explained. The measures of *Political Salience, Legal Salience, Have Majority, Chief Justice, Freshman Author, Author Expertise, End of Term,* and *Case Complexity* are identical to the measures used in the previous chapter. The *Author Distance* and *Cooperation* measures are identical to those employed in Chapter 3.

RESULTS

Table 5.3 reports the results of a Cox regression model with time-varying covariates in which the dependent variable is the "risk" that justices joined each draft of the majority opinion circulated in cases decided during the Burger Court. The highly significant chi-square enables us to reject confidently the null hypothesis that all of the independent variables jointly have no effect.[12] The parameter estimates (and significance levels) support our theoretical ar-

---

[12] After controlling for our independent variables, the baseline hazard suggests that, as more time elapses, justices are at slightly greater risk of joining the majority opinion.

Table 5.3. *Cox Regression of the Timing of Justices'*
Joining of Majority Opinions

Variables	Estimate	Robust Standard Error
Policy Preferences		
Author Distance	−.034***	.003
Coalition Distance	−.041***	.002
Dissent Distance	−.011***	.002
Conference Majority	1.610***	.071
Strategic Interaction		
Cooperation	1.003***	.261
Have Majority	.204*	.117
Number of Suggestions	−.187***	.018
Number of Waits	−.161***	.022
Number of Will Writes	−.128**	.047
First Drafts of Separate Opinions	−.106***	.012
Contextual Controls		
Political Salience	−.017***	.004
Legal Salience	−.065	.061
Case Complexity	−.151	.009
End of Term	−.002***	.000
Workload	−.018	.008
Chief Justice	−.109	.065
Freshman Author	.065	.048
Author Expertise	−.000	.008
Number of Observations	32,557	
Log-Likelihood	−106,178,39	
Chi-Square	153,908.72***	

*p ≤ .05; **p ≤ .01; ***p ≤ .001 (one–tail tests).

gument that justices decide to join based on the effect of that choice on securing their policy objectives. As we show in this chapter, the formation of the
majority coalition reflects justices' pursuit of their policy preferences within
the constraints of a case and the Court. Most importantly, the results show
that the collegial game influences justices' final votes in a case, which bolsters
our argument that the coalition formation process is interdependent, in part
animated by the evolving strategic context of each case.

Our first set of hypotheses posited that the timing of a justice's decision to join the majority opinion depends on the extent to which a draft majority opinion comports with a justice's policy preferences. The signs of both the *Author Distance* and *Coalition Distance* coefficients demonstrate that justices are at greater risk to join a draft of the majority opinion when they are ideologically closer to the author or to the opinion coalition supporting a draft opinion. For example, the hazard rate (the instantaneous risk that a justice will join a draft opinion) increases by 92.7 percent when a justice is ideologically aligned with, rather than distant from, the majority's author.[13] Additionally, the hazard rate increases more than threefold if a justice is more ideologically compatible with the emerging opinion coalition than not. In short, after an opinion draft is circulated, the hazard of a justice joining the opinion increases the closer a justice is ideologically to either the author or the emerging opinion coalition.

The influence of policy preferences is seen in two additional ways. Our Opinion Distance Hypothesis 3 suggested that the closer a justice is to authors of dissenting opinions, the lower is his or her risk of joining the majority. The coefficient for *Dissent Distance* supports this hypothesis: the hazard of joining drops by 79.5 percent when a justice is in ideological agreement, rather than disagreement, with the dissenting authors. We further suggested that members of the conference majority would be more receptive to joining a majority opinion draft. Our result for *Conference Majority* shows that the hazard of joining increases by 400 percent for members of the majority conference coalition. Taken together, these four variables indicate that a justice's decision to join an opinion is dramatically influenced by his or her policy goals.

A justice's decision to join is also influenced by the concurrent choices of his or her colleagues. These choices represent a central part of the collegial game and thus help structure the decisions other justices will make. In the Majority Status Hypothesis, we proposed that a justice's bargaining leverage affects his or her decision about joining a draft of the majority opinion. This idea captures an important dynamic element because, as justices decide to

---

[13] To calculate the impact of the covariates, we vary one variable. This produces the percentage change in the relative "risk" that a justice joins the majority given changes in the value of an explanatory factor. For the formula used to calculate these figures, see Box-Steffensmeier (1996, 367). For *Author Distance* we set the values at 0 and 78.1. The figures for *Coalition Distance* measures were set at −10.09 and 17.0; and the values for *Dissent Distance* were set at −69.5 and 78.1. The values for *Cooperation* were set at −.16 and .84. *Political Salience* was set at −.92 and 37.27. All other independent-variable values are listed in the text.

join the opinion, the coalition's size changes. The positive coefficient on *Have Majority* indicates that once a majority opinion coalition forms, the hazard of joining increases by 22.6 percent. This result shows that justices are more inclined to join a draft of the majority opinion once a coalition has formed and their leverage over the author has thus diminished.

Additional components of the collegial game include the signals sent by colleagues in the process of deciding cases. The use of each of these tactics (which are discussed at length in Chapter 3) signals to other justices that a particular draft is lacking in some way. Thus, we expect that when a justice signals disagreement with a draft opinion, other justices will be less amenable to joining it. The negative and statistically significant coefficient for our Signaling Hypotheses 1–4 supports these hypotheses. If a suggestion, wait statement, will write signal, or a first draft of a separate opinion is circulated in response to a draft opinion, then other justices are at less risk to join that draft.

For example, the coefficient for *Number of Suggestions* indicates that each additional suggestion submitted in response to a draft opinion decreases the hazard of any justice joining that draft by 17.1 percent. If a draft opinion receives the maximum number of suggestions in our data (11), as compared with no suggestions, the hazard rate lowers by 87.2 percent. Statements of uncertainty about a draft opinion have a similar effect. The hazard rate decreases by 14.9 percent for each additional justice stating his or her intention to await upcoming developments. If a justice either declares an intention to write separately or actually circulates a draft of a separate opinion, then the hazard of other justices joining also decreases. Each additional justice stating his or her intention to write separately or actually circulating the first draft of a separate opinion in response to a draft of the majority lowers the risk of other justices joining that draft by 12.0 and 10.1 percent, respectively.

A better sense of the substantive meaning of these hazard rates can be gleaned from Figures 5.1 and 5.2. Each figure shows the probability that a justice will not join a draft of the majority opinion (i.e., the survival curve), conditional on the responses of other justices to that draft opinion. Figure 5.1 indicates that when a justice sees one other justice signal an intention to await upcoming developments, he or she is much more likely to refrain from joining that draft of the majority. For example, if the first draft of the majority had been released 60 days ago, a justice has a 35.2 percent chance of *not* joining the current draft, provided no other justice had responded to that draft with a wait

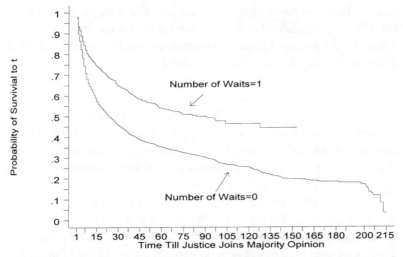

Figure 5.1. Influence of Wait Signals on Justices' Joining of Majority Opinions.

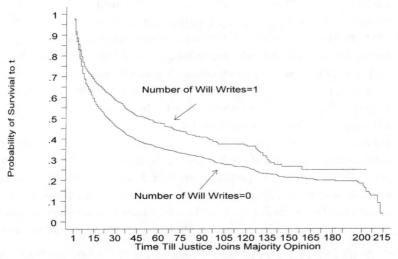

Figure 5.2. Influence of Will Write Signals on Justices' Joining of Majority Opinions.

signal.[14] If, by contrast, a justice witnesses one other justice signal that he or she will wait, the probability of his or her not joining the opinion draft increases to 53.8 percent. Figure 5.2 demonstrates that will write signals exert a similar influence. For instance, the probability of a justice choosing not to join a draft opinion, sixty days after the first draft of it was released, increases from 35.7 percent to 47.6 percent if one, as opposed to zero, justices respond to that draft by stating that they will write separately. These results clearly indicate that a justice is much less likely to join a majority opinion draft if other justices have criticized it in some way. We therefore find considerable evidence that a justice's final vote in a case depends in part on the concurrent choices made by his or her colleagues on the bench.

The final variable tapping strategic interdependencies on the Court is the past level of cooperation between the opinion author and a justice. The statistical results support the hypothesis that the greater the level of cooperation a justice received from an author in the past, the higher the risk he or she will join the majority opinion. The hazard of joining the opinion nearly triples if the author was previously uniformly cooperative rather than uncooperative with a justice. Further evidence of the importance of the collegial game appears in a log likelihood ratio test. This test shows that the model including the signaling, majority status, and cooperation hypotheses is a significant improvement over either a model that only includes the opinion distance variables (chi-square = 980.43; $p \leq .001$) or a model that includes all of the other covariates (chi-square = 755.28; $p \leq .001$).

The support we have found for the collegial game occurs in spite of the fact that we have controlled for the numerous contextual factors that may influence a justice's decision to join an opinion. Frequently, these variables are significant. In previous chapters we learned that the tactics of opinion assignors, majority opinion authors, and other justices on the Court vary by case salience and complexity. Thus, we hypothesized that in salient cases a justice will be at less risk to join a draft opinion. The negative coefficient for *Political Salience* indicates that the hazard of justices joining the majority opinion is lower in politically salient cases. In particular, the hazard rate drops by 48.3 percent when comparing an extremely politically salient case with a nonpolitically salient case. The coefficient for *Legal Salience*, although in the anticipated direction, is not statistically distinguishable from 0. Likewise, we did not find

---

[14]   We calculate these simulation numbers after controlling for all other variables at their mean values.

support for the hypothesis that justices would be less at risk to join a draft opinion if the case was legally complex.

An additional control we imposed taps the institutional positions occupied by justices. In previous chapters, for example, we have shown that Burger's position as chief justice affected his tendency to assign opinions to ideologically compatible justices, preemptively accommodate colleagues, and bargain with opinion authors. Here, however, we find no support for the conjecture that the chief justice is at any greater risk to join a draft opinion. We also do not confirm that justices deciding to join opinions written by expert authors will also manifest a higher hazard of joining. Neither do the data suggest that justices voting in cases authored by freshman justices would be more at risk to join. Institutional position, in short, appears not to matter in this setting.

We also tested the influence of two constraints that are related to the time a justice has to pursue an alternative to joining the majority opinion. First, consistent with our hypothesis, we find that justices respond to end-of-term pressures: the further away the end of the term, the lower the hazard of joining. If there are 178 days left in the term, as opposed to 38, then the hazard rate decreases by 25.7 percent. Contrary to our other workload expectation, however, justices were not more at risk to join when they had larger workloads.[15]

CONCLUSION

Our findings support the proposition that the opinion coalition formation process is dynamic and interdependent. A justice's decision to join the majority opinion results from his or her pursuit of policy preferences within the context and constraints of each case. Once again, preferences alone do not dictate behavior on the U.S. Supreme Court. A case's changing strategic environment, as well as a justice's policy preferences, play a central role in accounting for a justice's decision to join the majority opinion. Although it is clear that justices' votes on a case's disposition are largely determined by their policy preferences (see Segal and Spaeth 1993), the collaborative environment of the Court plays an important role in a justice's willingness to join the majority opinion.

---

[15] It may be that justices with heavier workloads concentrate on writing majority opinions and thus put off making decisions about whether to join other justices' majority opinions.

Our empirical results confirmed all of the hypotheses generated from our core theoretical argument. As outlined in Chapter 1, our perspective can be encapsulated in two postulates: justices prefer legal rules that comport with their policy goals (Outcome Postulate), and, given the Court's intrainstitutional rules, justices must often act strategically in order to secure their policy preferences (Collective Decision-Making Postulate). The timing and willingness of a justice's decision to join the majority opinion, we saw, was driven in large measure by these two factors.

First, justices' joining of majority opinions depends on the extent to which a draft opinion comports with a justice's policy preferences. Justices who are ideologically closer to the majority opinion author and the opinion coalition, ideologically distant from the dissenters, or members of the conference majority are more willing to sign the majority opinion. Second, justices take into consideration the strategic context of a case, namely the decisions made and signals sent by their colleagues. The timing and willingness of the decision to join the majority opinion vary along with the changing size of the majority opinion coalition, the concurrent bargaining tactics adopted by other justices, and the cooperative relationship each justice has with each of his or her colleagues.

Our results in this and the previous three chapters strikingly highlight the importance of the collegial game across the Supreme Court. First, opinion assignors' use of their policy preferences in assigning opinions is conditioned by the strategic setting of a case. Second, justices regularly attempt to entice the majority opinion author to adopt legal rules consistent with their policy preferences. Third, opinion authors themselves recognize that the collegial nature of the institution restricts their ability to pursue their own policy views, resulting in strategic accommodation of their colleagues' views. In this final empirical chapter, we see the end result of the collegial game. Justices take note of their colleagues' actions on each case and update their strategies accordingly as they decide whether and when to join the majority opinion. Some strategic maneuvers, such as the assembling of five votes for a majority, lead the remaining justices to join the majority. Other tactics, such as the sending of threats or circulation of separate opinions, deter justices from joining. Justices, we show, take seriously the signals sent during the collegial game – indeed, so seriously as to markedly influence their final action on each Supreme Court case. Strategic interdependence clearly shapes the politics of the collegial game.

6

Conclusion

In the introduction to his classic analysis of bargaining and compromise on the Supreme Court, Murphy (1964, 3) wrote: "While no writer of the traditional or behavioral persuasion has argued that a justice's range of choices and method of expression are limited to voting and writing opinions . . . neither – to my knowledge – has any scholar made a systematic effort to outline what other modes of expression are practically possible and what is the real range of choices open to a justice." Although Murphy set out to explain the choices justices make, he recognized that his work did not systematically test his notions of strategic interaction (1964, 3). Thirty-five years after publication of Murphy's book, scholars are just beginning to offer systematic theoretical and empirical treatments of the opinion-writing process on the Court.

By focusing our analysis on the opinion-writing process throughout the Burger Court, we have been able to demonstrate systematically and rigorously that preferences alone do not dictate the choices justices make. Instead, their decisions result from the pursuit of their policy preferences within constraints endogenous to the Court. These constraints primarily stem from intrainstitutional rules on the Court, which give the Court its collegial character.

In each of the key stages used to craft the majority opinion, we see that justices make decisions that are based on the behavior, signals, or preferences of their colleagues. Consistent with the second postulate articulated in Chapter 1, then, Court decision making is interdependent: the choices one justice makes in a case depend in part on the decisions being made by his or her colleagues on the bench. By taking these strategic factors into account, each justice is more likely to achieve his or her policy goals than by acting on preferences alone. Thus, we see the collegial game being played in the assignment of the majority opinion, in the writing of the majority opinion, in justices' choice of bargaining tactics, and, finally, in the decision of each justice to join the majority.

CONNECTIONS TO AND BREAKS FROM THE PAST

For decades, students of courts have vociferously disagreed on both how courts make decisions and how researchers should study them. On the one hand, those focusing on judicial behavior (mainly attitudinalists) pushed for a scientific, quantitative approach to understanding judicial outcomes (see Schubert 1959; Ulmer 1959; Spaeth 1965; Kort 1964). On the other hand, traditional, legally oriented scholars bemoaned the behavioral revolution and its attendant focus on judicial behavior, rather than court opinions (Mendelson 1963). These two distinct traditions are well illustrated by an exchange between Harold Spaeth and Wallace Mendelson in the 1960s. Spaeth, an attitudinalist, maintained that objective, scientific evidence about court decisions only resulted from the study of votes, rather than opinions, because "meaningful analysis is more likely if one focuses upon action, upon decision making, rather than upon what the actors say about what they have done" (Spaeth 1965, 879). Mendelson, a legalist, however, argued that to understand judicial decision making it is essential that one study legal discourse and the language of opinions (Mendelson 1963, 1964, 1966). Even thirty years after this debate, scholars still disagree about the appropriate way to go about studying judicial decision making. Some advocate a more traditional, legalistic orientation (Kahn 1994), whereas others continue to urge a more scientific and quantitative approach that focuses on the behavior of justices (Spaeth 1996; Segal and Spaeth 1993; Spaeth and Segal 1999).

In large part, this difference stems from three factors. First, judicial behavioralists and legal scholars each subscribe to a different paradigm. Whereas the former have tended to argue that justices' behavior stems from their personal policy preferences, the latter question any approach that ignores the role of law. Second, these two approaches have analyzed different aspects of decision making. Behaviorally oriented scholars have primarily turned their attention to discrete choices such as the granting of certiorari or the final votes on a case's merits, whereas legalists have maintained that it is the opinion of the Court that is most relevant. Undoubtedly, legal scholars see *Miranda v. Arizona* (1966) as important because of the implications of its opinion, not because Ernesto Miranda's conviction was reversed.[1] Third, for decades these two divergent orientations have talked past each other rather than recognize the possible connections between their research agendas.

In many respects, the collegial game represents a break from and a connection to both of these traditions. First, like the attitudinal model, central to the collegial game is the notion that policy preferences shape judicial behavior. Indeed, the first postulate on which our analysis rests argues that justices desire legal rulings that reflect their policy preferences. Thus, in each of our chapters we make the theoretical and empirical point that preferences influence the choices justices make as the Court crafts its opinions. Importantly, we also argue that preferences are not omnipotent. The behavior of justices depends on more than their preferences. Gillman and Clayton have recently argued that

any attempt to explain behavior with reference to beliefs but not to contexts such as institutional settings will inevitably be incomplete for at least two reasons. First, institutional settings are an omnipresent feature of our attempts to pursue a preferred course of action. It is not possible to imagine political behavior – or, for that matter, any purposeful human behavior – proceeding without some overt or tacit reference to the institutional arrangements and cultural contexts that give it shape, direction, and meaning. (Gillman and Clayton 1999, 3)

We concur.

Although our study conclusively demonstrates that preferences alone do not dictate justices' decisions, it is important to remind the reader that this does not mean the empirical contributions made by attitudinalists are misguided. As we stated in the Introduction, attitudinalists themselves have only claimed that preferences alone determine the final vote on a case's disposition. Spaeth's observation that "opinion coalitions and opinion writing may be a matter where nonattitudinal variables operate" (Spaeth 1995a, 314) suggests that attitudinalists would not necessarily disagree that the collegial game is an essential feature of opinion writing on the Court. Indeed, many advocates of the attitudinal model will inevitably take comfort in our finding that preferences shape behavior beyond the final vote on a case's disposition.

Second, consistent with most scholars who embrace a legal orientation, we believe that legal opinions are fundamentally important. Thus, our analytical

---

[1] Even though behavioralists often recognize the importance of Court opinions, they have consistently avoided studying them.

focus is on the choices justices make that help shape the Court's final opinions. By coupling this empirical emphasis on opinion writing with our theoretical focus on the way institutional rules can constrain choice and thus lead to bargaining, negotiation, and compromise, we hope to provide one possible way to bring some unification to these two seemingly disparate research traditions. We, for instance, have shown that one can adopt a scientific approach to the study of the process of opinion writing and the formation of legal doctrine.

Third, this book makes an important departure from both traditions in that, instead of studying final outcomes – final votes for attitudinalists and final opinions for legalists – we focus on the political process by which votes and opinions are formed.[2] Indeed, our theoretical orientation, with its emphasis on the strategic interdependencies on the Court, suggests that one cannot fully understand the decision making of any collegial court without researching the dynamics of judicial process and politics. We therefore turn our attention to the choices justices make in the opinion-writing process. These choices constitute the justices' efforts to shape the content of the legal rules and policies contained in the Court's opinions. Our empirical results, moreover, convincingly show that these choices regularly turn on strategic considerations of the collegial game. As Chief Justice Rehnquist put it, "There must be an effort to get an opinion for at least a majority of the Court. . . . To accomplish this, some give and take is inevitable, and doctrinal purity may be muddied in the process" (Rehnquist 1992, 270). Consequently, if one wishes to ultimately understand, for example, the development of Court opinions and change in the law over time, it is necessary to couple a study of outcomes with a discussion of the internal dynamics of the process. In this way, a richer and more complete portrait of judicial decision making will emerge.

SCIENCE AND THE STUDY OF COURTS

The first, and arguably the most important, component of good social science is the development of a logical and compelling theoretical orientation that yields testable hypotheses. Toward this end, Chapter 1 articulated two postu-

---

[2] Obviously, not every legal scholar focuses exclusively on final opinions. Many judicial biographies, for example, discuss intra-Court interactions (see Mason 1956; see also Howard 1971).

lates that are central to our argument. Taken together, they contend that a justice's principal objective is to produce legal rulings comporting as closely as possible with his or her policy preferences, but in order to do so a justice must respond to constraints placed on him or her by the collegial nature of Court decision making. These constraints largely derive from various institutional rules – most notably that legal precedent is set only if a majority of the justices agree to an opinion – that affect the choices available to a justice. Decision making, in short, is interdependent because of these institutional rules.

Yet our theoretical emphasis on the collegial game is not all-encompassing. Although we suspect, and hope, that legal scholars will appreciate our analytical focus, they may question why we do not systematically test the extent to which the decisions and actions of justices are shaped by legal considerations, rather than the collegial game. Such criticism is well founded. As we stated in the conclusion to our first chapter, we do not test every possible explanation for behavior. We have no doubt that a justice may send a suggestion to the majority opinion author or that the majority opinion author may circulate a new draft because he or she has become aware of a precedent or statute that should guide the Court. Such a focus, however, is beyond the scope of this book, and we urge future research to examine the constraining role of legal norms, such as precedent, on justices' decisions (see Spriggs and Hansford 1998; Knight and Epstein 1996b).

Nevertheless, our models do contain a variety of variables whose aim is to control for alternative explanations for the behavior we explain. Indeed, some scholars may actually criticize this book not for omitting variables but for including others. Specifically, they may submit that our contextual variables – case salience, a justice's institutional position, time constraints justices encounter, and the legal complexity of a case – are more akin to conjectures than theoretically derived predictions. We, in fact, recognize that these contextual variables do not directly emanate from our collegial game argument. Such controls are necessary, however, to ensure that our statistical results for those variables directly testing our collegial game hypotheses are as robust as possible. Excluding such factors could result in a model that was both underspecified and difficult to interpret. Leaving them out could thus distort our conclusions.

Good science also requires rigorous empirical testing of hypotheses. To accomplish this objective, we have consistently tried to develop research designs and use statistical modeling techniques that accurately reflect the processes we are trying to explain. In addition, strong social scientific findings depend on the use of reasonable measures of theoretical concepts. When one is trying to develop quantitative measures to understand a process that does not always result in easily observable choices (such as preemptive accommodation) or is trying to get at concepts (such as expertise), rather than concrete facts (such as whether a justice is the chief justice) data choices are not self-evident. For this reason, we have attempted to demonstrate the validity and reliability of our measures in Appendixes 1 and 3. We are confident that our measures are reasonable representations of their corresponding concepts.

Generalizable empirical results are another hallmark of good science. Throughout this book, we have supplemented case examples with a rigorous analysis of the decisions made by all of the justices during the crafting of the 2,293 cases where an opinion assignment was made or a signed opinion was released during the Burger Court (1969–1985 terms). These opinions involved almost every subject matter that the Court addresses. Although our decision to focus on the seventeen years that comprise the Burger Court stemmed from the availability of data for this period, such an extensive record enables us to make claims that will help predict judicial behavior in cases outside of this period.

SMALL STEPS

Although we present a theoretical and empirical case for the factors that shape judicial behavior, it is important to note that we have not made the final step: explaining the actual content of Court opinions. This task we leave to the future. Before explaining why an opinion says what it does, though, we need a clear understanding of the tactics individual justices pursue and a comprehension of why and under what conditions they choose them. Such knowledge has been the motivation for this book. The conclusions one should draw from our empirical results suggest that a model of Court opinions must incorporate the role of intrainstitutional rules and how they can encourage bargaining, negotiation, and compromise. Such a model will, at a minimum, need to recognize not only the central role that individual preferences play in shaping outcomes but also the role of strategic calculation.

Appendix 1
Data Reliability

We have made extensive use of data derived from archival resources. Although we primarily use the papers of Justice Brennan, we also relied on the papers of Justices Douglas, Marshall, and Powell. Justices Brennan, Douglas, and Marshall donated their papers to the Manuscript Division of the Library of Congress, Washington, D.C. Justice Powell's papers are housed at Washington and Lee University, Lexington, Virginia.

We have used Brennan's docket sheets as the source of the justices' conference votes,[1] Brennan's copy of the assignment sheets circulated by Chief Justice Burger for opinion assignment choices, and Justice Brennan's circulation records for information on the actions taken and choices made by justices during the course of the deliberative process. We have attached as Figure A1.1 a copy of Justice Brennan's docket sheet in *O'Shea v. Littleton* (1974). As one can see from this docket sheet, Brennan noted that Justices Rehnquist, Powell, Blackmun, White, and Stewart and Chief Justice Burger voted in the majority in favor of reversing the lower court decision, whereas Justices Marshall, Brennan, and Douglas instead favored affirming that decision. Figure A1.2 is a copy of the assignment sheet circulated on October 23, 1973, that assigned *O'Shea* to Byron White. This sheet also includes examples of assignments by associate justices: Stewart and Brennan both received assignments from Justice Douglas.

Turning to Figure A1.3, a copy of Brennan's circulation record in *O'Shea*, one sees the choices and behavior of justices during the writing of the opinions. The circulation record notes that Justice White was the assigned author and that he circulated majority opinion drafts on November 27, 1973, January 5, 1974, and January 9, 1974. The first opinion draft prompted several

---

[1]   If we could not locate a docket sheet in Brennan's files, we used Douglas's docket sheets.

Court ......CA – 7......   Voted on..................., 19...

Argued ...., 19...   Assigned ...., 19...   No.72-953

Submitted ...., 19...   Announced ...., 19...(Vide 72-955)

MICHAEL O'SHEA, AS MAGISTRATE OF THE CIRCUIT COURT FOR ALEXANDER COUNTY, ILLINOIS, AND DOROTHY SPOMER, AS ASSOCIATE CIRCUIT JUDGE FOR ALEXANDER COUNTY, ILLINOIS, Petitioners

vs.

EZELL LITTLETON, ET AL.

1/3/73 Cert. filed.

	953	955	1107
CJ	G	G & reversed on rehearing	D
WOD	G	G	Hold
WJB	G	G	"
PS	D	G	"
BRW	G	G	"
TM	G	G & reversed	"
HAB	G	G	"
LP	G	G	"
WR	G	G	↳

Together with No. 72-955- Spomer v. Littleton
No. 72-1107- BerBLing v. Littleton

	HOLD FOR	CERT.		JURISDICTIONAL STATEMENT				MERITS		MOTION		AB-SENT	NOT VOT-ING
		G	D	N	POST	DIS	AFF	REV	AFF	G	D		
Rehnquist, J.								✓					
Powell, J.								✓					
Blackmun, J.								✓					
Marshall, J.									✓	delation, ga illeal			
White, J.								✓					
Stewart, J.								✓					
Brennan, J.									✓	with new definitions as to guidelines			
Douglas, J.								✓		"			
Burger, Ch. J.								✓		"			

Figure A1.1. Brennan's Docket Sheet for *O'Shea v. Littleton*.

OCTOBER TERM, A. D. 19..73

................................October 23................, 19...73

JUSTICE REHNQUIST....	72-1148 - Cupp v. Naughten ....
" POWELL	72-782 - Gateway Coal Co. v. UMW ....
" BLACKMUN ...	72-822 - Renegotiation Bd. v. Bannercraft Clothing
" MARSHALL....	72-397 - Bonelli Cattle Co. v. Arizona ....
" WHITE	72-888 - Zahn v. Intl. Paper Co. .... (72-953 - O'Shea v. Littleton (72-955 - Spomar v. Littleton ....
" STEWART	(72-777 - Cleveland Bd. of Education v. LaFleur (assgned by WOD) (72-1129 - Cohen v. Chesterfield Cty. Sch. Bd. (assigned by WOD)
" BRENNAN	72-1040 - Communist Party of Ind. v. Whitcomb (assigned by WOD)
" DOUGLAS	
CHIEF JUSTICE	
PER CURIAM	72-922 - Paschall v. Christie-Stewart, Inc. (HAB) 72-5881 - Marshall v. U. S. (WEB)..............

Figure A1.2. Assignment Sheet for *O'Shea v. Littleton*.

No. ___72-953___ , ___O'Shea v. Littleton___

Argued: ___October 17, 1973___   Announced: ___4/5/74___

Assigned: ___White, J.___   Date: ___October 23, 1973___

Vote: Affirm: ___TM, WJB & WOD___

       Reverse: ___WHR, LFP, HAB, BRW, PS & WEB___

       Out: _____

	Date:	Print:
Circulated:	11-27-73	1
	1-5-74	2
	1-9-74	3

Replies:	Date:	Print:	Remarks:
The Chief Justice	12/11/73		Cegree
Mr. Justice Douglas:	11/29/73	&	Jype do—
	12/8/73	3	do—
	12/3/73	2	do—
	12/3/73	4	do—
	12/29/73	5	do— jn lg w JB+TM
	1-11-74	6	" " " "
Mr. Justice Brennan:	12/10/73		jn WOD's do—

Figure A1.3. Brennan's Circulation Record for *O'Shea v. Littleton*.

Replies:	Date:	Print:	Remarks:
Mr. Justice Stewart:	11/28/73		*agrees with app*
Mr. Justice White:			
Mr. Justice Marshall:	12/27/73		*in wods le —*
Mr. Justice Blackmun:	1/3/73		*agrees ___ PS.*
	1/7/74		
	1/9/74		
	1/17/74	1	
	1-14-74		
Mr. Justice Powell:	1/4/73		*Agrees with Op.*
Mr. Justice Rehnquist:	12/3/73		*Agree*

Figure A1.3 (continued).

responses: Justice Stewart agreed with (i.e., "joined") the opinion but simultaneously made a suggestion; Justices Blackmun and Powell supported Stewart's suggestion; Justice Rehnquist and Chief Justice Burger joined White's majority opinion draft without other comment; and Justice Douglas, on November 29, notified White that he planned to write a dissent. Douglas subsequently circulated five drafts of his dissenting opinion beginning with the first on December 3. In the weeks that followed, Justice Brennan joined Douglas's dissent (December 10), as did Justice Marshall (December 27). After White circulated the second draft of his majority opinion, Blackmun informed him that he planned to write a concurrence, and, on January 9, Blackmun circulated the first of three drafts of such an opinion.

THE RELIABILITY OF THE HISTORICAL RECORD

While judicial scholars have made increasing use of data gleaned from the justices' personal papers (see Caldeira, Wright, and Zorn 1997; Dorff and Brenner 1992; Maltzman and Wahlbeck 1996b; Wood and Gansle 1997), scholars have publicly and privately expressed their concerns with the reliability of the justices' papers (Ulmer 1973b, 1990; Palmer and Brenner 1989; Palmer 1990). Indeed, there is some consensus among scholars who use historical records that different accounts and sources pose the danger of selection bias (Lustick 1996; see also Gates 1990; Johnson 1987b).

Most notably, in a collection of personal papers, one might reasonably fear that the justices have edited their papers' content in an attempt to shape history's view of events or justices. In Justice Douglas's case file for *Brown v. Board of Education* (1954), he included a memo to the file that details the positions taken by justices in the 1952 term that gives the impression that, had the Vinson Court decided *Brown*, it would have upheld segregation (Douglas 1954). In contrast, other justices removed items from their files. Ulmer (1973b, 296) reports that Chief Justice Hughes destroyed large numbers of documents in order, perhaps, to project a particular image. The most vivid example is the burning of Justice Black's conference notes after he was admitted to Bethesda Naval Hospital shortly before his death (Ulmer 1990, 194). Although Black may have destroyed his conference notes to prevent the public from learning what occurred, some justices, like Justice Powell, who discarded his certiorari memos and votes in cases where certiorari ultimately was denied, are likely to have thought that such material would not interest scholars.

What are the results of such possible selection effects? If justices systematically destroy some of their records, while retaining others, the conclusions one draws may reflect data availability, not actual events. Inferences drawn from an incomplete historical record may be wrong. Each justice's records may represent variations from the actual events that result from "the extraneous circumstances of measurement, the hidden idiosyncrasies of individual analysts" (Krippendorff 1980, 129). Because the likelihood of trustworthy conclusions is directly proportional to the accuracy of the data, one must determine whether the data are valid and reliable.

In thinking about the integrity of the data used in this book, two issues arise. First, we must demonstrate that the measures we draw from the justices' papers actually capture the underlying behavior of interest. If, for example, Brennan's circulation records fail to record certain types of memos then our measures would be invalid – that is, our indicators would not measure what they purport to represent. This type of accuracy is thus analogous to ascertaining the validity of a measure (see Krippendorff 1980; Carmines and Zeller 1979). We examine this type of data accuracy in two ways: (1) we ascertain whether Brennan's docket sheets correctly record the conference votes of the justices; and (2) we test whether Brennan's circulation records provide a systematic recording of the actions taken by justices during the writing of opinions. Second, we must be confident that our coding of Brennan's circulation records is reliable. A measure is reliable if other researchers can replicate it (see Krippendorff 1980; Carmines and Zeller 1979). Thus, to test for our coding reliability, we compared the extent to which the coding decisions of one of the authors agree with the coding decisions of a second coder (a graduate student in political science).

CONFERENCE VOTES

To test the accuracy of Brennan's record of the conference vote, we used original docket sheets of William Douglas, William Brennan, and Lewis Powell for the 1973 term to identify how each justice initially voted on the merits.[2] As

---

[2] This portion of Appendix 1 is derived in part from Maltzman and Wahlbeck (1996c). We examine records in cases that were orally argued and for which a signed opinion was assigned or published. We exclude votes on the cases for which the Court exercised original jurisdiction – only Justice Powell's papers contained a completed docket sheet, and the recorded positions were noted in unusual categories – approve master's report or disapprove report. We do not include the conference votes recorded by Thurgood Marshall. Marshall's papers include his

one can see from Figure A1.1, the justices' docket sheet contains a grid of justices and their votes on certiorari, jurisdiction, merits, and other motions.[3] For the vote on the merits, which we examine here, the form has a column for each of two positions, affirm and reverse. In most cases, the recording justice simply places a check in the appropriate box to represent each justice's vote. On occasion, the justice also places a note next to a justice's vote on the merits to indicate differing grounds for the vote or to indicate a position other than affirmation or reversal.[4] Justices sometimes place additional columns in the grid to allow for votes in multiple issues or dockets.

We test the precision of the data in two different ways. First, we examine the reliability of the justices' records of votes. Taking as a given that each justice accurately assesses his own position, we compare that record with the vote recorded by other justices. If the other justices agree with the stated position of the voting justice himself, we can conclude that their records accurately reflect the views stated at conference. We also examine the reliability of the justices' records on all votes cast at conference by all nine justices. Both the accuracy of the data and intercoder reliability are assessed by a measure of intercoder reliability.

How accurate are the justices' appraisals of their colleagues' positions? To the extent that a justice's mind is made up at conference, we have an accurate portrayal of the three recording justices' stances at conference.[5] The accuracy of the justices' records can be measured by the agreement between each justice's record of his own vote and other justices' records of that vote. We examine, for instance, the rate of agreement between Brennan's record of Douglas's vote and Douglas's record of his own vote. If the two records agree, we conclude that Brennan's record is an accurate depiction of Douglas's vote at conference.

---

    docket sheets in the case files, but he has retained the docket sheets in only 12 of the 143 cases decided during the 1973 term.

[3] Powell did not record the conference vote on the docket sheet. Instead, Powell indicated each justice's position in his notes from the conference discussion. Consequently, his record of conference positions is more detailed than either Douglas or Brennan. He notes, as does Douglas to a lesser extent, the shifts in position that occur during the conference. For instance, he notes that Chief Justice Burger passed on the first vote before he announced his position on the second vote. Brennan, however, just records the ultimate position taken by each justice without regard for an initial position.

[4] There are several other outcomes not presented on the docket sheet: dismiss as improvidently granted, dismiss, vacate, remand, modify, reargue, and hold. Justices also note reasons for no vote. In particular, Brennan usually notes on the docket sheet whether a justice is participating, but passes, or is out. Out is also another column on the docket sheet.

[5] Of course, the justices do not have to come to a firm conclusion at the conference. Indicative of this is Powell's practice to occasionally put the word "tentatively" next to the vote.

To assess the rate of agreement, we use the kappa statistic. Essentially, kappa tests the null hypothesis that the observed level of agreement might occur by chance. More specifically, in the form used in this portion of our analysis, kappa is the proportional reduction of the rate of expected disagreement among coders. If there is perfect agreement, kappa equals 1; otherwise, the level of agreement that ca. ᴴ᾿ observed by chance is denoted by kappa equal to 0, while kappa less than 0 indicates agreement at less than the rate expected by chance (Cohen 1960; Landis and Koch 1977).

The degree of agreement across the justices ranges from substantial, at worst, to almost perfect. The rates of agreement among Douglas, Brennan, and Powell, presented in Table A1.1, range between 85.1 and 97.6 percent. Of these four justices, Justice Powell has the highest overall rate of agreement – 97.5 and 94.6 percent agreement with Douglas and Brennan, respectively. Uniformly, the justices' agreement rate exceeds that expected by chance. Powell has the highest rate of reduction of the expected rate of disagreement, as indicated by the kappa statistic. The accuracy of each justice's conference record, however, is fairly comparable. A difference-of-proportions test indicates that the overall accuracy of Brennan's record is indistinguishable from that of either colleague.[6] In any event, all three justices seem to portray accurately their fellow justices' votes.[7]

Given the significant pairwise agreement on votes cast at conference, do the docket sheets of Douglas, Brennan, and Powell record the same vote for all nine justices? We can assess this by examining the votes of all nine justices recorded by our three justices. Again, we use kappa as a measure of intercoder reliability. In this form, kappa compares the number of coders who associate a justice with a particular outcome and the total number of coders. The kappa statistic is then calculated for each outcome, like affirm, reverse, and so on, and for the combined outcomes. This form of kappa has the advantage of accounting for multiple coders and multiple outcomes.

Two outcomes are explicitly presented on the printed docket sheet, affirm

---

[6] The difference-of-proportions test yields a probability of .16 for the comparison between Brennan and Powell and .054 for the Brennan-Douglas comparison. The only comparison that produced a significant difference was between Douglas and Powell where Powell's records were significantly more accurate than Douglas's records (p < .01).

[7] A problem, however, arises, in that the voting categories that justices use on their docket sheets are not mutually exclusive, which reduces reliability. To resolve this problem, if one recording justice described a justice's vote as a pass or out, we recoded votes originally recorded no vote to pass or out. Moreover, in a number of cases, a justice recorded a vote as more than a simple affirm, such as an affirm and remand or a reverse and remand. In these instances, we coded these votes as just affirm or just reverse.

Table A1.1. *Accuracy of Recorded Conference Votes*

Recording Justice	Voting Justice	Rate of Agreement	Kappa
Douglas	Brennan[a]	95.20%	.9131***
	Powell[b]	85.12%	.7244***
Brennan	Douglas[a]	97.60%	.9570***
	Powell[c]	90.70%	.8260***
Powell	Douglas[b]	97.52%	.9561***
	Brennan[c]	94.57%	.9011***

[a] n = 125. [b] n = 121. [c] n = 129. *** p < .0001.

and reverse. Not surprisingly, there is a high degree of intercoder agreement for these two outcomes.[8] Indeed, as reflected in Table A1.2, there is almost perfect agreement when the outcome takes one of these two values as the kappa statistic is, respectively, .9230 and .9125. The only other outcome that has this degree of reliability is when the justice did not participate in the case (kappa = .9569). For most of the other dispositions, there is moderate agreement, at best, on the justices' votes. Intuitively, one would expect greater disagreement for these outcomes since, in order to record a vote for an alternative outcome, the justice has to either make a note on the sheet or alter the heading on the column from, say, reverse to remand (see Holsti 1969; Krippendorff 1980). Nevertheless, as seen in the kappa for all outcomes combined, there is substantial agreement among the recording justices on the outcome supported by each of the nine justices.[9]

In summary, Justice Brennan's docket sheets provide a reliable source of data for the positions taken by the justices at conference. This bolsters the validity of our measures for whether a justice voted with the majority or minority conference coalition.

---

[8] For this analysis, we exclude the records of the justice who voted if he is one of the three recording justices. This is done to prevent biasing the reliability results since presumably, if we used the records of the voting justice, those will be accurate.

[9] Unfortunately, when the number of coders varies across cases, as happens when justices do not have a vote recorded because of absence or confusion, we technically cannot test the null hypothesis of chance agreement. Some have argued that showing that the estimate differs from zero does not have much meaning, given that we are mainly concerned with how much above zero it is (Cohen 1968, 217).

Table A1.2. *Intercoder Reliability of Conference Vote on Merits*

Outcome	Kappa
Affirm	.9230
Reverse	.9125
Affirm in Part/Reverse in Part	.1872
No Vote	.4595
Pass	.7805
Out	.9569
Dismiss	.5727
DIG	.5248
DIG or Reverse	.0313
Remand	.4328
Remand or Affirm	−.1067
Remand or Reverse	−.1067
Vacate	−.0796
Vacate and Dismiss	−.0151
Vacate and Remand	.2589
Modify	.0892
Reargue	−.1067
Combined	.8537

Notes: n = 1,852. DIG = dismiss as improvidentally granted.

CIRCULATION RECORDS

To what extent do Justice Brennan's circulation records comprise an accurate and complete portrait of the activity that occurs during the course of writing opinions? Do they include all actions or do they systematically exclude documents of interest? In order to assess the comprehensiveness of Brennan's circulation records, we conducted a review of the case files and circulation records found in the papers of Justices Brennan, Douglas, Marshall, and Powell in the 1973 term. First, we identified all documents contained in the case files or circulation records and coded whether they were, for example, a draft majority opinion, a separate opinion draft, a suggestion, a threat. We found 2,306 documents in total.[10] Of these items, 235 (10.2 percent) did not fall into

---

[10] This includes only verified documents: those items of which we found a physical copy or that were referenced in more than one circulation record. The circulation records contain some administration errors. In all, we found reference to sixty-four documents that we could not

any of our coding categories. For instance, we found memos related to the assignment decision, cover memos accompanying opinion drafts, and other miscellaneous notes. Of the 2,071 documents that fell into one of our coding categories, 52 notes (2.5 percent) were not sent to all of the justices, but were sent privately to one or more justices. Because Justice Brennan's circulation records do not consistently record private memos, we excluded them from our analysis. First, when private correspondence is recorded, Brennan's circulation sheets only reference memos either sent by or to Brennan. Second, his circulation records do not list private memos until the Court's 1982 term, and they do not appear to be systematically recorded until the 1983 term. Thus, using these private memos would introduce bias both because they only appear beginning with the 1983 term and they only pertain to Brennan. We, however, recognize that we somewhat underestimate the total amount of bargaining occurring on the Court.

Justice Brennan's circulation records include reference to 1,924 of the 2,019 (95.3 percent) nonprivate documents. The coverage of Brennan's records is the most comprehensive set of documents of all the sources. Indeed, Brennan's circulation records are significantly more comprehensive than all but one of the other sources; Marshall's case files are not significantly less complete, although they contain 1,908 (94.5 percent) of the documents. More specifically, we conducted a series of difference-of-proportions tests to ascertain whether Brennan's circulation records provide a more comprehensive source of data than the justices' case files or other circulation records. That is, we compare the proportion of items found in Brennan's circulation records with the proportion of documents found in the other sources. As Table A1.3 indicates, Brennan's circulation records are significantly better than five of the six other sources.

This analysis suggests that Brennan's circulation records are one of the most comprehensive sources for documents circulated among the justices during the opinion-writing process. But what are the ninety-five omitted documents from Justice Brennan's circulation records? Most of the missing documents are opinion drafts (n = 50) or memos joining those opinions (n = 37). Of these, the most frequently absent items are memos joining the majority opinion (n = 25), and this is followed by majority opinion drafts themselves

locate in any case file. Justice Douglas's circulation records had the most erroneous additions, twenty-seven. Justice Brennan's circulation record referenced fourteen documents that we could not locate in any other source. We also excluded *United States v. Nixon* (1974) inasmuch as this case was heard during a special oral argument session in July 1974, and we could not find a circulation record for this case. Our data for *Nixon*, consequently, were derived entirely from case files.

Table A1.3. *Reliability of Brennan's Circulation Records*

Justice	Type of Record	Contains Proportion of All Documents	Probability That Brennan Circulation Proportion Is Not Greater Than Proportion from Other Sources
Brennan	Circulation	.953	—
Brennan	Case Files	.910	0.000
Douglas	Circulation	.424	0.000
Douglas	Case Files	.932	0.002
Marshall	Case Files	.945	0.126
Powell	Circulation	.916	0.000
Powell	Case Files	.682	0.000

(n = 21). Very few missing items are bargaining memos, which tap what we have termed our signaling hypotheses. There were, for example, one threat and four suggestions missing from Brennan's circulation sheets. Of course, the missing items do not constitute a substantial share of these types of documents. The missing join memos, for example, comprise only 3.1 percent of the 802 join memos that were sent to majority opinion authors during the 1973 term. We should note that if we were missing an action by a justice (e.g., there was no memo recorded for a justice), we examined the available case files for evidence of the justice's decision.

From this analysis, we conclude that Brennan's circulation records present a reliable and comprehensive record of the actions taken by the justices. This, in turn, allows us to develop valid measures of the actions justices take in the process of writing opinions.

CODING ACTIONS FROM BRENNAN'S CIRCULATION RECORDS

Another important issue is whether our coding of the information contained in Brennan's circulation records is replicable. That is, we must ensure that our coding procedures will result in similar results over repeated measurements. To ascertain the reliability of our coding protocols, we employed a second person to code the circulation sheets for two randomly selected terms, 1973 and

Table A1.4. *Intercoder Reliability of the Coding
of Brennan's Circulation Records*

Type of Memo	Rate of Agreement	Kappa
Join Majority	98.6	.97***
Wait	99.5	.92***
Will Write	99.2	.91***
Suggestion	98.9	.58***
Threat	99.3	.72***
Concur	99.1	.93***
Dissent	98.5	.93***

Note: N = 4,542.
*** p < .0001.

1984. In particular, we ascertained whether the two coders agreed that the notations on Brennan's sheets referred to a join memo, wait statement, suggestion, threat, will write signal, draft concurrence, or draft dissent. Although other types of memos exist (e.g., reargue a case), they are not herein analyzed because we did not incorporate any of them into the book's analysis. As before, we use the kappa statistic to ascertain the level of intercoder agreement above that expected by chance. We present the results in Table A1.4

Table A1.4 makes clear that our coding of Brennan's circulation records is highly reliable. The rate of agreement between the two coders ranged from a low of 98.5 percent for dissents to a high of 99.5 percent for wait statements. As the kappa statistics indicate, moreover, this level of intercoder agreement is significantly better than one would expect to occur by chance. Consider the result for statements that a justice will write separately. The two coders agreed that an entry on Brennan's circulation records referred to such a memo 99.2 percent of the time. The kappa for this type of memo, at .91 (p < .0001), shows that this rate of agreement is, according to Landis and Koch (1977) "almost perfect." The two coders agree at a rate of 91 percent above chance agreement. The 98.9 percent agreement for suggestions, with a kappa of .58 (p < .0001) shows that this agreement rate is 58 percent better than random agreement.[11] In short, this analysis confirms that our coding of Brennan's circulation sheets is reliable.

[11] The kappa statistic for suggestions is in part lower than that for other actions because relatively few suggestions were circulated, and thus the rate of expected agreement is higher.

Appendix 2
Summary Statistics for Independent Variables

Table A2.1. *Summary Statistics for Independent Variables in Chief Justice Opinion Assignment Model (Chapter 2)*

Variable	Mean	Standard Deviation	Minimum	Maximum
Ideology	15.82	15.67	0	69.50
Self-Assignment	.15	.35	0	1
Ideology * Winning Margin	36.82	48.39	−49.1	278
Ideology * Political Salience	17.32	68.56	−55.28	1450.56
Ideology * Legal Salience	1.79	7.85	0	69.50
Self-Assignment * Political Salience	.18	1.34	−.92	52.54
Self-Assignment * Legal Salience	.01	.11	0	1
Equity	.33	.87	0	8
Expertise	−.01	.93	−2.11	2.67
Freshman	.08	.27	0	1
Freshman * Case Complexity	.003	.28	−.92	5.52
Workload	.002	.92	−2.43	2.67
Ideology * End of Term	2,536.16	2,947.74	−556	17,931

Table A2.2. *Summary Statistics for Independent Variables in Associate Justice Opinion Assignment Model (Chapter 2)*

Variable	Mean	Standard Deviation	Minimum	Maximum
Ideology	16.67	16.14	0	74
Self-Assignment	.18	.39	0	1
Ideology * Winning Margin	11.98	24.51	−49	193.80
Ideology * Political Salience	20.99	72.84	−54.15	861.01
Ideology * Legal Salience	3.27	9.87	0	60.50
Self-Assignment * Political Salience	.25	1.51	−.92	29.29
Self-Assignment * Legal Salience	.04	.19	0	1
Equity	.21	.69	0	6
Expertise	.08	.96	−1.91	2.67
Freshman	.05	.22	0	1
Freshman * Case Complexity	.01	.27	−.92	7.26
Workload	−.01	.91	−2.67	2.67
Ideology * End of Term	2,715.43	3,051.91	0	18,179

Table A2.3. *Summary Statistics for Independent Variables Used in Models of Justices' Bargaining Tactics (Chapter 3)*

Variable	Mean	Standard Deviation	Minimum	Maximum
Author Distance	18.72	14.70	0	78.10
Coalition Distance	11.70	8.97	0	52.02
Winning Margin	2.01	1.46	−3	4
Cooperation	.004	.12	−.16	.84
Political Salience	1.20	3.13	−.92	37.27
Legal Salience	.10	.31	0	1
Case Complexity	−.009	.99	−.53	6.89
End of Term	113.70	69.68	−9	261
Workload	8.75	3.95	0	26
Chief Justice	.13	.33	0	1
Freshman Author	.07	.26	0	1
Expertise	−.008	.93	−2.11	2.67

Table A2.4. *Summary Statistics for Independent Variables in Model of Preemptive Accommodation (Chapter 4)*

Variable	Mean	Standard Deviation	Minimum	Maximum
Conference Coalition Distance	14.98	10.72	0	63.28
Conference Coalition Heterogeneity	14.53	6.49	0	34.56
Winning Margin	1.59	1.52	−4	4
Cooperation	.003	.07	−.14	.26
Political Salience	1.66	3.60	−.92	52.54
Legal Salience	.10	.31	0	1
Case Complexity	−.001	1.0	−.92	7.26
End of Term	160.69	67.56	−8	271
Workload	8.85	3.99	0	25
Chief Justice Author	.11	.32	0	1
Freshman Author	.08	.27	0	1
Author Expertise	.01	.92	−1.96	2.67

Table A2.5. *Summary Statistics for Independent Variables in Model of Responsive Accommodation (Chapter 4)*

Variable	Mean	Standard Deviation	Minimum	Maximum
Distance from Nonjoiners	13.44	15.35	0	74.0
Heterogeneity of Nonjoiners	6.19	9.23	0	52.33
Winning Margin	1.45	1.52	−4	4
Cooperation of Nonjoiners	−.01	.05	−.20	.43
Have Majority	.67	.47	0	1
Number of Suggestions	.12	.47	0	11
Number of Waits	.06	.27	0	4
Number of Will Writes	.23	.49	0	5
First Draft of Separate Opinions	.59	.84	0	6
Political Salience	1.79	3.81	−.92	52.54
Legal Salience	.11	.31	0	1
Case Complexity	.08	1.02	−.92	7.26
End of Term	102.87	70.09	−22	261
Workload	8.59	4.12	0	25
Chief Justice Author	.11	.32	0	1
Freshman Author	.07	.26	0	1
Author Expertise	.03	.93	−1.96	2.67

Table A2.6. *Summary Statistics for Independent Variables in Model of Justices' Joining of Majority Opinions (Chapter 5)*

Variable	Mean	Standard Deviation	Minimum	Maximum
Author Distance	22.85	17.06	0	78.1
Coalition Distance	3.47	13.56	−69.5	55.9
Dissent Distance	4.51	17.94	−69.5	78.1
Conference Majority	.60	.49	0	1
Cooperation	−.007	.11	−.16	.84
Have Majority	.15	.36	0	1
Number of Suggestions	.15	.50	0	11
Number of Waits	.20	.54	0	5
Number of Will Writes	.27	.52	0	5
First Draft of Separate Opinions	.52	.77	0	6
Political Salience	1.77	3.57	−.92	37.27
Legal Salience	.11	.31	0	1
Case Complexity	.11	1.02	−.92	7.26
End of Term	107.71	70.20	−9	514
Workload	8.57	3.80	0	27
Chief Justice	.11	.31	0	1
Freshman Author	.07	.25	0	1
Author Expertise	.03	.93	−1.96	2.67

Appendix 3
Measuring Preemptive
Accommodation

In Chapter 4, we model when authors preemptively accommodate their colleagues. Our statistical results show that the amount of effort authors put into accommodating their brethren varies with, among other factors, the strategic environment. To capture an author's efforts at preemptive accommodation, we examine the length of time in days that it takes an author to circulate the first draft of the opinion after it is assigned to him or her. While our duration model's dependent variable is technically the hazard rate – the risk that an author will circulate the first opinion draft given that he or she had not already done so – our underlying measure is the time it takes to write that first draft. In other words, we assume that, as long as one controls for other factors that may influence the amount of time needed to circulate the first draft (namely, our contextual control variables), the length of time required to write the first draft is a reasonable indication of preemptive accommodation. We use this proxy in large part because preemptive accommodation is unobservable. As we note in Chapter 4, preemptive accommodation is unobservable and, in fact, rests on a counterfactual that the author would have acted differently if he or she had not preemptively accommodated.

The assumption that the amount of time needed to circulate the first draft reflects an author's attempt to accommodate is not necessarily self-evident. It is possible, of course, that the amount of time needed to circulate a first draft taps something that we fail to control for in our model of preemptive accommodation (see Table 4.3). Thus, it is imperative that we establish the validity of our measure. We can ascertain our measure's validity by examining justices' reactions to the initial draft. If time elapsed measures an author's efforts at preemptive accommodation, we would expect that the longer it takes to issue a first draft, the higher the number of justices who will join the first draft. This approach is thus analogous to construct validity (see Krippendorff 1980), which "is concerned with the extent to which a particular measure relates to other measures consistent with theoretically derived hypotheses concerning the concepts (or constructs) that are being measured" (Carmines and Zeller 1979, 23).

To test for construct validity, we created a variable, *Acceptable First Draft*. This measure tells us whether the initial draft is acceptable to all of the justices who initially voted with the conference majority, to some of the justices who voted with the conference majority, or to more than the number of justices who voted with the conference majority. The variable ranges from −8 to +4. If fewer justices join the first draft than were in the conference majority, it takes on a negative value and is a count of the number of justices who supported the disposition favored by the majority but did not join the first draft. Thus, if the initial vote on a case's merits is 7–2 and no one joins the first draft, the *Acceptable First Draft* variable is equal to −6.[1] On the other hand, if more justices join the first draft than voted with the majority, it takes on a positive value. Thus, if each of the author's eight colleagues found the first draft acceptable in spite of the fact that the initial conference majority only had seven justices (7–2), the *Acceptable First Draft* variable is equal to +2. In this case, the author preemptively accommodated the other eight justices. Table A3.1 shows the distribution of this variable for the 2,293 cases where an opinion assignment was made or a signed opinion was released during the Burger Court.

Because Table A3.1 suggests a normal distribution and has twelve values, we use ordinary least squares and regress *Acceptable First Draft* on the amount of time an author takes to circulate the first draft (*Drafting Time*). We can therefore see whether authors who preemptively accommodate their brethren do indeed write opinions that are more acceptable. Because the amount of time an author has to craft the first draft differs over the course of a Court term, our independent variable is the ratio of the time taken to circulate the first draft (after an opinion is assigned) to the number of days between the assignment date and July 1. This *Drafting Time* variable is the independent variable that tests the validity of our preemptive accommodation measure.[2]

To control for other variables that might influence how many justices eventually join the first draft, we include in our model the same measures of *Con-*

---

[1]   We exclude the author from the calculation of this variable.

[2]   In the preemptive accommodation model in Chapter 4, we also control for the number of days left in the term.

Table A3.1. *Crafting an Acceptable First Draft*

Acceptable First Draft	Frequency	Percentage
−8	21	0.92
−7	69	3.01
−6	95	4.14
−5	161	7.02
−4	284	12.39
−3	360	15.70
−2	370	16.14
−1	357	15.57
0	401	17.49
1	103	4.49
2	43	1.88
3	22	0.96
4	7	0.31

Table A3.2. *Regression of Acceptable First Draft*

Variable	Estimate	Robust Standard Error
Drafting Time	.752***	.208
Conference Coalition Distance	−.013*	.006
Conference Coalition Heterogeneity	−.026**	.011
Winning Margin	−.517	.045
Cooperation	−.157	1.107
Political Salience	−.040**	.014
Legal Salience	.046	.149
Case Complexity	−.336***	.033
Workload	.011	.012
Chief Justice Author	−.011	.106
Freshman Author	.463**	.182
Author Expertise	−.101	.071
Constant	−2.134***	.247
Number of Observations	2,293	
R^2	.180	
F	95.8***	

*p ≤ .05; **p ≤ .01; ***p ≤ .001.

ference Coalition Heterogeneity, Winning Margin, Cooperation, Political Salience, Legal Salience, Case Complexity, Workload, Chief Justice Author, Freshman Author, and *Author Expertise* employed in Chapter 4. In addition to these variables, we include a measure to tap the opinion author's ideological extremity. We expect extreme authors to preemptively accommodate fewer of their colleagues. This measure is based on the same issue-specific ideology score we employed throughout the book.[3]

Table A3.2 contains the results for our model predicting how many justices found the first draft acceptable. Even after controlling for other factors that might influence whether a justice finds the first draft acceptable, it is clear that the *Drafting Time* variable is statistically significant. In other words, authors who take longer to compose the first draft of an opinion are more likely to have crafted an opinion that is acceptable to the other justices. Time elapsed, in other words, is a reasonably valid (though certainly not perfect) measure of preemptive accommodation.

---

[3]   More specifically, the measure is based on the twelve value areas identified by Spaeth (1994). For each justice, we calculated the absolute difference between his or her ideology score and 50.

References

Ake v. Oklahoma. 1985. 470 U.S. 68.

Aldrich, John H., and Forrest D. Nelson. 1984. *Linear Probability, Logit, and Probit Models.* Newbury Park, CA: Sage.

Alexander v. Choate. 1985. 469 U.S. 287.

Allison, Paul D. 1984. *Event History Analysis: Regression for Longitudinal Event Data.* Newbury Park, CA: Sage.

Alt, James E., and Kenneth A. Shepsle, eds. 1990. *Perspectives on Positive Political Economy.* Cambridge: Cambridge University Press.

Alvarez, Michael R., and Jonathan Nagler. 1998. "When Politics and Models Collide: Estimating Models of Multiparty Elections." *American Journal of Political Science* 42 (January): 55–96.

Arrow, Kenneth J. 1951. *Social Choice and Individual Values.* New Haven: Yale University Press.

Astrup v. Immigration and Naturalization Service. 1971. 402 U.S. 509.

Atkins, Burton M. 1970. "Some Theoretical Effects of the Decision-Making Rules on the United States Courts of Appeals." *Jurimetrics Journal* 11 (September): 13–23.

——— 1972. "Decision-Making Rules and Judicial Strategy on the United States Courts of Appeals." *Western Political Quarterly* 25 (December): 626–642.

Atkins, Burton M., and William Zavoina. 1974. "Judicial Leadership on the Court of Appeals: A Probability Analysis of Panel Assignment in Race Relations Cases on the Fifth Circuit." *American Journal of Political Science* 18 (November): 701–711.

Austen-Smith, David, and William H. Riker. 1987. "Asymmetric Information and the Coherence of Legislation." *American Political Science Review* 81 (September): 897–918.

Axelrod, Robert. 1970. *Conflict of Interest: A Theory of Divergent Goals with Applications to Politics.* Chicago: Markham.

1984. *The Evolution of Cooperation.* New York: Basic Books.

Baron, David P., and John A. Ferejohn. 1989. "Bargaining in Legislatures." *American Political Science Review* 83 (December): 1181–1206.

Baum, Lawrence. 1985. *The Supreme Court.* 2d ed. Washington, DC: CQ Press.

1997. *The Puzzle of Judicial Behavior.* Ann Arbor: University of Michigan Press.

1998. *The Supreme Court.* 6th ed. Washington, DC: CQ Press.

Beck, Nathaniel, Jonathan N. Katz, and Richard Tucker. 1998. "Taking Time Seriously: Time-Series–Cross-Section Analysis with a Binary Dependent Variable." *American Journal of Political Science* 42 (October): 1260–1288.

Bentley, A. Lee. 1985. Memo to Justice Marshall, February 12. Papers of Justice Thurgood Marshall. Washington, DC: Library of Congress Manuscript Division.

Berelson, Bernard R., Paul F. Lazarsfeld, and William N. McPhee. 1954. *Voting.* Chicago: University of Chicago Press.

Berkemer v. McCarty. 1984. 468 U.S. 420.

Berry, Frances Stokes, and William D. Berry. 1990. "State Lottery Adoptions as Policy Innovations: An Event History Analysis." *American Political Science Review* 84 (June): 395–415.

1992. "Tax Innovation in the States: Capitalizing on Political Opportunity." *American Journal of Political Science* 36 (August): 715–742.

1994. "The Politics of Tax Increases in the States." *American Journal of Political Science* 38 (August): 855–859.

Bhat, Chandra R. 1995. "A Heteroscedastic Extreme Value Model of Intercity Travel Mode Choice." *Transportation Research* 29B (February): 471–483.

Binder, Sarah, Eric Lawrence, and Forrest Maltzman. 1999. "Uncovering the Hidden Effect of Party." *Journal of Politics* 61 (August): 815–831.

Binmore, Kenneth. 1986. "Bargaining and Coalitions." In *Game Theoretic Models of Bargaining,* ed. Alvin E. Roth, 269–304. Cambridge: Cambridge University Press.

Biskupic, Joan. 1995. "As Deadline Nears, Court Leaders Pin Hopes on 'Holding 5.'" *Washington Post,* June 7.

Black, Hugo L. 1970. Letter to William J. Brennan Jr., March 26. Papers of Justice William J. Brennan Jr. Washington, DC: Library of Congress Manuscript Division.

Blackmun, Harry A. 1973. Letter to Thurgood Marshall, April 2. Papers of Justice William J. Brennan Jr. Washington, DC: Library of Congress Manuscript Division.

1975. Letter to William H. Rehnquist, December 3. Papers of Justice William J. Brennan Jr. Washington, DC: Library of Congress Manuscript Division.

1980a. Letter to Lewis F. Powell Jr., May 16. Papers of Justice William J. Brennan Jr. Washington, DC: Library of Congress Manuscript Division.

1980b. Memorandum to the Conference, May 21. Papers of Justice William J. Brennan Jr. Washington, DC: Library of Congress Manuscript Division.

1980c. Letter to Lewis F. Powell Jr., June 12. Papers of Justice William J. Brennan Jr. Washington, DC: Library of Congress Manuscript Division.

1984. Letter to Sandra Day O'Connor, December 4. Papers of Justice William J. Brennan Jr. Washington, DC: Library of Congress Manuscript Division.

Blalock, Hubert M., Jr. 1979. *Social Statistics.* Rev. ed. New York: McGraw-Hill.

Box-Steffensmeier, Janet M. 1996. "A Dynamic Analysis of the Role of War Chests in Campaign Strategy." *American Journal of Political Science* 40 (May): 352–371.

Box-Steffensmeier, Janet M., Laura W. Arnold, and Christopher J. W. Zorn. 1997. "The Strategic Timing of Position Taking in Congress: A Study of the North American Free Trade Agreement." *American Political Science Review* 91 (June): 324–338.

Box-Steffensmeier, Janet M., and Bradford Jones. 1997. "Time Is of the Essence: Event History Models in Political Science." *American Journal of Political Science* 41 (October): 1414–1461.

Brace, Paul, and Melinda Gann Hall. 1990. "Neo-Institutionalism and Dissent in State Supreme Courts." *Journal of Politics* 52 (February): 54–70.

1993. "Integrated Models of Judicial Dissent." *Journal of Politics* 55 (November): 914–935.

1995. "Studying Courts Comparatively: The View from the American States." *Political Research Quarterly* 48 (March): 5–29.

Brennan, William J., Jr. 1960. "State Court Decisions and the Supreme Court." *Pennsylvania Bar Association Quarterly* 31 (June): 393–407.

1963. "How the Supreme Court Arrives at Decisions." *New York Times*, October 12.

1973a. Memorandum to the Conference, February 14. Papers of Justice William J. Brennan Jr. Washington, DC: Library of Congress Manuscript Division.

1973b. Memorandum to the Conference, February 28. Papers of Justice William J. Brennan Jr. Washington, DC: Library of Congress Manuscript Division.

1984a. Letter to Sandra Day O'Connor, December 10. Papers of Justice William J. Brennan Jr. Washington, DC: Library of Congress Manuscript Division.

1984b. Letter to Sandra Day O'Connor, December 12. Papers of Justice William J. Brennan Jr. Washington, DC: Library of Congress Manuscript Division.

1986. "In Defense of Dissents." *Hastings Law Journal* 37 (January): 427–438.

1990a. Letter to Thurgood Marshall, June 7. Papers of Justice Thurgood Marshall. Washington, DC: Library of Congress Manuscript Division.

1990b. First Majority Opinion Draft, May 31. Papers of Justice Thurgood Marshall. Washington, DC: Library of Congress Manuscript Division.

1990c. Second Majority Opinion Draft, June 6. Papers of Justice Thurgood Marshall. Washington, DC: Library of Congress Manuscript Division.

1990d. Letter to Thurgood Marshall, June 13. Papers of Justice Thurgood Marshall. Washington, DC: Library of Congress Manuscript Division.

1990e. Memorandum to the Conference, May 31. Papers of Justice Thurgood Marshall. Washington, DC: Library of Congress Manuscript Division.

Brenner, Saul. 1982. "Strategic Choice and Opinion Assignment on the U.S. Supreme Court: A Reexamination." *Western Political Quarterly* 35 (June): 204–211.

1984. "Issue Specialization as a Variable in Opinion Assignment." *Journal of Politics* 46 (November): 1217–1225.

1985. "Is Competence Related to Majority Opinion Assignment on the United States Supreme Court?" *Capital University Law Review* 15 (Fall): 35–41.

1990. "Measuring Policy Leadership on the U.S. Supreme Court: A Focus on Majority Opinion Authorship." In *Studies in U.S. Supreme Court Behavior*, ed. Harold J. Spaeth and Saul Brenner, 136–148. New York: Garland.

1993. "The Chief Justice's Self Assignment of Majority Opinions in Salient Cases." *Social Science Journal* 30 (2): 143–150.

1995. "Fluidity in Voting on the United States Supreme Court: A Bibliographic Overview of the Studies." *Law Library Journal* 87 (Spring): 380–386.

1998. "Measuring the Importance of Supreme Court Decisions." *Law Library Journal* 90 (Summer): 183–192.

Brenner, Saul, and Timothy M. Hagle. 1996. "Opinion Writing and the Acclimation Effect." *Political Behavior* 18 (September): 235–261.

Brenner, Saul, Timothy M. Hagle, and Harold J. Spaeth. 1989. "The Defection of the Marginal Justice on the Warren Court." *Western Political Quarterly* 42 (September): 409–425.

1990. "Increasing the Size of Minimum Winning Coalitions on the Warren Court." *Polity* 23 (Winter): 309–318.

Brenner, Saul, and Jan Palmer. 1988. "The Time Taken to Write Opinions as a Determinant of Opinion Assignments. *Judicature* 88 (October–November): 179–184.

Brenner, Saul, and Harold J. Spaeth. 1986. "Issue Specialization in Majority Opinion Assignment on the Burger Court." *Western Political Quarterly* 39 (September): 520–527.

1988a. "Majority Opinion Assignment and the Maintenance of the Original Coalition on the Warren Court." *American Journal of Political Science* 32 (February): 72–81.

Briscoe v. Bell. 1977. 432 U.S. 404.

Brown v. Board of Education. 1954. 347 U.S. 483.

Burger, Warren E. 1971a. Memorandum to the Conference, February 5. Papers of Justice William J. Brennan Jr. Washington, DC: Library of Congress Manuscript Division.

1971b. Letter to William O. Douglas, December 20. Papers of Justice William J. Brennan Jr. Washington, DC: Library of Congress Manuscript Division.

1977. Memorandum to the Conference, April 4. Papers of Justice William J. Brennan Jr. Washington, DC: Library of Congress Manuscript Division.

1980. Letter to Harry A. Blackmun, June 4. Papers of Justice William J. Brennan Jr. Washington, DC: Library of Congress Manuscript Division.

1983. Memorandum to the Conference, May 10. Papers of Justice William J. Brennan Jr. Washington, DC: Library of Congress Manuscript Division.

1984a. Letter to Thurgood Marshall, May 31. Papers of Justice William J. Brennan Jr. Washington, DC: Library of Congress Manuscript Division.

1984b. Letter to Sandra Day O'Connor, December 21. Papers of Justice William J. Brennan Jr. Washington, DC: Library of Congress Manuscript Division.

1985a. Letter to Sandra Day O'Connor, January 29. Papers of Justice William J. Brennan Jr. Washington, DC: Library of Congress Manuscript Division.

Caldeira, Gregory A., and John R. Wright. 1988. "Organized Interests and Agenda Setting in the U.S. Supreme Court." *American Political Science Review* 82 (December): 1109–1127.

Caldeira, Gregory A., John R. Wright, and Christopher J. W. Zorn. 1997. "Sophisticated Judicial Behavior: Agenda Setting via the Discuss List." Paper presented at the annual meeting of the American Political Science Association, Washington, DC, August 28–31.

Caldeira, Gregory A., and Christopher J. W. Zorn. 1998. "Of Time and Consensual Norms in the Supreme Court." *American Journal of Political Science* 42 (July): 874–902.

Campbell, Angus, Philip E. Converse, Warren E. Miller, and Donald E. Stokes. 1960. *The American Voter.* New York: Wiley.

Carmines, Edward G., and Richard A. Zeller. 1979. *Reliability and Validity Assessment.* Beverly Hills, CA: Sage.

Clark, Tom C. 1959. "Internal Operation of the United States Supreme Court." *Judicature* 43 (August): 45–51.

Clayton, Cornell W. 1999. "The Supreme Court and Political Jurisprudence: New and Old Institutionalisms." In *Supreme Court Decision-Making: New Institutionalist Approaches,* ed. Cornell W. Clayton and Howard Gillman, 15–41. Chicago: University of Chicago Press.

Clayton, Cornell W., and Howard Gillman, eds. 1999. *Supreme Court Decision-Making: New Institutionalist Approaches.* Chicago: University of Chicago Press.

Cohen, Jacob. 1960. "A Coefficient of Agreement for Nominal Scales." *Educational and Psychological Measurement* 20 (1): 37–46.

1968. "Weighted Kappa: Nominal Scale Agreement with Provision for Scaled Disagreement or Partial Credit." *Psychological Bulletin* 70 (4): 213–220.

Coleman v. Alabama. 1970. 399 U.S. 1.

Cook, Beverly B. 1993. "Measuring the Significance of U.S. Supreme Court Decisions." *Journal of Politics* 55 (November): 1127–1139.

Crawford, Vincent P. 1990. "Explicit Communication and Bargaining Outcome." *American Economic Review* 80 (May): 213–219.

Crawford, Vincent P., and Joel Sobel. 1982. "Strategic Information Transmission." *Econometrica* 50 (November): 1431–1451.

Dahl, Robert. 1961. "The Behavioral Approach in Political Science." *American Political Science Review* 55 (December): 763–772.

Danelski, David J. 1968. "The Influence of the Chief Justice in the Decisional Process of the Supreme Court." In *The Federal Judicial System: Readings in Process and Behavior,* ed. Thomas P. Jahnige and Sheldon Goldman, 147–160. New York: Holt, Rinehart and Winston.

1986. "Causes and Consequences of Conflict and Its Resolution in the Supreme Court." In *Judicial Conflict and Consensus: Behavioral Studies of American Appellate Courts,* ed. Charles M. Lamb and Sheldon Goldman, 21–49. Lexington: University Press of Kentucky.

Davis, Sue. 1990. "Power on the Court: Chief Justice Rehnquist's Opinion Assignments." *Judicature* 74 (August–September): 66–72.

Department of Justice v. Tax Analysts. 1989. 492 U.S. 136.

De Swann, Abraham. 1970. "An Empirical Model of Coalition Formation as an N-Person Game of Policy Distance Minimization." In *The Study of Coalition Behavior: Theoretical Perspectives and Cases from Four Continents,* ed. Sven Groennings, E. W. Kelley, and Michael Leiserson, 424–444. New York: Holt, Rinehart, and Winston.

Dewey v. Reynolds Metals. 1971. 402 U.S. 689.

Dorff, Robert H., and Saul Brenner. 1992. "Conformity Voting on the United States Supreme Court." *Journal of Politics* 54 (August): 762–775.

Douglas, William O. 1954. Memorandum for the File *in re Segregation Cases,* May 17. Papers of Justice William O. Douglas. Washington, DC: Library of Congress Manuscript Division.

1970. Memo to William J. Brennan Jr., January 8. Papers of Justice William J. Brennan Jr. Washington, DC: Library of Congress Manuscript Division.

1971. Memo to Warren E. Burger, December 18. Papers of Justice William J. Brennan Jr. Washington, DC: Library of Congress Manuscript Division.

1972a. Memorandum from Mr. Justice Douglas, June 2. Papers of Justice William O. Douglas. Washington, DC: Library of Congress Manuscript Division.

1972b. Memo to Warren E. Burger, August 7. Papers of Justice William O. Douglas. Washington, DC: Library of Congress Manuscript Division.

Eastland v. United States Servicemen's Fund. 1975. 421 U.S. 491.

Elster, Jon. 1986. Introduction. In *Rational Choice,* ed. Jon Elster, 1–33. New York: New York University Press.

Epstein, Lee, Valerie J. Hoekstra, Jeffrey A. Segal, and Harold J. Spaeth. 1998. "Do Political Preferences Change? A Longitudinal Study of U.S. Supreme Court Justices." *Journal of Politics* 60 (August): 801–818.

Epstein, Lee, and Jack Knight. 1995. "Documenting Strategic Interaction on the U.S. Supreme Court." Paper presented at the annual meeting of the American Political Science Association, Chicago, August 31–September 3.

———. 1998. *The Choices Justices Make.* Washington, DC: CQ Press.

Epstein, Lee, and Jeffrey A. Segal. Forthcoming. "Measuring Issue Salience." *American Journal of Political Science.*

Epstein, Lee, Jeffrey A. Segal, Harold J. Spaeth, and Thomas G. Walker. 1994. *The Supreme Court Compendium: Data, Decisions and Developments.* Washington, DC: CQ Press.

Eskridge, William N. 1991a. "Overriding Supreme Court Statutory Decisions." *Yale Law Journal* 101 (November): 331–450.

———. 1991b. "Reneging on History? Playing the Court/Congress/President Civil Rights Game." *California Law Review* 79 (May): 613–684.

Farrell, Joseph, and Robert Gibbons. 1989. "Cheap Talk Can Matter in Bargaining." *Journal of Economic Theory* 48 (June): 221–237.

Feldman, Jim. 1984. Memorandum to Justice Brennan, December 1. Papers of Justice William J. Brennan Jr. Washington, DC: Library of Congress Manuscript Division.

Fenno, Richard F., Jr. 1962. "The House Appropriations Committee as a Political System: The Problem of Integration." *American Political Science Review* 56 (June): 310–324.

———. 1966. *Power of the Purse.* Boston: Little, Brown.

———. 1986. "Observation, Context, and Sequence in the Study of Politics." *American Political Science Review* 80 (March): 3–15.

Fleming, Thomas R., and David P. Harrington. 1991. *Counting Processes and Survival Analysis.* New York: John Wiley and Sons.

Fortas, Abe. 1975. "Chief Justice Warren: The Enigma of Leadership." *Yale Law Journal* 84 (January): 405–412.

Frankfurter, Felix. 1949. "'The Administrative Side' of Chief Justice Hughes." *Harvard Law Review* 63 (November): 1–4.

Friedrich, Robert J. 1982. "In Defense of Multiplicative Terms in Multiple Regression Equations." *American Journal of Political Science* 26 (November): 797–833.

Frontiero v. Richardson. 1973. 411 U.S. 677.

Garrow, David J. 1996. "The Rehnquist Reins." *New York Times Magazine,* October 6.

Gates, John B. 1990. "Content Analysis: Possibilities and Limits for Qualitative Data." *Judicature* 73 (December–January): 202–203.

George, Tracey E., and Lee Epstein. 1992. "On the Nature of Supreme Court Decision Making." *American Political Science Review* 86 (June): 323–337.

Giannelli, Paul C. 1993. "Junk Science: The Criminal Cases." *Journal of Criminal Law and Criminology* 84 (Spring): 105–128.

Gibson, James. 1997. *United States Supreme Court Judicial Data Base – Phase II: 1953–1993.* Ann Arbor, MI: Inter-University Consortium for Political and Social Research.

Gilligan, Thomas W., and Keith Krehbiel. 1989. "Asymmetric Information and Legislative Rules with a Heterogeneous Committee." *American Journal of Political Science* 33 (May): 459–490.

———. 1990. "Organization of Informative Committees by a Rational Legislature." *American Journal of Political Science* 34 (May): 531–564.

Gillman, Howard, and Cornell W. Clayton. 1999. "Beyond Judicial Attitudes: Institutional Approaches to Supreme Court Decision-Making." In *Supreme Court Decision-Making: New Institutionalist Approaches,* ed. Cornell W. Clayton and Howard Gillman, 1–12. Chicago: University of Chicago Press.

Ginsburg, Ruth Bader. 1990. "Remarks on Writing Separately." *Washington Law Review* 65 (January): 133–150.

———. 1994. "Remarks for American Law Institute Annual Dinner May 19, 1994." *Saint Louis University Law Journal* 38 (Summer): 881–888.

———. 1995. "Communicating and Commenting on the Court's Work." *Georgetown Law Journal* 83 (July): 2119–2129.

Ginter, James L., and Greg M. Allenby. 1995. "The Effects of In-Store Displays and Feature Advertising on Consideration Sets." *International Journal of Research in Marketing* 12 (May): 67–80.

Green, Donald P., and Ira Shapiro. 1994. *Pathologies of Rational Choice Theory: A Critique of Applications in Political Science.* New Haven: Yale University Press.

Greenbelt v. Bresler. 1970. 398 U.S. 6.

Greene, William H. 1997. *Econometric Analysis.* 3d ed. New York: Macmillan.

———. 1998. *Limdep: Version 7.0 User's Manual.* Plainview, NY: Econometric Software.

Griggs v. Duke Power Co. 1971. 401 U.S. 424.

Hagle, Timothy M. 1993. "'Freshmen Effects' for Supreme Court Justices." *American Journal of Political Science* 37 (November): 1142–1157.

Hagle, Timothy M., and Harold J. Spaeth. 1991. "Voting Fluidity and the Attitudinal Model of Supreme Court Decision Making." *Western Political Quarterly* 44 (March): 119–128.

———. 1992. "The Emergence of a New Ideology: The Business Decisions of the Burger Court." *Journal of Politics* 54 (February): 120–134.

1993. "Ideological Patterns in the Justices' Voting in the Burger Court's Business Cases." *Journal of Politics* 55 (May): 492–505.

Hall, Melinda Gann, and Paul Brace. 1989. "Order in the Courts: A Neo-Institutional Approach to Judicial Consensus." *Western Political Quarterly* 42 (September): 391–407.

1992. "Toward an Integrated Model of Judicial Voting Behavior." *American Politics Quarterly* 20 (April): 147–168.

Hall, Richard L., and Bernard Grofman. 1990. "The Committee Assignment Process and the Conditional Nature of Committee Bias." *American Political Science Review* 84 (December): 1149–1166.

Hammond, Thomas H. 1986. "Agenda Control, Organizational Structure, and Bureaucratic Politics." *American Journal of Political Science* 30 (May): 379–420.

Hansford, Thomas G., and David F. Damore. Forthcoming. "Congressional Preferences, Perceptions of Threat, and Supreme Court Decision Making." *American Politics Quarterly.*

Harlan, John M. 1970a. Letter to Potter Stewart, April 23. Papers of Justice William J. Brennan Jr. Washington, DC: Library of Congress Manuscript Division.

1970b. Memorandum to the Conference, March 16. Papers of Justice William J. Brennan Jr. Washington, DC: Library of Congress Manuscript Division.

1971a. Memo to Warren E. Burger, June 7. Papers of Justice William J. Brennan Jr. Washington, DC: Library of Congress Manuscript Division.

1971b. Letter to Warren E. Burger, June 18. Papers of Justice William J. Brennan Jr. Washington, DC: Library of Congress Manuscript Division.

1971c. Letter to Warren E. Burger, June 7. Papers of Justice William J. Brennan Jr. Washington, DC: Library of Congress Manuscript Division.

Hausman, Jerry, and Daniel McFadden. 1984. "Specification Tests for the Multinomial Logit Model." *Econometrica* 52 (September): 1219–1240

Hays, William L. 1994. *Statistics.* 5th ed. Forth Worth, TX: Harcourt Brace.

Heffron v. International Society for Krishna Consciousness. 1981. 452 U.S. 640.

Holsti, Ole. 1969. *Content Analysis for the Social Sciences and Humanities.* Reading, MA: Addison-Wesley.

Howard, J. Woodford, Jr. 1968. "On the Fluidity of Judicial Choice." *American Political Science Review* 62 (March): 43–56.

1971. "Judicial Biography and the Behavioral Persuasion." *American Political Science Review* 65 (September): 704–715.

Hughes, Charles Evans. 1966. *The Supreme Court of the United States: Its Foundation, Methods, and Achievements: An Interpretation.* New York: Columbia University Press.

Hurst, James Willard. 1956. *Law and the Conditions of Freedom in the Nineteenth-Century United States.* Madison: University of Wisconsin Press.

Ignagni, Joseph, and James Meernik. 1994. "Explaining Congressional Attempts to Reverse Supreme Court Decisions." *Political Research Quarterly* 47 (June): 353–371.

James v. Valtierra. 1971. 402 U.S. 137.

Johnson, Charles A. 1987a. "Law, Politics, and Judicial Decision Making: Lower Federal Court Uses of Supreme Court Decisions." *Law and Society Review* 21 (2): 325–340.

———. 1987b. "Content-Analytic Techniques and Judicial Research." *American Politics Quarterly* 15 (January): 169–197.

Johnson, Charles A., and Bradley C. Canon. 1984. *Judicial Policies: Implementation and Impact.* Washington, DC: CQ Press.

Johnstone, Sandra. 1992. "In the Shadow of the Chief: William J. Brennan and the Role of the Senior Associate Justice on the Supreme Court." Paper presented at the annual meeting of the American Political Science Association, Chicago, September 3–6.

Julnes, George, and Lawrence B. Mohr. 1989. "Analysis of No-Difference Findings in Evaluation Research." *Evaluation Review* 13 (December): 628–655.

Kahn, Ronald. 1994. *The Supreme Court and Constitutional Theory, 1953–1993.* Lawrence: University Press of Kansas.

Kennedy, Peter. 1992. *A Guide to Econometrics.* 3d ed. Cambridge, MA: MIT Press.

King, Gary. 1989. *Unifying Political Methodology: The Likelihood Theory of Statistical Inference.* Cambridge: Cambridge University Press.

Kingdon, John W. 1981. *Congressmen's Voting Decisions.* 2d ed. New York: Harper and Row.

Knight, Jack. 1992. *Institutions and Social Conflict.* Cambridge: Cambridge University Press.

———. 1993. "Interpretation as Social Interaction." Paper presented at the Political Economy of the Law Conference, Wallis Institute, University of Rochester, October 15–16.

———. 1994. "Symposium: The Supreme Court and the Attitudinal Model." *Law and Courts* 4 (Spring): 5–6.

Knight, Jack, and Lee Epstein. 1996a. "On the Struggle for Judicial Supremacy." *Law and Society Review* 30: 87–120.

———. 1996b. "The Norm of Stare Decisis." *American Journal of Political Science* 40 (November): 1018–1035.

Knight, Jack, and Itai Sened, eds. 1995. *Explaining Social Institutions.* Ann Arbor: University of Michigan Press.

Kort, Fred. 1964. "Comment on 'The Untroubled World of Jurimetrics.'" *Journal of Politics* 26 (November): 923–926.

Krehbiel, Keith. 1991. *Information and Legislative Organization.* Ann Arbor: University of Michigan Press.

Krippendorff, Klaus. 1980. *Content Analysis: An Introduction to Its Methodology.* Beverly Hills, CA: Sage.

Landis, J. Richard, and Gary G. Koch. 1977. "The Measurement of Observer Agreement for Categorical Data." *Biometrics* 33 (March): 159–174.

Larson v. Valente. 1982. 456 U.S. 228.

Levi, Edward H. 1949. *An Introduction to Legal Reasoning.* Chicago: University of Chicago Press.

Lin, D. Y., and L. J. Wei. 1989. "The Robust Inference for the Cox Proportional Hazards Model." *Journal of the American Statistical Association* 84 (December): 1074–1078.

Logue v. United States. 1973. 412 U.S. 521.

Lustick, Ian S. 1996. "History, Historiography, and Political Science: Multiple Historical Records and the Problem of Selection Bias." *American Political Science Review* 90 (September): 605–618.

Maddala, G. S. 1983. *Limited-Dependent and Qualitative Variables in Econometrics.* Cambridge: Cambridge University Press.

Maltzman, Forrest, and Paul J. Wahlbeck. 1996a. "Strategic Policy Considerations and Voting Fluidity on the Burger Court." *American Political Science Review* 90 (September): 581–592.

1996b. "May It Please the Chief? Opinion Assignments in the Rehnquist Court." *American Journal of Political Science* 40 (May): 421–433.

1996c. "Inside the U.S. Supreme Court: The Reliability of the Justices' Conference Records." *Journal of Politics* 58 (May): 528–539.

Mancusi v. Stubbs. 1972. 408 U.S. 204.

Manley, John F. 1970. *The Politics of Finance: The House Committee on Ways and Means.* Boston: Little, Brown.

March, James G., and Johan P. Olsen. 1984. "The New Institutionalism: Organizational Factors in Political Life." *American Political Science Review* 78 (September): 734–749.

1989. *Rediscovering Institutions: The Organizational Basis of Politics.* New York: Free Press.

Marks v. United States. 1977. 430 U.S. 188.

Marrese v. American Academy of Orthopaedic Surgeons. 1985. 470 U.S. 373.

Marshall, Thurgood. 1971. Letter to Potter Stewart, April 7. Papers of Justice William J. Brennan Jr. Washington, DC: Library of Congress Manuscript Division.

1985. Memorandum to Justices Brennan, White, Blackmun, Powell, Stevens, and O'Connor, January 3. Papers of Justice Thurgood Marshall. Washington, DC: Library of Congress Manuscript Division.

Mason, Alpheus T. 1956. *Harlan Fiske Stone: Pillar of the Law.* New York: Viking Press.

Matthews, Donald R. 1960. *U.S. Senators and Their World.* New York: Vintage Books.

McGuire, Kevin T. 1993a. "Lawyers and the U.S. Supreme Court: The Washington Community and Legal Elites." *American Journal of Political Science* 37 (May): 365–390.

———. 1993b. *The Supreme Court Bar: Legal Elites in the Washington Community.* Charlottesville: University Press of Virginia.

McGuire, Kevin T., and Gregory A. Caldeira. 1993. "Lawyers, Organized Interests, and the Law of Obscenity: Agenda Setting in the Supreme Court." *American Political Science Review* 87 (September): 717–726.

McGuire, Kevin T., and Barbara Palmer. 1995. "Issue Fluidity on the U.S. Supreme Court." *American Political Science Review* 89 (September): 691–702.

McLauchlan, William P. 1972. "Research Note: Ideology and Conflict in Supreme Court Opinion Assignment, 1946–1962." *Western Political Quarterly* 25 (March): 16–27.

Medine, David. 1990. "The Constitutional Right to Expert Assistance for Indigents in Civil Cases." *Hastings Law Journal* 41 (January): 281–349.

Mendelson, Wallace. 1963. "The Neo-Behavioral Approach to the Judicial Process: A Critique." *American Political Science Review* 57 (September): 593–603.

———. 1964. "The Untroubled World of Jurimetrics." *Journal of Politics* 26 (November): 914–922.

———. 1966. "An Open Letter to Professor Spaeth and His Jurimetric Colleagues." *Journal of Politics* 28 (May): 429–432.

Michelin Tire Corp. v. Wages. 1976. 423 U.S. 276.

Mintrom, Michael. 1997. "Policy Entrepreneurs and the Diffusion of Innovation." *American Journal of Political Science* 41 (July): 738–770.

Miranda v. Arizona. 1966. 384 U.S. 436.

Mulloy v. United States. 1970. 398 U.S. 410.

Murphy, Walter F. 1964. *Elements of Judicial Strategy.* Chicago: University of Chicago Press.

Myers, Daniel J. 1997. "Racial Rioting in the 1960s: An Event History Analysis of Local Conditions." *American Sociological Review* 62 (1): 94–112.

Nagel, Stuart S. 1961. "Political Party Affiliation and Judges' Decisions." *American Political Science Review* 55 (September): 844–850.

———. 1962. "Ethnic Affiliations and Judicial Propensities." *Journal of Politics* 24 (February): 94–110.

North, Douglass C. 1990. *Institutions, Institutional Change and Economic Performance.* Cambridge: Cambridge University Press.

O'Brien, David M. 1996. *Storm Center: The Supreme Court in American Politics.* 4th ed. New York: Norton.

O'Connor, Sandra Day. 1984a. Letter to William J. Brennan Jr., June 19. Papers of Justice William J. Brennan Jr. Washington, DC: Library of Congress Manuscript Division.

1984b. Letter to Byron R. White, May 25. Papers of Justice William J. Brennan Jr. Washington, DC: Library of Congress Manuscript Division.

1984c. Letter to William H. Rehnquist, May 23. Papers of Justice William J. Brennan Jr. Washington, DC: Library of Congress Manuscript Division.

1984d. Letter to John Paul Stevens, November 30. Papers of Justice William J. Brennan Jr. Washington, DC: Library of Congress Manuscript Division.

1984e. Letter to William J. Brennan Jr., December 11. Papers of Justice William J. Brennan Jr. Washington, DC: Library of Congress Manuscript Division.

1985a. Letter to Warren E. Burger, January 2. Papers of Justice William J. Brennan Jr. Washington, DC: Library of Congress Manuscript Division.

1985b. Letter to Thurgood Marshall, January 4. Papers of Justice Thurgood Marshall. Washington, DC: Library of Congress Manuscript Division.

1990. Memorandum to William J. Brennan Jr., June 4. Papers of Justice Thurgood Marshall. Washington, DC: Library of Congress Manuscript Division.

Ohio v. Roberts. 1980. 448 U.S. 56.

Orren, Karen, and Stephen Skowronek. 1994. "Beyond the Iconography: Notes for a 'New Institutionalism.'" In *The Dynamics of American Politics*, ed. Lawrence C. Dodd and Calvin Jillson, 311–330. Boulder, CO: Westview Press.

O'Shea v. Littleton. 1974. 414 U.S. 488.

Palmer, Jan. 1990. *The Vinson Court Era: The Supreme Court's Conference Votes.* New York: AMS Press.

Palmer, Jan, and Saul Brenner. 1989. "Working with Supreme Court Docket Books." *Law Library Journal* 81 (Winter): 41–46.

1990. "Determinants of the Amount of Time Taken by the Vinson Court to Process Its Full Court Opinions." *Journal of Supreme Court History* 1990: 142–151.

Paris Adult Theater I v. Slaton. 1973. 413 U.S. 49.

Parmar, Mahesh K. B., and David Machin. 1995. *Survival Analysis: A Practical Approach.* New York: John Wiley.

Pennsylvania v. Muniz. 1990. 496 U.S. 582.

Perry, H. W. 1991. *Deciding to Decide: Agenda Setting in the U.S. Supreme Court.* Cambridge, MA: Harvard University Press.

Polsby, Nelson W., Robert A. Dentler, and Paul A. Smith. 1963. "A Brief Introduction to the Scientific Study of Political Behavior." In *Politics and Social Life: An Introduction to Political Behavior,* ed. Nelson W. Polsby, Robert A. Dentler, and Paul A. Smith, 1–14. Boston: Houghton Mifflin.

Powell, Lewis F., Jr. 1973. Letter to Thurgood Marshall, April 16. Papers of Justice William J. Brennan Jr. Washington, DC: Library of Congress Manuscript Division.

1975. Office Manual. Papers of Justice Lewis F. Powell Jr. Lexington, VA: Washington and Lee Law Library.

1976. Report to the Labor Law Section of the American Bar Association, Atlanta, August 11.

1980a. Letter to Harry A. Blackmun, May 15. Papers of Justice William J. Brennan Jr. Washington, DC: Library of Congress Manuscript Division.

1980b. Letter to Harry A. Blackmun, May 21. Papers of Justice William J. Brennan Jr. Washington, DC: Library of Congress Manuscript Division.

1980c. Letter to Harry A. Blackmun, May 21. Papers of Justice William J. Brennan Jr. Washington, DC: Library of Congress Manuscript Division.

1984a. Briefing Notes Law Clerks. Papers of Justice Lewis F. Powell Jr. Lexington, VA: Washington and Lee Law Library.

1984b. Letter to Thurgood Marshall, December 19. Papers of Justice Lewis F. Powell Jr. Lexington, VA: Washington and Lee University.

1986. Letter to William H. Rehnquist, February 10. Papers of Justice Lewis F. Powell Jr. Lexington, VA: Washington and Lee University.

Pritchett, C. Herman. 1948. *The Roosevelt Court: A Study in Judicial Politics and Values, 1937–1947.* New York: Macmillan.

Provine, Doris Marie. 1980. *Case Selection in the U.S. Supreme Court.* Chicago: University of Chicago Press.

Rathjen, Gregory James. 1974. "Policy Goals, Strategic Choice and Majority Opinion Assignments in the U.S. Supreme Court: A Replication." *American Journal of Political Science* 18 (November): 713–724.

1980. "Time and Dissension on the United States Supreme Court." *Ohio Northern University Law Review* 7 (2): 227–258.

Regents of the University of California v. Bakke. 1978. 438 U.S. 265.

Rehnquist, William H. 1973. Memorandum to the Conference, May 9. Papers of Justice William J. Brennan Jr. Washington, DC: Library of Congress Manuscript Division.

1976. "Chief Justices I Never Knew." *Hastings Constitutional Law Quarterly* 3 (Summer): 637–655.

1978. Letter to William J. Brennan Jr., June 1. Papers of Justice William J. Brennan Jr. Washington, DC: Library of Congress Manuscript Division.

1984a. Letter to Harry A. Blackmun, June 12. Papers of Justice William J. Brennan Jr. Washington, DC: Library of Congress Manuscript Division.

1984b. Letter to Thurgood Marshall, December 10. Papers of Justice William J. Brennan Jr. Washington, DC: Library of Congress Manuscript Division.

1987. *The Supreme Court: How It Was, How It Is.* New York: Morrow.

1989. Memorandum to the Conference: Policy Regarding Assignments, November 24. Papers of Justice Thurgood Marshall. Washington, DC: Library of Congress Manuscript Division.

1992. "Remarks on the Process of Judging." *Washington and Lee Law Review* 49 (Spring): 263–270.

Richey, Mary Ellen. 1980a. Memorandum to Lewis F. Powell Jr., May 16. Papers of
Justice Lewis F. Powell Jr. Lexington, VA: Washington and Lee University.

1980b. Memorandum to Lewis F. Powell Jr., June 12. Papers of Justice Lewis F.
Powell Jr. Lexington, VA: Washington and Lee University.

Richmond Newspapers v. Virginia. 1980. 448 U.S. 555.

Riker, William H. 1962. *The Theory of Political Coalitions.* New Haven: Yale University Press.

1982. *Liberalism against Populism: A Confrontation between the Theory of Democracy
and the Theory of Social Choice.* San Francisco: W. H. Freeman.

1986. *The Art of Political Manipulation.* New Haven: Yale University Press.

Riker, William H., and Donald Niemi. 1962. "The Stability of Coalitions on Roll Calls
in the House of Representatives." *American Political Science Review* 56 (March):
58–65.

Roberts v. United States Jaycees. 1984. 468 U.S. 609.

Roe v. Wade. 1973. 410 U.S. 113.

Rohde, David W. 1972a. "Policy Goals, Strategic Choice and Majority Opinion Assignments in the U.S. Supreme Court." *Midwest Journal of Political Science* 16
(November): 652–682.

1972b. "Policy Goals and Opinion Coalitions in the Supreme Court." *Midwest
Journal of Political Science* 16 (May): 208–224.

1972c. "A Theory of the Formation of Opinion Coalitions in the U.S. Supreme
Court." In *Probability Models of Collective Decision Making,* ed. Richard
G. Niemi and Herbert F. Weisberg, 165–178. Columbus, OH: Charles E.
Merrill.

Rohde, David W., and Harold J. Spaeth. 1976. *Supreme Court Decision Making.* San
Francisco: W. H. Freeman.

Rosenberg v. Yee Chien Woo. 1971. 402 U.S. 49.

Rubinstein, Ariel. 1982. "Perfect Equilibrium in a Bargaining Model." *Econometrica*
50 (January): 97–109.

Ruckelshaus v. Monsanto Company. 1984. 467 U.S. 986.

Scalia, Antonin. 1994. "The Dissenting Opinion." *Journal of Supreme Court History*
1994: 33–44.

Schmidhauser, John R. 1961. "Judicial Behavior and the Sectional Crisis of
1837–1860." *Journal of Politics* 23 (November): 615–640.

Schubert, Glendon. 1959. *Quantitative Analysis of Judicial Behavior.* Glencoe, IL: Free
Press.

1961. "A Psychometric Model of the Supreme Court." *American Behavioral Sci-
entist* 5 (November): 14–18.

1962. "The 1960 Term of the Supreme Court: A Psychological Analysis." *American Political Science Review* 56 (March): 90–107.

1965. *The Judicial Mind.* New York: Free Press.

1974. *The Judicial Mind Revisited: Psychometric Analysis of Supreme Court Ideology.* New York: Oxford University Press.

Schwartz, Bernard. 1985. *The Unpublished Opinions of the Warren Court.* New York: Oxford University Press.

1988. *The Unpublished Opinions of the Burger Court.* New York: Oxford University Press.

1993. *A History of the Supreme Court.* New York: Oxford University Press.

1996. *Decision: How the Supreme Court Decides Cases.* New York: Oxford University Press.

Schwartz, Edward P. 1996. "The Proliferation of Concurring Opinions on the U.S. Supreme Court: Politics Killed the Norm." Paper presented at the annual meeting of the Midwest Political Science Association, Chicago, April 18–20.

Segal, Jeffrey A. 1984. "Predicting Supreme Court Decisions Probabilistically: The Search and Seizure Cases." *American Political Science Review* 78 (December): 891–900.

1997. "Separation-of-Powers Games in the Positive Theory of Congress and Courts." *American Political Science Review* 91: 28–44.

Segal, Jeffrey A., Charles M. Cameron, and Albert D. Cover. 1992. "A Spatial Model of Roll Call Voting: Senators, Constituents, Presidents, and Interest Groups in Supreme Court Confirmations." *American Journal of Political Science* 36 (February): 96–121.

Segal, Jeffrey A., and Albert D. Cover. 1989. "Ideological Values and the Votes of U.S. Supreme Court Justices." *American Political Science Review* 83 (June): 557–565.

Segal, Jeffrey A., Lee Epstein, Charles M. Cameron, and Harold J. Spaeth. 1995. "Ideological Values and the Votes of U.S. Supreme Court Justices Revisited." *Journal of Politics* 57 (August): 812–823.

Segal, Jeffrey A., and Harold J. Spaeth. 1993. *The Supreme Court and the Attitudinal Model.* Cambridge: Cambridge University Press.

1994. "The Authors Respond." *Law and Courts* 4 (Spring): 10–12.

Shepsle, Kenneth A. 1989. "Studying Institutions: Some Lessons from the Rational Choice Approach." *Journal of Theoretical Politics* 1 (April): 131–147.

Shepsle, Kenneth A., and Barry R. Weingast. 1987. "The Institutional Foundations of Committee Power." *American Political Science Review* 81 (March): 85–104.

Sigelman, Lee. 1984. "Doing Discriminant Analysis: Some Problems and Solutions." *Political Methodology* 10 (1): 67–80.

Singer, Judith D., and John B. Willett. 1993. "It's about Time: Using Discrete-Time Survival Analysis to Study Duration and the Timing of Events." *Journal of Educational Statistics* 18 (Summer): 155–195.

Slotnick, Elliot E. 1978. "The Chief Justices and Self-Assignment of Majority Opinions: A Research Note." *Western Political Quarterly* 31 (June): 219–225.

1979a. "Who Speaks for the Court? Majority Opinion Assignments from Taft to Burger." *American Journal of Political Science* 23 (February): 60–77.

1979b. "The Equality Principle and Majority Opinion Assignment on the United States Supreme Court." *Polity* 12 (Winter): 318–332.

1979c. "Judicial Career Patterns and Majority Opinion Assignment on the Supreme Court." *Journal of Politics* 41 (May): 640–648.

Smith, Rogers M. 1988. "Political Jurisprudence, the 'New Institutionalism,' and the Future of Public Law." *American Political Science Review* 82 (March): 89–108.

1996. "Science, Non-Science and Politics." In *The Historic Turn in Human Science,* ed. Terrence J. McDonald, 119–159. Ann Arbor: University of Michigan Press.

Snyder, Eloise C. 1958. "The Supreme Court as a Small Group." *Social Forces* 36: 232–238.

Songer, Donald R., Jeffrey A. Segal, and Charles M. Cameron. 1994. "The Hierarchy of Justice: Testing a Principal-Agent Model of Supreme Court–Circuit Court Interactions." *American Journal of Political Science* 38 (August): 673–696.

Spaeth, Harold J. 1961. "An Approach to the Study of Attitudinal Differences as an Aspect of Judicial Behavior." *Midwest Journal of Political Science* 5 (May): 165–180

1963. "An Analysis of Judicial Attitudes in the Labor Relations Decisions of the Warren Court." *Journal of Politics* 25 (May): 290–311.

1965. "Jurimetrics and Professor Mendelson: A Troubled Relationship." *Journal of Politics* 27 (November): 875–880.

1984. "Distributive Justice: Majority Opinion Assignments in the Burger Court." *Judicature* 67 (December–January): 299–304.

1994. *United States Supreme Court Judicial Database, 1953–1992 Terms.* 5th ed. Ann Arbor, MI: Inter-University Consortium for Political and Social Research.

1995a. "The Attitudinal Model." In *Contemplating Courts,* ed. Lee Epstein, 296–314. Washington, DC: CQ Press.

1995b. *Expanded United States Supreme Court Judicial Database, 1946–1968 Terms.* Ann Arbor, MI: Inter-University Consortium for Political and Social Research.

1996. "Different Strokes for Different Folks: A Reply to Professor Shapiro's Assessment of the Subfield." *Law and Courts* 6 (Spring): 11–13.

1998. *United States Supreme Court Judicial Database, 1953–1996 Terms.* 8th ed. Ann Arbor, MI: Inter-University Consortium for Political and Social Research.

Spaeth, Harold J., and Jeffrey A. Segal. 1999. *Majority Rule or Minority Will: Adherence to Precedent on the U.S. Supreme Court.* Cambridge: Cambridge University Press.

Spriggs, James F., II. 1996. "The Supreme Court and Federal Administrative Agencies: A Resource-Based Theory and Analysis of Judicial Impact." *American Journal of Political Science* 40 (November): 1122–1151.

1997. "Explaining Bureaucratic Compliance with Supreme Court Opinions." *Political Research Quarterly* 50 (September): 567–593.

Spriggs, James F., II, and Thomas G. Hansford. 1998. "Explaining the Overturning of U.S. Supreme Court Precedent." Paper presented at the annual meeting of the Midwest Political Science Association, Chicago, April 23–25.

1999. "Measuring Legal Change: The Reliability and Validity of *Shepard's Citations.*" University of California, Davis. Photocopy.

Spriggs, James F., II, Forrest Maltzman, and Paul J. Wahlbeck. 1999. "Bargaining on the U.S. Supreme Court: Justices' Responses to Majority Opinion Drafts." *Journal of Politics* 61 (May): 485–506.

Steamer, Robert J. 1986. *Chief Justice: Leadership and the Supreme Court.* Columbia: University of South Carolina Press.

Stevens, John P. 1984. Letter to Sandra Day O'Connor, November 29. Papers of Justice William J. Brennan Jr. Washington, DC: Library of Congress Manuscript Division.

1985. Letter to Thurgood Marshall, January 3. Papers of Justice Thurgood Marshall. Washington, DC: Library of Congress Manuscript Division.

1989. Letter to William R. Rehnquist, December 19. Papers of Justice Thurgood Marshall. Washington, DC: Library of Congress Manuscript Division.

Stewart, Potter. 1970. Memorandum to the Conference, April 23. Papers of Justice William J. Brennan Jr. Washington, DC: Library of Congress Manuscript Division.

1971. Letter to Warren E. Burger, January 28. Papers of Justice William J. Brennan Jr. Washington, DC: Library of Congress Manuscript Division.

1980. Letter to Harry A. Blackmun, May 15. Papers of Justice William J. Brennan Jr. Washington, DC: Library of Congress Manuscript Division.

Stimson, James A. 1985. "Regression in Space and Time: A Statistical Essay." *American Journal of Political Science* 29 (November): 914–947.

Strøm, Kaare, and Jørn Y. Leipart. 1993. "Policy, Institutions, and Coalition Avoidance: Norwegian Governments, 1945–1990." *American Political Science Review* 87 (December): 870–887.

Tanenhaus, Joseph, Marvin Schick, Matthew Muraskin, and Daniel Rosen. 1963. "The Supreme Court's Certiorari Jurisdiction: Cue Theory." In *Judicial Decision-Making,* ed. Glendon Schubert, 111–132. New York: Free Press.

Terry v. Ohio. 1968. 392 U.S. 1.

Thurmon, Mark A. 1992. "When the Court Divides: Reconsidering the Precedential Value of Supreme Court Plurality Decisions." *Duke Law Journal* 42 (November): 419–468.

Trans Alaska Pipeline Cases. 1978. 436 U.S. 631.

Ulmer, S. Sidney. 1959. "An Empirical Analysis of Selected Aspects of Lawmaking of the United States Supreme Court." *Journal of Public Law* 8 (Fall): 414–436.

1965. "Toward a Theory of Sub-Group Formation in the United States Supreme Court." *Journal of Politics* 27 (February): 133–152.

1970a. "The Use of Power in the Supreme Court: The Opinion Assignments of Earl Warren, 1953–1960." *Journal of Public Law* 19 (Winter): 49–67.

1970b. "Dissent Behavior and the Social Background of Supreme Court Justices." *Journal of Politics* 32 (August): 580–598.

1973a. "Social Background as an Indicator to the Votes of Supreme Court Justices in Criminal Cases: 1947–1956 Terms." *American Journal of Political Science* 17 (August): 622–630.

1973b. "Bricolage and Assorted Thoughts on Working in the Papers of Supreme Court Justices." *Journal of Politics* 35 (May): 286–310.

1984. "The Supreme Court's Certiorari Decisions: Conflict as a Predictive Variable." *American Political Science Review* 78 (December): 901–911.

1986. "Exploring the Dissent Patterns of the Chief Justices: John Marshall to Warren Burger." In *Judicial Conflict and Consensus: Behavioral Studies of American Appellate Courts*, ed. Sheldon Goldman and Charles M. Lamb, 50–67. Lexington: University of Kentucky Press.

1990. "Further Reflections on Working in the Papers of Supreme Court Justices." *Judicature* 73 (December–January): 193–196.

United States v. Albertini. 1985. 472 U.S. 675.

United States v. Hensley. 1985. 469 U.S. 221.

United States v. Johnson. 1971a. 403 U.S. 956.

United States v. Johnson. 1971b. 404 U.S. 802.

United States v. Karo. 1984. 468 U.S. 705.

United States v. Koecher. 1986. 475 U.S. 133.

United States v. Leon. 1984. 468 U.S. 897.

United States v. Nixon. 1974. 418 U.S. 683.

Vines, Kenneth N. 1964. "Federal District Judges and Race Relations Cases in the South." *Journal of Politics* 26 (May): 337–357.

Wahlbeck, Paul J. 1997. "The Life of the Law: Judicial Politics and Legal Change." *Journal of Politics* 59 (August): 778–802.

1998. "The Development of a Legal Rule: The Federal Common Law of Public Nuisance." *Law and Society Review* 32 (3): 613–637.

Wahlbeck, Paul J., James F. Spriggs II, and Forrest Maltzman. 1998. "Marshalling the Court: Bargaining and Accommodation on the U.S. Supreme Court." *American Journal of Political Science* 42 (January): 294–315.

1999. "The Politics of Dissents and Concurrences on the U.S. Supreme Court." *American Politics Quarterly* 27 (October): 488–514.

Wahlbeck, Paul J., James F. Spriggs II, and Lee Sigelman. 1999. "Ghostwriters on the Court? A Stylistic Analysis of U.S. Supreme Court Opinion Drafts." Paper presented at the annual meeting of the Midwest Political Science Association, Chicago, April 15–17.

Walker, Thomas G., Lee Epstein, and William J. Dixon. 1988. "On the Mysterious Demise of Consensual Norms in the United States Supreme Court." *Journal of Politics* 50 (May): 361–389.

Wardius v. Oregon. 1973. 412 U.S. 470.

Weinberger v. Rossi. 1982. 456 U.S. 25.

Welsh v. United States. 1970. 398 U.S. 333.

Wenzel, James P. 1994. "Modelling Value Conflict in the Supreme Court." Paper presented at the annual meeting of the Midwest Political Science Association, Chicago, April 14–16.

White, Byron R. 1985. Letter to Thurgood Marshall, January 4. Papers of Justice Thurgood Marshall. Washington, DC: Library of Congress Manuscript Division.

1989. Letter to Thurgood Marshall, June 5. Papers of Justice Thurgood Marshall. Washington, DC: Library of Congress Manuscript Division.

White, Halbert. 1980. "A Heteroskedasticity-Consistent Covariance Matrix Estimator and a Direct Test for Heteroskedasticity." *Econometrica* 48 (May): 817–838.

Wood, Sandra L., and Gary M. Gansle. 1997. "Seeking a Strategy: William J. Brennan's Dissent Assignments." *Judicature* 81 (September–October): 73–75.

Wood, Sandra L., Linda Camp Keith, Drew Noble Lanier, and Ayo Ogundele. 1998. "'Acclimation Effects' for Supreme Court Justices: A Cross-Validation, 1888–1940." *American Journal of Political Science* 42 (April): 690–697.

Forthcoming. "The Opinion Assignments of the Chief Justices, 1888–1940." *Social Science Quarterly.*

Woodward, Bob, and Scott Armstrong. 1979. *The Brethren: Inside the Supreme Court.* New York: Simon and Schuster.

Yamaguchi, Kazuo. 1991. *Event History Analysis.* Newbury Park, CA: Sage.

Zhang, Junsen, and Saul D. Hoffman. 1993. "Discrete-Choice Logit Models: Testing the IIA Property." *Sociological Methods and Research* 22 (November): 193–213.

Author Index

Aldrich, John, 41n12
Allenby, Greg, 41n12
Allison, Paul, 109
Alt, James, 14n8
Alvarez, Michael, 41n12
Armstrong, Scott, 6, 25
Arnold, Laura, 129n3
Arrow, Kenneth, 91
Atkins, Burton, 14n10
Austen-Smith, David, 20
Axelrod, Robert, 19, 21, 100

Baron, David, 24
Baum, Lawrence, 12, 13, 15, 21, 35, 37
Beck, Nathaniel, 110
Bentley, A. Lee, 95n1
Berelson, Bernard, 11
Berry, Frances, 109n11
Berry, William, 109n11
Bhat, Chandra, 41n12
Binder, Sarah, 129n3
Binmore, Kenneth, 24, 103
Biskupic, Joan, 25
Black, Hugo, 22, 24, 135–6
Blackmun, Harry, 59–61, 63, 68, 94, 127
Blalock, Hubert, Jr., 54
Box-Steffensmeier, Janet, 118n22, 129n3, 138n6, 143n13
Brace, Paul, 12, 14n10
Brennan, William, 3, 7, 9–10, 34, 63, 69, 94, 97, 107, 127–28
Brenner, Saul, 7, 23, 36, 37, 38, 39, 40, 44nn16,17, 101, 102, 128, 160
Burger, Warren, 22, 29, 38, 39, 47, 60, 65, 67, 95, 99, 125

Caldeira, Gregory, 6, 14n10, 33, 160
Cameron, Charles, 5, 139n7

Campbell, Angus, 11
Canon, Bradley, 5, 16
Carmines, Edward, 161, 174
Clark, Tom, 7, 10
Clayton, Cornell, 11, 12, 151
Cohen, Jacob, 163, 164n9
Cook, Beverly, 37
Cover, Albert, 6, 10, 139n7
Crawford, Vincent, 7, 9, 20

Dahl, Robert, 11
Damore, David, 13n7
Danelski, David, 8, 23, 32, 36, 40
Davis, Sue, 35, 37
Dentler, Robert, 11
De Swann, Abraham, 100
Dixon, William, 14n10
Dorff, Robert, 7, 160
Douglas, William, 29–30, 69, 160

Elster, Jon, 14n9
Epstein, Lee, 5, 12, 13nn6,7, 15, 22, 25, 26, 28, 32, 38, 43, 44n18, 45n23, 51n33, 58n1, 65n4, 79, 96n2, 109, 140n10, 153
Eskridge, William, 5

Farrell, Joseph, 7
Feldman, Jim, 128
Fenno, Richard F., Jr., 11, 139
Ferejohn, John, 24
Fleming, Thomas, 109
Fortas, Abe, 8
Frankfurter, Felix, 7
Friedrich, Robert, 49n30

Gansle, Gary, 160
Garrow, David, 135
Gates, John, 160

Subject Index